Dark E

Book VII

Panthera

by

K. M. Ashman

Copyright K. M. Ashman, January 2025

All rights are reserved. No part of this publication may be reproduced, stored, or transmitted in any form or by any means without prior written permission of the copyright owner. All characters depicted within this publication are fictitious, and any resemblance to any real person, living or dead, is entirely coincidental.

Character Names

The Occultum
- **Seneca** - Tribune, Unit Commander
- **Marcus** – Ex Centurion
- **Falco** - Former Gladiator
- **Sica** - Syrian Assassin
- **Decimus** - Veteran
- **Talorcan** - Belgic Scout
- **Veteranus** – Ex member of the Occultum

Roman Military Leadership
- **Gaius Cornelius Flavus** - Legatus Legionis (Legion Commander)
- **Scipio** - Camp Prefect
- **Senator Lepidus** – Senator and liaison to the Occultum

Indigenous Leaders and Peoples
- **Panthera** - Chieftain, City Ruler
- **Khaemwaset** - Senior Nubian Guide
- **Kesi** - Local Guide
- **The Makatani** - Tribal Warriors

Background Characters
- **Corvus** - Optio, Sole Survivor of Twenty-First Rapax
- **Tiberius** - Centurion

Africa

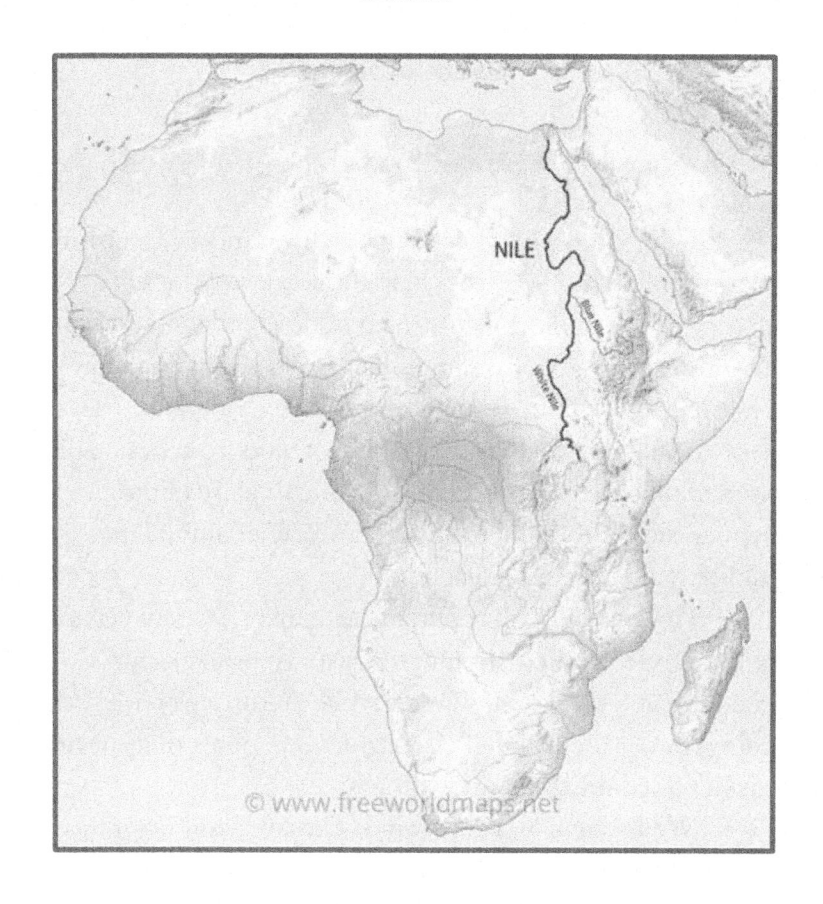

Prologue

South of Syene

Egypt

The vultures had been circling for hours as Centurion Tiberius pulled his horse to a halt at the crest of the rocky outcrop. In this godforsaken stretch of desert that marked the southernmost edge of Roman influence, scavengers usually meant only one thing: something was dying, or already dead.

'What do you think?' asked his Optio from beside him, his scarred face squinting against the harsh glare of the Egyptian sun. 'Probably just another caravan animal that couldn't make the crossing?'

Tiberius didn't respond immediately. Twenty years of frontier service had taught him to trust his instincts, and something about this felt different. The vultures weren't feeding, they were waiting, circling in lazy spirals that suggested their intended meal still drew breath.

'We'll take a look,' he said eventually, and urged his horse forward towards the descending vultures.

The patrol rode down into the shallow wadi where the scavengers had focused their attention, the horses picking their way carefully across stones that radiated heat like forge coals. What they found defied explanation.

A man lay sprawled in the meagre shade of a stunted acacia tree, his body so emaciated that his ribs showed clearly through skin burned black by the merciless sun. A few rotting rags clung to his skeletal frame, barely covering his nakedness, offering no clue to his identity or origin. He might have been Egyptian, Nubian, or from any of the countless peoples who dwelt beyond Rome's southern borders.

But it was what the man clutched against his chest that stopped the centurion's breath in his throat. Even dulled by sand and exposure, the necklace blazed with inner fire. Gold work of extraordinary craftsmanship formed intricate patterns that seemed to shift and writhe in the harsh light, while precious stones the size of dove eggs caught the sun and threw it back in dazzling fragments of green, blue, and crimson. It was a king's ransom wrought in metal and gems, beautiful beyond anything Tiberius had ever seen.

'Jupiter's balls,' whispered one of the soldiers. 'Where did he get that?'

The dying man's eyes fluttered open at the sound of Latin voices. They were fever-bright, sunken deep in a face that had been carved gaunt by starvation and thirst, but they fixed on Tiberius with desperate intensity.

'Water,' he croaked, his voice like wind through dry reeds.

Tiberius dismounted and dropped to his knees, before lifting his waterskin to the stranger's cracked lips.

'Easy,' Tiberius murmured, supporting the man's head. 'You're safe now.' He looked down at the jewelled necklace still clutched tightly to the man's chest. 'This necklace, where did you get it from?'

The man's fingers tightened convulsively around the necklace, holding it against his chest like a talisman. His lips moved soundlessly, and the centurion leaned closer, trying to understand as the stranger's eyes focused one final time, burning with the intensity of a man desperate to deliver a message before death claimed him. He struggled to raise himself, his skeletal hand reaching toward the Centurion with trembling fingers.

'*Panthera,*' he whispered, painfully. '*Beware... Panthera.*'

The light faded from his eyes like a candle flame guttering out and as Tiberius tried to decipher the last words, the nameless wanderer drew his final breath beneath the pitiless Egyptian sun, taking his secrets with him into whatever darkness awaited beyond.

Tiberius sat back on his heels, staring at the corpse while his mind raced through the implications. A dying man who spoke Latin, a warning about something called Panthera and clutched in dead fingers, a treasure that suggested unimaginable wealth hidden somewhere in the trackless wilderness.

'Centurio?' ventured the Optio quietly. 'What do we do?'

As Tiberius carefully pried the necklace from the corpse's death grip, feeling its surprising weight, something caught his eye. There, on the man's right forearm, barely visible beneath layers of grime and sun damage, was the fading outline of a tattoo.

He poured liquid from his own waterskin and gently cleaned the dead man's arm. Slowly, like an image emerging from morning mist, the tattoo became clear. A Roman eagle, its wings spread in the classic pose of imperial authority, talons gripping a banner. And below it, numbers so faded they were barely legible: XII. Tiberius's blood turned to ice.

'Sweet Jupiter,' he breathed.

The Optio leaned closer, studying the faded marks.

'Is that what I think it is?' he said.

'It looks like the mark of the Twenty-first Rapax,' replied Tiberius, 'but what this man is doing out here I have no idea. As far as I know, the Rapax have never been deployed this far south.'

'He could be a deserter or even a veterani seeking his fortune,' said the Optio.

'Well whatever the reason,' said Tiberius, 'it seems he was successful, though little good it has done him.'

Tiberius carefully placed the necklace in his cloak, his mind racing at the implications. Whatever this fellow Roman was doing out here, beyond the edges of the known world, he had somehow managed to cross hundreds of miles of hostile desert clutching a fortune in gold and precious gems, and he couldn't help but wonder what else could be out there.

'We report this to Alexandria immediately,' he said finally. 'And we say nothing to the men about what we just heard. This stays between us until someone with authority decides what it means.'

The two men joined their comrades to ride away, and once they had crested the hill, Tiberius took one last look back at the body of the unknown soldier now covered with squabbling vultures.

The man had somehow survived everything the desert gods had thrown at him, all to deliver a priceless artifact, and the threat of something that would turn out to be far more dangerous than gold… *Panthera.*

Chapter One

The Outskirts of Rome

The morning sun cast long shadows across the crumbling courtyard of the Castra Veterana, its pale light doing little to improve the appearance of the military barracks that had seen better days under Augustus. Weeds sprouted between the broken stones of the parade ground, and the wooden buildings sagged with the weight of decades of neglect. It was, as Falco had observed on their first day, exactly the sort of place where Rome sent people it wanted to forget.

'Three weeks,' Marcus muttered, adjusting the linen sling that supported his left arm. The bone had knitted well during their journey from Britannia, but the limb still ached in the damp Roman weather. 'Three weeks of sitting in this cesspit while Lepidus vanishes into the bowels of the Palatine.'

He sat on a wooden bench beside the barracks, methodically working his injured fingers through a series of exercises the Greek physician had prescribed. The movements were painful but necessary if he hoped to regain full use of the arm that had been shattered during their final battle with the Shadow Walkers.

Across the courtyard, Sica emerged from the modest bath house they had constructed from salvaged materials. Steam rose from his dark skin as he towelled himself dry, the network of scars that covered his torso standing out like a map of violence survived.

'Any word from our illustrious Senator?' he asked, settling onto the bench beside Marcus.

'Nothing,' replied Marcus with obvious frustration. 'Not a single message since he disappeared into whatever hole

Senatorial privilege affords.'

Nearby, Decimus sat in the shade of a collapsed portico, carefully oiling and sharpening his gladius with the methodical precision that marked him as a veteran of countless campaigns. The blade gleamed in the morning light, its edge honed to deadly perfection despite having seen hard use in the forests of Britannia.

'Maybe he's trying to convince Claudius that we didn't completely balls up the mission,' he suggested without looking up from his work. 'Though I suspect that's a difficult argument to make when the man we were sent to kill is still breathing.'

'We made the right choice,' said Talorcan firmly, emerging from the armoury where he had been repairing equipment damaged during their ordeal. The Belgic scout's face still bore the faint scars of his desperate escape from the Silures settlement, but his eyes held no regret about their decisions in enemy territory.

As Talorcan took a seat near the others, Decimus glanced around the courtyard with a frown.

'Where's Veteranus?' he asked, noting the absence of their newest member. 'I haven't seen him for days.'

Seneca looked up from adjusting his sling.

'I gave him leave to head into Rome,' he replied. 'He had a personal matter that required attention.'

Decimus's eyebrows shot up in genuine surprise.

'Personal matter?' he repeated, clearly taken aback. 'I thought Veteranus was a lone wolf, no ties anywhere. That's certainly the impression he's given us.'

'You'd be surprised,' Seneca said simply, returning his attention to his injured arm. His tone carried a note of finality that suggested the subject was closed.

Decimus studied his commander's face for a moment,

recognizing the subtle signals that indicated no further explanation would be forthcoming. In their years together, he had learned to read Seneca's moods, and this was clearly one of those situations where discretion was valued above curiosity.

Marcus looked up from his own equipment maintenance.

'Strange timing though,' he observed. 'Just when it seems like our situation might be resolved one way or another, he disappears.'

'Perhaps that's exactly why the timing matters,' Seneca suggested, his voice carrying implications he didn't elaborate upon. 'Anyway, it is what it is.'

The conversation returned to their actions in Britannia, as it had countless times over the past three weeks, but it was interrupted by a sound that was becoming the almost daily morning entertainment: Falco's voice raised in indignant protest from somewhere inside the main barracks building.

'You mangy, flea-bitten son of a diseased whore!' the former gladiator's roar echoed across the courtyard. *'Get away from my gear!'*

Moments later, he appeared in the doorway, totally naked and wielding a wooden training sword like a man preparing for mortal combat. His massive frame also bore the evidence of their recent trials, fresh scars layering over old ones in a tapestry of violence survived. But it was his expression of outraged dignity that drew grins from his watching comrades.

'What's the matter, Falco?' called Decimus with barely concealed amusement. 'Finally found an opponent that matches your fighting skills?'

'That cursed rat,' Falco snarled, pointing the wooden blade toward the barracks interior, 'has been stealing my rations. Every morning, I wake to find my bread gnawed and my cheese riddled with holes. It's conducting a campaign of sabotage against my breakfast.'

'Maybe it's tired of listening to your snoring,' Sica suggested helpfully. 'I know I am.'

Falco fixed him with a baleful glare.

'My snoring is the sound of a warrior at rest, Syrian. It's musical. Heroic. Like distant thunder announcing the approach of victory.'

'It's like a wounded boar drowning in mud,' Marcus corrected. 'I've been considering requesting a transfer to quieter accommodations. Perhaps somewhere near a pig farm or an erupting volcano.'

'You're all ungrateful bastards,' Falco declared, warming to his theme. 'Here I am, recovering from grievous wounds suffered in service to the Empire, and instead of the gratitude and admiration I deserve, I'm subjected to rodent harassment and mockery from my supposed brothers-in-arms.' He struck a heroic pose, the wooden sword raised toward the sky. 'In the arena, he continued, 'crowds cheered my name. Women threw flowers at my feet and Senators offered fortunes for the privilege of witnessing my prowess. And now? Now I'm reduced to single combat with a rat in a barracks that probably housed goats before they decided to warehouse unwanted soldiers here.'

'The goats probably had better table manners,' Talorcan observed, which earned appreciative chuckles from the others.

'Mock me if you will,' Falco continued, lowering his weapon and settling onto a nearby stone block, 'but mark my words. When we're finally called to account for our actions in Britannia, when we're standing before Claudius explaining why we chose to rescue a princess instead of killing a druid, you'll

11

wish we had spent this time preparing proper speeches instead of lounging about like invalids at a bathhouse.'

The mention of their eventual reckoning cast a shadow over the group's mood. Each man had been avoiding the subject, focusing instead on their recovery and the comfortable routine they had established in their temporary exile. But Falco's words brought their situation into sharp focus.

'We prevented a war,' said Marcus quietly, flexing his injured fingers. 'The marriage alliance between the Brigantes and Ordovices would have collapsed if Rhiannon had died in captivity. The resulting conflict would have driven the western tribes into Caratacus's arms.'

'And in doing so, we let Mordred escape,' Decimus countered, testing his sword's edge with practiced care. 'The most dangerous druid in Britannia, the man who nearly killed the emperor, walks free because we chose political expedience over military objectives.'

'Mordred was trying to heal Caratacus,' said Talorcan, 'and surrounded by warriors. We had no guarantee we could have reached him even if we had tried.'

'We had no guarantee we could rescue the girl either,' Sica added. 'But we managed that well enough.'

The debate that had consumed them for weeks threatened to resume, each man defending the choices they had made while privately wondering if they had chosen correctly. They had prevented one disaster while possibly enabling another, and the uncertainty of their decision's consequences gnawed at them.

Their discussion was interrupted by the appearance of a figure at the barracks gate. A young man in the white tunic of an imperial messenger. He paused at the courtyard's edge, studying the group with obvious uncertainty.

'I seek the men called the Occultum,' he announced formally. 'I bear a message from Senator Lepidus.'

Silence greeted this pronouncement, each man feeling the weight of the moment settle upon him. After three weeks of waiting, wondering, and worrying, the reckoning had finally arrived.

Seneca emerged from the barracks' shadowed interior, his weathered face betraying nothing as he approached the messenger. As their leader, he had borne the greatest weight during their exile, knowing that whatever judgment awaited them would fall most heavily upon his shoulders.

'I am Seneca,' he said simply. 'These are my men. What does the Senator require?'

The messenger produced a scroll sealed with red wax, extending it with the ceremonial precision required for official communications.

'You are summoned to appear before Senator Lepidus at the villa of Marcus Cornelius Flavus at the sixth hour. Come armed and equipped for travel.'

The young man departed without waiting for acknowledgment, leaving the Occultum to contemplate the implications of their summons. Armed and equipped for travel suggested they might be departing Rome soon, but whether for a new mission or permanent exile remained unclear.

'Well,' said Falco, rising to his feet with theatrical resignation, 'it appears our holiday is over.'

'At least we'll finally know what's expected of us,' replied Marcus, struggling to his feet and working his injured arm carefully. 'This waiting has been worse than the uncertainty.'

As they prepared for their appointment with whatever fate awaited them, each man checked his equipment. Weapons

13

were inspected and personal effects secured. They dressed not as men going to their execution, but as professionals preparing for duty.

'Whatever happens,' said Seneca as they formed up in the courtyard, 'I alone will take responsibility for the choices we made. The rest of you were just following orders.'

'Hah, we'll see about that,' replied Marcus. 'As far as I am concerned, we stand or fall as one.'

Seneca knew it would be pointless arguing with his men, but he would do what he could to protect them, and as they left the Castra Veterana, he knew they would meet their fate as they had met every challenge before, together, with the bonds forged in shared danger stronger than any fear of imperial displeasure.

Chapter Two

The Villa

The villa of Marcus Cornelius Flavus stood in sharp contrast to the squalor of their temporary barracks, its marble columns and manicured gardens speaking of wealth that flowed as freely as wine at a Senator's banquet. Seneca led his men through the atrium, their hobnailed boots echoing against polished floors that probably cost more than most soldiers earned in a lifetime.

A steward, his tunic immaculate despite the afternoon heat, guided them through corridors lined with frescoes depicting scenes from Homer's epics. The painted warriors seemed to watch their passage with knowing eyes, as if recognising kindred spirits in these scarred veterans of Rome's frontier wars.

They were shown into a spacious dining room where a long table had been set with simple fare: bread, olives, cheese, and watered wine. The food was good quality but deliberately modest, suggesting that this was business rather than pleasure.

The Occultum took their places around the table, each man settling into the familiar routine of shared meals that had sustained them through countless campaigns. The conversation was muted, each aware that their fate would soon be decided within these elegant walls.

As they ate, Falco's attention turned onto one of the serving girls, a young woman with dark hair bound in an elaborate style that suggested she held some status within the household. Her movements were graceful as she refilled their wine cups, and when she leant close to pour Falco's drink, the former gladiator's eyes lit up with familiar interest.

'My thanks, beautiful one,' he said in his most charming voice, flashing the smile that had allegedly won hearts across the Empire. 'Tell me, do you serve here often? Because I find myself in sudden need of... regular refreshment.'

The girl's cheeks coloured slightly, but she maintained her professional composure as she moved to the next cup. Falco, undeterred by this apparent lack of enthusiasm, shifted in his seat to maintain eye contact.

'Perhaps you've heard tales of gladiatorial prowess?' he continued, 'I am Falco, victor of a hundred arena contests, slayer of wild beasts, defender of the innocent. Surely such achievements merit at least a smile?'

Marcus cleared his throat meaningfully, while Sica shook his head in obvious disapproval. Talorcan focused intently on his bread, as if the grain's origins were a matter of vital military intelligence.

'The girl is working, Falco,' said Decimus quietly. 'Leave her be.'

'I'm merely being friendly,' Falco protested, though he continued to track the servant's movements around the room. 'It's called civilised conversation. Perhaps you've heard of it? We've been buried in that military cesspit for weeks, surrounded by nothing but ugly soldiers and uglier rats. Surely you can't blame a man for appreciating feminine beauty when it finally graces his presence?'

'I can blame a man for making a fool of himself,' replied Marcus dryly. 'Especially when we're about to learn whether we still have a future to worry about.'

Seneca was about to add his own rebuke when the sound of approaching footsteps echoed from the corridor beyond. The conversation died instantly as Senator Lepidus entered the dining room, his expression grave enough to silence even Falco's romantic ambitions.

The Senator looked older than when they had last seen him. His toga was immaculate as always, but there was something in his bearing that suggested sleepless nights and difficult conversations.

He took his place at the head of the table without ceremony, selecting a piece of bread and picking at it absently while his eyes studied each man in turn. The silence stretched uncomfortably, broken only by the soft footfalls of servants who seemed to sense the tension and moved even more quietly than before.

Finally, Falco's patience snapped.

'By Jupiter's hairy arse, what's going on?' he demanded, his voice cutting through the oppressive quiet. 'We've been rotting in that barracks for three weeks without so much as a word from you, and now you sit there picking at bread like a nervous bride at her wedding feast. Are we to be disbanded? Exiled? Fed to the lions for entertainment? Just tell us!'

'Falco,' Seneca's voice carried a sharp reproach, 'mind your tongue.'

But Lepidus raised his hand, the gesture carrying enough authority to silence both men.

'No, Seneca. Your man's frustration is understandable. I've kept you waiting long enough, and you deserve answers.' He set down his bread and met each man's gaze directly. 'I have much to impart, and none of it will be easy to hear or understand.'

The words hung in the air as Marcus leant forward slightly, his veteran's instincts reading the gravity in the Senator's voice.

'First things first,' he said quietly. 'Are we to be disbanded?'

Lepidus looked at him for a long moment, and when he spoke, his voice carried something almost approaching reverence.

'No. Far from it.'

The relief that washed over the table was almost palpable, though it was quickly tempered by wariness. If they weren't being disbanded, if their failure to kill Mordred hadn't cost them their positions, then something else was coming. Something that required their particular skills.

'You've been given a new mission,' Lepidus continued, his tone growing more serious with each word. 'And this one is different to anything you've ever done before. In every sense of the word.'

The silence that followed was heavy with anticipation and dread. Each man understood that missions described as 'different' usually meant impossible, and impossible missions had a tendency to become fatal very quickly.

'How different?' asked Seneca.

Lepidus reached inside his toga and withdrew a scroll sealed with purple wax, the imperial seal that marked it as coming directly from Claudius himself. He placed it on the table between them like a weapon being laid down before combat.

'Different enough that the emperor has taken personal interest. Different enough that failure is not merely discouraged, it is unthinkable.' His eyes swept around the table once more. 'Different enough that some of you may not return from where you're going.'

The serving girl who had attracted Falco's attention earlier chose that moment to refill his cup, but the former gladiator didn't even glance in her direction. His attention, like that of all his comrades, was fixed entirely on the scroll that would determine their fate.

Whatever came next, whatever impossible task Claudius had in mind for them, their comfortable exile was about to end. The Occultum were going back to work, and from the expression on Lepidus's face, they were going to earn every coin of their imperial wages.

The only question was whether they would live long enough to spend them.

Chapter Three

Rome

Lepidus set the scroll aside without opening it, his weathered hands clasped before him on the polished table.

'Several years ago,' he began, 'during the reign of Caligula an expedition was dispatched deep into Africa, further than any Roman had ventured before.' He paused, allowing this information to settle before continuing. 'The mission was one of discovery and trade, penetrating beyond our southernmost borders to establish contact with peoples unknown to civilised men. Over three hundred souls set out from Alexandria, including two hundred legionaries of the Twenty-First Rapax, along with guides, interpreters, traders, and enough supplies for a journey of many months.'

Sica leant forward slightly, his dark eyes fixed on the Senator's face.

'What happened to them?'

'We don't know,' replied Lepidus. 'Nothing was ever heard from them again. They vanished into the wilderness as completely as if the earth had swallowed them. For years, the only trace of their passage was a single helmet that appeared in an Alexandrian market, sold by a Nubian trader who claimed to have found it beside a dried riverbed far to the south.'

Marcus shifted in his seat, his injured arm still tender from their recent ordeal.

'But something's changed,' he observed. 'Otherwise we wouldn't be sitting here.'

'Indeed.' Lepidus's expression grew more serious. 'Six months ago, a frontier patrol discovered a dying man in the desert beyond Syene. He was barely alive, burned by the sun and starved to the point of death. At first, he appeared to be nothing more than another desert wanderer who had succumbed to the wilderness.' The Senator paused, reaching for his wine cup and taking a measured sip before continuing. 'However, when the patrol examined the body more closely, he discovered something remarkable. A tattoo, faded but still visible, marking the man as a legionary of the Twenty-First Rapax.'

The silence that followed was profound. Each member of the Occultum understood the implications immediately. After years of assuming the entire expedition had perished, here was proof that at least one man had survived whatever catastrophe had befallen them.

'One survivor,' said Talorcan slowly. 'After all this time.'

'One survivor who managed to cross hundreds of miles of hostile territory to reach Roman soil,' Lepidus confirmed.

Falco leant across the table, his earlier frivolity completely forgotten.

'What did he say exactly?'

'Little that made sense,' Lepidus admitted. 'Fever talk, mostly. But if he survived then there may be others and the possibility that some of the Twenty-First Rapax might still be alive has captured the emperor's attention.'

Decimus cut to the heart of the matter.

'So Claudius wants to mount another expedition to find out what happened to the first one and bring back any survivors.'

'Precisely.' Lepidus nodded. 'The emperor believes that Roman soldiers, however few might remain, should not be abandoned to die in foreign lands when rescue might still be possible. Your reputation has grown considerably within the corridors of power and despite the complications surrounding your recent mission in Britannia, Claudius recognises your unique capabilities.'

Marcus frowned, working through the tactical implications.

'Are we to go alone? Six men searching for survivors in unknown territory seems optimistic, even for us.'

Lepidus shook his head, and when he spoke, his words shocked them into stunned silence.

'No. This time, the emperor is sending a legion.'

The implications crashed over them like a tide. A full legion meant four to five thousand men, along with all the support personnel, equipment, and supplies necessary for an extended campaign in hostile territory.

'A legion?' Talorcan repeated, his voice betraying his astonishment.

'Which legion?' Seneca asked.

'That will be explained in due course,' replied Lepidus. 'What matters for now is that you understand the scale of what's being planned. This isn't a reconnaissance mission or a quick strike into enemy territory. This is a full-scale expedition of discovery, and the Occultum will be attached to ensure its success.' He leant back in his chair, studying their faces as they processed this information. 'You have ten days to prepare. Sort out any equipment you may need, see to outstanding personal affairs, and anything else you need to settle before departing Rome. After that, you join the expedition and venture further into the unknown than any Roman has gone before.'

Lepidus reached for the scroll he had set aside earlier, breaking the wax seal with deliberate care. As he unrolled the parchment, he continued speaking.

'This is all we have to guide you.'

He passed the document to Seneca, who studied it with growing resignation. The map showed the familiar course of the Nile as it flowed north from Syene through the cataracts, every bend and landmark carefully marked by generations of Roman cartographers. But further south, beyond Syene, beyond the reach of Roman influence, the detail vanished. Only a thin line indicated the river's continuing course, marked with barely any features or settlements, leading south to what appeared to be a substantial body of water.

Seneca looked up from the map, his weathered face showing the strain of command.

'Where exactly is our target?'

'We don't know,' Lepidus admitted. 'We believe it's somewhere around the lake region shown there, but we can't be certain.'

'How far?' Marcus asked.

'We don't know.'

'What route should we take?'

'We don't know.'

'How long will the expedition take?'

'We don't know.'

Falco leant back in his chair with obvious exasperation.

'Is there anything you do know?'

Lepidus met his gaze steadily.

'The dying man spoke one word clearly. Probably a place. Panthera. We believe that's where we'll find whatever remains of the Twenty-First Rapax.'

Seneca sighed and looked around at his men, seeing his own thoughts reflected in their faces. An impossible mission into unknown territory, following vague directions to find survivors who might not exist, in a place they couldn't locate on their only map.

'It isn't much,' he said finally.

'No,' Lepidus agreed. 'But it's exactly the sort of thing you're used to doing.'

'I have a question,' said Falco. 'Veteranus still hasn't returned, and we have received any word from him. Do we wait?'

'You do not,' said Lepidus. 'If he is not back in time then you will proceed without him.'

Despite everything, Seneca found himself smiling grimly. The Senator was right. Impossible missions with inadequate intelligence were exactly what the Occultum did best. At least this time they wouldn't be doing it alone.

'Ten days,' he said, rolling up the map carefully.

'Ten days,' Lepidus confirmed. 'And then you march south, into the unknown.'

A commotion from the corridor interrupted the heavy silence that had followed Lepidus's briefing. Hurried footsteps approached, and a young messenger appeared in the doorway, his face flushed with the urgency of his errand.

'Senator Lepidus,' the youth called breathlessly, 'The emperor requires your immediate attendance. There's been developments regarding the situation in Germania.'

Lepidus rose from the table and looked around the group.

'Gentlemen, you'll excuse me. We'll speak again before your departure.' He paused at the doorway, looking back at the six men seated around the table. 'Use this time to consider what lies ahead. Ten days isn't long to prepare for what may be the longest journey any of you will ever make.' And with that, he departed, leaving the Occultum alone with their thoughts and the weight of what they had just learned.

For several moments, nobody spoke. The serving girl who had attracted Falco's earlier attention continued to move quietly around the room, but even she seemed to sense the gravity of the conversation that had just concluded. Finally, Falco broke the silence with characteristic directness.

'Well, that's something different, isn't it? No more skulking through British forests being rained on by clouds that apparently never empty. No more eating half-rotten meat in freezing bogs while painted savages try to gut us with rusty spears.' He reached for his wine cup, taking a generous swallow before continuing. 'Africa means sunshine and plenty of it. Proper heat that warms a man's bones instead of a damp Britannic climate that makes my old arena injuries ache. And the food down there, exotic spices, fruits we've never tasted, and women with skin like polished bronze...'

'It also means desert,' Sica interrupted quietly. 'Endless stretches of sand where the sun can kill a man in hours. Scorpions, snakes, and tribes who've never seen Romans before and probably won't welcome the introduction.'

Marcus nodded agreement, working his injured fingers through their exercises.

'The Twenty-First Rapax were no fools. If two hundred experienced legionaries with proper equipment and local guides couldn't survive whatever's down there, what makes anyone think we'll fare better?'

'Because we are the Occultum,' said Seneca thoughtfully, studying the map that still lay open before him, 'and are not bound by normal tactics. We have always succeeded by adapting to circumstances that would destroy conventional forces.'

Talorcan leant forward, his Belgic pragmatism cutting

through the speculation.

'But this time we're not going alone. We'll be part of something much larger, much more visible. That changes everything about how we operate.'

'Does it?' Decimus asked. 'Or does it just give us better resources to work with? A legion can go places and do things that six men alone never could.'

'A legion can also get bogged down in logistics, politics, and procedure,' Marcus countered. 'How many times have we succeeded precisely because we could move fast and make decisions without consulting a command structure?'

Falco drained his wine cup and gestured for a refill from the hovering serving girl.

'Personally, I'd rather have four thousand legionaries watching my back when we're facing whatever killed two hundred men of the Twenty-First. There's something to be said for overwhelming force when the alternative is ending up as bleached bones in some African wasteland.'

'If we can find them,' Sica observed darkly. 'That map shows nothing useful beyond Syene. We'll be marching into territory that might as well be the edge of the world, following rumours and the fevered dreams of a dying man.'

'Panthera,' said Seneca the word quietly, as if testing its weight. 'Whatever that means, wherever it is, that's our destination. A place that supposedly holds survivors of an expedition that vanished years ago.'

The conversation lapsed into contemplative silence as each man considered the magnitude of what lay ahead. Outside, the sounds of Roman life continued, citizens going about their daily business while unaware that within this elegant villa, six men were contemplating a journey that would take them further from civilisation than any Roman had gone before.

'Do we have a choice?' Decimus asked finally, voicing the question they had all been avoiding.

'There's always a choice,' replied Seneca. 'We could refuse the mission and accept whatever consequences that brought.'

'Disbandment,' said Marcus flatly. 'Exile if we're fortunate. Execution if Claudius decides we've become unreliable.'

'So not really a choice at all,' Talorcan observed.

Falco set down his empty cup with more force than necessary.

'Then why are we even debating it? We've been given a mission by the emperor himself. It's a chance to redeem ourselves after the complications in Britannia with a full legion to support us instead of operating alone in hostile territory.'

'And possibly death in unknown lands,' Sica added quietly.

'We've faced that possibility before,' said Seneca, rolling up the map with careful precision. 'It comes with what we do.'

He looked around the table at his men, seeing his own resignation reflected in their faces. This wasn't the mission any of them would have chosen, but it was the mission they had been given. And despite the risks, despite the unknowns, despite the very real possibility that they might join the Twenty-First Rapax in whatever fate had befallen them, they would accept it. It was, as Lepidus had observed, exactly what the Occultum did best.

Chapter Four

Alexandria

The Mediterranean crossing had been mercifully calm, allowing the Occultum to recover from their hurried departure from Rome whilst enjoying the luxury of a properly provisioned military transport. The sea air and decent rations had done much to restore their spirits after the frustrating weeks of uncertainty in the crumbling Castra Veterana.

Alexandria's harbour greeted them with its familiar chaos of merchant vessels, military transports, and fishing boats, all competing for space along the massive stone quays that had made the city one of the empire's greatest trading centres. The smell of tar, fish, and exotic spices filled the air as they disembarked, their boots echoing against stones worn smooth by countless previous arrivals.

'It hasn't changed much since we were last here?' said Marcus, scanning the harbour.

'I agree,' said Seneca, noting the same mix of Roman efficiency and Egyptian commerce that had characterised the port during their previous visit. 'Though I suspect we'll have fewer complications this time.'

Falco grinned at the memory.

'No secret societies trying to murder us in our beds. No mysterious cults worshipping beetles in underground temples. Just a straightforward mission into unexplored territory with a full legion for support. This should be positively relaxing.'

Sica's expression remained impassive, but his eyes swept the crowds carefully, remembering how dangerous Alexandria could be beneath its civilised veneer. Their previous encounter with the Scarab conspiracy had taught them all that Egypt's apparent tranquillity could hide deadly currents.

'What about you?' Decimus asked, noticing Talorcan studying their surroundings with obvious unfamiliarity. 'Is this your first time in the jewel of the east?'

'It is,' said Talorcan, his gaze taking in the massive lighthouse that dominated the harbour approach. 'Though I've heard enough stories from the rest of you to feel as if I know it already.'

A thin man in a crisp tunic bearing the insignia of imperial administration waited at the harbour's edge, his sharp eyes identifying them without difficulty despite the crowds of soldiers and merchants moving through the port.

'Are you the men sent from Rome?' he asked without preamble. 'I am Gaius Scribonius Libo, secretary to Senator Lepidus. You are to accompany me immediately.'

Seneca nodded acknowledgement and they followed him through Alexandria's crowded streets, past the marble facades of temples and public buildings that proclaimed the city's wealth and Roman authority. For Seneca, Marcus, Falco, Sica, and Decimus, the route held familiar landmarks from their previous mission, though this time they walked openly rather than skulking through shadows in pursuit of conspirators. Talorcan, however, had not been with them then, and he found the place fascinating.

'Different when you're not hunting cultists,' Falco observed quietly as they passed a temple they had once surveyed. 'Almost civilised.'

'Let's hope it stays that way,' replied Seneca, remembering the violence that had marked their last visit to the city.

The route led away from the harbour district's commercial bustle toward a more orderly section where administrative necessity took precedence over architectural grandeur. The complex they entered sprawled across several acres, its high walls enclosing a miniature city dedicated to the efficient governance of Egypt.

'I don't remember this place,' said Sica, studying the well-ordered compound with interest.

'We never had reason to visit the administrative centre before,' Seneca explained. 'Our business was with darker corners of the city.'

Guard towers at regular intervals housed sentries whose vigilance seemed routine rather than urgent, their attention focused outward toward potential threats rather than inward toward the controlled chaos of imperial administration.

Within the walls, the compound buzzed with activity. Scribes hurried between buildings carrying scrolls and tablets, their arms full of the documentation that kept an empire functioning while slaves and freedmen hauled loads of supplies toward massive warehouses that stretched along the compound's eastern wall, their contents destined for outposts scattered across the African frontier.

'This is where Egypt is actually governed,' Libo explained as they walked between the orderly rows of buildings. 'The Governor has his palace across the city for ceremonial functions and entertaining. Here we handle the real work of keeping the province functioning.'

They passed a training ground where a cohort of legionaries conducted their morning exercises, their movements sharp and disciplined despite the growing heat. These were garrison troops, men whose primary concern was maintaining order and protecting the administrative apparatus rather than conducting active campaigning.

'How long has Egypt been peaceful?' Talorcan asked,

noting the relaxed atmosphere that pervaded the compound.

'Truly peaceful? Since Augustus incorporated it into the Empire,' Libo replied. 'There have been occasional disturbances, tribal raids from the south, disputes over trade routes, but nothing that threatened Roman control. Egypt understands the benefits of cooperation.'

Seneca, listening to this assessment, glanced at his more experienced comrades who exchanged knowing looks. They had seen firsthand how deceptive Alexandria's apparent tranquillity could be and how ancient resentments and foreign conspiracies could lurk beneath the surface of Roman order.

The truth of Libo's words, however, was evident everywhere they looked. Caravans moved freely through the compound's gates, their guards carrying weapons openly without causing alarm amongst the administrators who processed their papers. Egyptian merchants conducted business alongside Roman traders, their conversations conducted in the mixture of Latin, Greek, and local dialects that characterised a truly integrated province.

They paused before a substantial warehouse where workers loaded amphorae of wine onto ox-drawn carts whilst others unloaded bales of cotton and spices from pack animals still dusty from desert travel. The efficiency of the operation spoke of decades of established routine, and procedures refined through constant repetition.

'Supplies flow both directions,' Libo noted, following their gaze. 'Luxuries from Rome and the eastern provinces come south to our frontier garrisons, whilst African goods travel north to markets throughout the empire. It's a profitable arrangement for everyone involved.'

The barracks block they were assigned stood near the compound's centre, positioned to provide quick access to the administrative buildings whilst remaining separate from the main garrison facilities. It was a pragmatic choice that reflected their ambiguous status as elite operatives attached to imperial administration rather than conventional military forces.

The quarters themselves were designed for a standard contubernium, eight men sharing a common room with individual sleeping spaces arranged around a central area for equipment and social activities. For six men accustomed to far worse accommodations, it represented luxury approaching that of officers' quarters.

'You'll remain here until Senator Lepidus arrives to brief you further,' said Libo. 'Food will be provided from the garrison kitchens. Everything else you require can be obtained through proper channels, but you are not to leave the compound without authorisation.'

Marcus tested one of the sleeping couches, finding it substantially more comfortable than anything they had enjoyed since leaving Rome.

'How long until Lepidus arrives?' he asked.

'That hasn't been communicated to me,' replied Libo. 'My instructions are to ensure your comfort and security until he chooses to make contact. Beyond that, I know nothing of your purpose here.'

After their guide departed, the Occultum settled into their new quarters with something approaching enthusiasm. Equipment was again checked and organised, personal items arranged according to individual preference, and the familiar routines of military life reasserted themselves.

'Better than the rat-infested barracks in Rome,' Falco observed, stretching out on his assigned couch with obvious satisfaction. 'And considerably more pleasant than our last accommodation in this city. No underground chambers, no beetle-worshipping madmen, just proper Roman efficiency.'

'Don't get too comfortable,' Seneca warned, though he too appreciated their improved circumstances. 'This is just a way station. Whatever we're really here to do won't involve lounging in administrative compounds.'

Through the open windows, they could hear the constant activity of the compound continuing around them. Voices calling orders, cart wheels rumbling across stone, the distant sound of marching feet as guard details conducted their rounds. It was the sound of an empire at work, efficient and confident in its authority.

As evening approached and lamps were lit throughout the complex, the Occultum prepared for another period of waiting. They had grown accustomed to the intervals between missions, the bureaucratic delays that preceded action, the careful planning that attempted to anticipate unknown dangers.

But they knew that somewhere in this bustling administrative centre, decisions were being made that would determine their fate. Maps were being studied, supplies allocated, and orders written and sealed with imperial authority. Soon enough, they would learn what role they were expected to play in whatever grand design had brought them to Egypt, but for now, they could only wait and prepare themselves for whatever challenges lay ahead in the vast territories beyond Alexandria's walls.

Chapter Five

Alexandria

Two days passed in restless anticipation and Seneca found himself pacing the narrow confines of their shared quarters like a caged leopard. His men had taken to dice games and idle conversation, but the forced inactivity was wearing on them all. They were soldiers, not merchants waiting for favourable winds.

The message they had been waiting for arrived at midday, carried by a dust-covered courier. Seneca broke the seal with eager fingers, recognizing Lepidus's familiar hand.

Seneca – I have proceeded south to Syene to organize the legion you are to accompany. Situation more complex than anticipated. Secure passage south immediately. Time is of the essence. – Lepidus

Seneca read the brief message twice, then crumpled it in frustration.

'More complex than anticipated' - what did that mean? Were they walking into a trap? A full-scale revolt? The Senator's 's usual verbose style had been replaced by military brevity that told him nothing of what lay ahead.

'So? asked Falco, noting his commander's expression.

'We're to find our own passage south to Syene,' said Seneca. 'Lepidus has gone ahead.'

Falco picked up the crumpled message and passed it to his comrades to read. After weeks of following orders they barely understood, being kept in the dark had become a particular source of irritation.

'Well,' said Falco, 'at least it means we have some time

to ourselves before we sail. We could go into the city and see something of Alexandria beyond these warehouse walls.'

Seneca shook his head immediately.

'Too risky. We don't know who might be watching, and we can't afford to draw attention.'

But even as he spoke, he could see the disappointed faces around him. Marcus shifted uncomfortably while Decimus let out a barely audible sigh of disappointment. Even Sica looked as though he might actually argue the point.

'Come now, Seneca,' Falco pressed, his tone carefully respectful but persuasive. 'We've had a difficult few months. We've been beaten up by barbarians, cooped up like prisoners, and are about to head off to our deaths in some unknown corner of a world. Surely we deserve some time off?'

'Falco's right,' Marcus added quietly. 'We've earned it.'

The others nodded agreement, and Seneca found himself facing what amounted to a gentle mutiny. He looked at their faces, good soldiers all, who had followed him without question through situations that would have broken lesser men. Perhaps they did deserve better than to spend their last free hours staring at warehouse walls.

'Very well,' he said finally, raising a hand to forestall their celebrations. 'But only after we've secured passage. And I want everyone ready to move at a moment's notice.'

The transformation was immediate. Shoulders straightened, spirits lifted, and suddenly the cramped quarters seemed less oppressive. They set about packing their kit with renewed energy, placing everything ready for departure the following day before making their way toward the docks.

The harbour district of Alexandria assaulted the senses, a maze of warehouses, counting houses, and taverns that serviced the greatest port in the Mediterranean. The air was thick with the smell of tar, fish, and exotic spices, while the babel of voices spoke in a dozen languages. Seneca moved through the chaos with practiced efficiency, seeking a captain willing to take passengers south along the Nile.

It took the better part of an hour, but eventually he found what he needed, a grain barge making the return journey to Syene, her captain willing to take paying passengers for the right price. The negotiations were brief but expensive; river travel was not cheap, and the captain had recognised Roman military bearing despite their civilian clothes.

'Dawn departure,' the captain had confirmed, pocketing Seneca's silver. 'And any man not aboard when we cast off stays behind.'

Seneca rejoined his men at a nearby tavern, a respectable establishment that catered to merchants and ship captains rather than the rougher waterfront crowd. The wine was good, the food edible, and the atmosphere relaxed. As he settled beside Falco at a corner table, he caught the look in his comrade's eye, a familiar gleam that usually preceded trouble.

'Whatever you're planning,' said Seneca quietly, 'don't.'

Falco adopted an expression of wounded innocence.

'Me? I am offended by your insinuation. I'm merely contemplating the excellent vintage of my wine and the pleasant company of my fellow soldiers.'

'Falco…' responded Seneca, his tone an unmistakable warning.

'I swear by all the gods,' said Falco, 'I'll be on my best behaviour. Just a cup of good wine, two at the most and we'll be back at the barracks with plenty of time to spare.'

Seneca studied Falco's face, noting the careful sincerity that didn't quite reach his eyes. In their years together, he had learned to read Falco's moods like a weather-wise sailor reads the sky. The man was planning something, but what?

'Two cups,' said Seneca finally. 'And I'm holding you to that oath. We sail at dawn, and I won't have you swimming out to catch the barge because you were too drunk to walk.'

'You have my word,' replied Falco. 'Best behaviour.'

Seneca remained dubious, but there was little more he could do. He took Falco at his word, settled back in his chair, and tried to ignore the growing certainty that before the night was over, that word would be thoroughly tested.

Three hours later, Seneca's certainty proved entirely justified. The tavern had filled as evening approached, drawing merchants and sailors seeking good wine and better company after long days of honest labour. The atmosphere had grown convivial, with conversations flowing as freely as the wine, and somewhere in that pleasant haze of alcohol and camaraderie, Falco's promise of restraint had evaporated like morning mist.

'Two cups,' Marcus muttered, watching Falco attempt to charm a serving girl whilst simultaneously engaging two Alexandrian merchants in increasingly boisterous conversation. 'He's had at least ten, and that's only what I've counted.'

'Look at him,' said Decimus with a mixture of admiration and concern. 'He's telling them about the time he fought three lions in the Circus Flavius.'

'Did he ever actually fight three lions?' asked Talorcan.

'Not simultaneously,' Sica replied. 'And they were quite small lions. Practically cubs, really.'

Seneca watched with growing alarm as Falco demonstrated his supposed lion-fighting technique, using a wine cup as an improvised shield whilst wielding a piece of bread as a gladius. The merchants were laughing

37

appreciatively, but several other patrons had begun to take notice of the loud Roman who was steadily commandeering more of the tavern's attention.

'Perhaps we should suggest a return to quarters,' said Marcus diplomatically.

Before Seneca could respond, Falco's voice boomed across the tavern.

'And then,' he declared, climbing unsteadily up onto his chair, 'the crowd rose as one man! *Falco!*' they cried. 'Falco the Magnificent! Falco the Unconquerable! The emperor himself threw down his purple cloak as tribute to my prowess!'

'Which Emperor was this?' asked one of the merchants with suspicious politeness.

'All of them!' replied Falco expansively. 'Every Emperor who ever lived came to witness my legendary skills! Even the dead ones rose from their graves to applaud!'

Seneca closed his eyes. This was precisely the sort of attention they couldn't afford.

'I think,' he said quietly, 'it's time to collect our hero and depart.'

But as he rose from his seat, Falco chose that moment to attempt an elaborate gladiatorial manoeuvre that involved spinning dramatically whilst still balanced on his chair.

The chair collapsed, sending him tumbling backwards into a table occupied by several large men whose clothing and bearing suggested they earned their living through less than civilised means. Wine cups flew, food scattered, and suddenly the tavern's pleasant atmosphere transformed into something considerably more dangerous.

'You clumsy Roman pig!' snarled the largest of the men, a Nubian whose muscles suggested he could probably lift a small building. 'Look what you've done to our dinner!'

Falco, sprawled amongst the wreckage of the table, attempted to focus his wine-addled vision on his accuser. When he spoke, his words carried the careful precision of a very drunk man trying to sound sober.

'My profound apologies, good sir. Allow me to purchase replacement refreshments for you and your... distinguished colleagues.'

'You'll purchase nothing, you drunken fool,' replied the man, 'you'll crawl out of here on your belly like the worm you are!'

The suggestion did not sit well with Falco's inebriated sense of dignity.

'Crawl?' he repeated, struggling to his feet with obvious difficulty. 'Did you just suggest that Falco the Magnificent should crawl? Falco, whose very name strikes terror into the hearts of gladiators throughout the Empire?'

'I've never heard of you,' the Nubian replied flatly.

'Then clearly your education has been sadly neglected!' Falco declared, swaying dangerously as he attempted another dramatic pose. 'Perhaps I should provide a practical demonstration of my legendary prowess!'

He swung a wild punch that missed his target by several feet and instead connected solidly with an entirely innocent merchant who had been trying to edge away from the developing confrontation. The merchant staggered backwards into another table, which promptly collapsed under his weight, sending more food and drink flying.

'Oh, wonderful,' Marcus muttered. 'Now we have a proper riot starting.'

Within moments, the tavern erupted into complete chaos. Men who had been enjoying peaceful drinks suddenly found themselves ducking flying furniture whilst others enthusiastically joined the brawl for reasons that had nothing to do with the original insult. Falco, meanwhile, stood in the centre of the maelstrom like a drunken colossus, swinging enthusiastically at anyone within reach whilst remaining blissfully unaware that most of his punches were connecting with empty air.

'Should we help?' asked Talorcan, watching him attempt to grapple with a man half his size whilst a much larger opponent prepared to club him with a wooden stool.

'We should get him out of here before the vigiles arrive,' replied Seneca grimly, noting that someone near the tavern's entrance was already shouting for the authorities.

The Occultum moved through the melee, carving a path through towards their beleaguered comrade. Marcus grabbed a wine pitcher and used it to discourage an overly enthusiastic brawler, whilst Decimus, who over the years had taken part in more than his fair share of bar fights, used a broken chair leg to clear a route towards Falco's position.

'Time to go!' Seneca shouted over the din, seizing Falco's arm and attempting to guide him towards the door.

'Go?' replied Falco indignantly, his words badly slurred. 'But I'm winning! Look how they flee before my mighty prowess!'

The men in question were not so much fleeing as regrouping for a coordinated assault, but before they could implement their strategy, the sound of military boots on stone announced the arrival of the city watch.

'Roman guards!' someone shouted near the entrance. 'The vigiles are coming!'

'Now we really need to leave,' said Marcus urgently.

They half-carried, half-dragged Falco towards the tavern's rear exit, leaving behind a scene of magnificent destruction that would be talked about in Alexandria's drinking establishments for years to come. Tables lay overturned, wine stained the floors in abstract patterns, and several dozen men continued to punch each other with the dedicated enthusiasm of people who had found an excellent excuse to settle old grievances.

The cool night air hit them like a blessing as they emerged into the alley behind the tavern though Falco swayed dangerously, squinting at his surroundings in confusion.

'Did we win?' he asked hopefully.

'Gloriously,' Sica replied dryly. 'Your legend grows by the hour.'

'Excellent!' Falco declared, then promptly staggered sideways into a wall.

They moved quickly through Alexandria's winding streets, staying to the shadows whilst the sounds of continued conflict echoed from the tavern behind them. Seneca found himself caught between genuine concern for their situation and an almost irrepressible urge to laugh at the absurdity of it all.

'At least he kept his promise about the wine,' Decimus observed as they navigated a narrow side street. 'He did say two cups. He just didn't specify the size of the cups.'

'Those weren't cups,' Marcus corrected. 'Those were amphorae disguised as drinking vessels.'

'Details,' Falco mumbled, listing heavily against Talorcan's supporting arm. 'Technical details. The important thing is that I maintained my dignity throughout the entire proceedings.'

They paused at the edge of the administrative compound, its gates still open but guarded by sentries who would certainly notice their condition. In the distance, they could hear shouts and the clash of weapons as the vigiles dealt with the continuing tavern brawl.

Seneca thought frantically, realising the true scope of their problem. Falco, even in his current dishevelled state, was an unmistakable figure. His size, his scars, his general appearance, everything about him would make him easily identifiable to anyone who cared to investigate the evening's disturbances.

'Sica,' he said quietly, his mind racing through the implications. 'Get him out of here. Clean him up, sober him up, and meet us at the boat tomorrow morning. Whatever you have to do, just make sure he's not connected to tonight's entertainment.'

Sica nodded his understanding, already calculating routes through the city that would avoid the main thoroughfares where patrols might be searching for drunken Romans.

'What about you?' he asked.

'We'll return to quarters like responsible soldiers who spent a quiet evening discussing family life,' replied Seneca. 'With any luck, no one will think to question men who were clearly never involved in tavern brawls.'

'Tavern brawl?' Falco repeated, focusing on the conversation with obvious difficulty. 'Did someone mention a tavern brawl? Because I should probably point out that I am undefeated in tavern brawls. Legendary, even. There was this one time in Gaul...'

'Save the stories for tomorrow,' said Sica firmly, taking charge of their inebriated comrade. 'Right now, we need to make you disappear.'

As the two men melted into Alexandria's shadows, Seneca led the rest of his team back towards the compound gates. Behind them, the sounds of conflict were gradually subsiding as the vigiles restored order to the district.

'Think he'll be all right?' Marcus asked as they approached the sentries.

'It's Falco,' replied Seneca. 'He's survived everything from arena lions to British druids. I suspect one evening of Alexandrian hospitality won't be the end of him.'

'And if they connect him to the fight?'

'Then we'll deal with that problem when it arises,' said Seneca firmly. 'For now, we're just soldiers returning from a quiet evening of cultural appreciation.'

The guards nodded respectfully as they passed through the gates, their professional bearing suggesting nothing more interesting than a group of ordinary legionaries returning to quarters. Behind them, Alexandria's night continued its ancient rhythms, albeit with one more evening of chaos and mayhem added to the city's endless collection of stories.

Somewhere in the darkness, Sica was undoubtedly explaining to Falco exactly why discretion was currently more important than legend-building, and tomorrow, they would all sail south towards whatever destiny awaited them beyond the cataracts. But for now, Seneca reflected as they made their way back to their barracks, at least they had one final reminder of why life with the Occultum was never boring.

Chapter Six

Alexandria

The pre-dawn air carried a chill that would soon be burned away by the Egyptian sun, but for now it provided welcome relief from the oppressive heat that would dominate the day ahead. Seneca stood on the dock beside their hired barge, watching the captain's crew make their final preparations for departure whilst keeping one eye on the approaches to the harbour.

The grain barge *Isis* was a practical vessel built for commerce rather than comfort, her broad beam designed to carry maximum cargo with minimum draught for navigating the Nile's seasonal variations. Amphorae of wine and oil were being secured in the hold alongside bales of cotton and other trade goods destined for the markets upriver.

'Any sign of them?' Marcus asked quietly, settling his sarcina amongst the supplies they had loaded aboard.

'None,' replied Seneca. 'But they'll appear when they need to. They always do.'

The captain, a weathered Egyptian whose skin had been turned to leather by decades of river work, approached to talk to Seneca.

'We leave with the morning breeze,' he announced in heavily accented Latin, gesturing towards the eastern horizon where the first hints of dawn were beginning to show. 'River conditions are good.'

Seneca nodded acknowledgement whilst continuing to scan the dock area. Somewhere in Alexandria's maze of streets, Sica was presumably dealing with whatever state Falco had achieved after his evening of cultural appreciation. The Syrian's resourcefulness was legendary, but even he might be challenged by Falco's capacity for creating complicated situations out of thin air.

Among the cargo already loaded, carefully concealed beneath rolls of sailcloth and coils of rope, lay two extra sets of military equipment. Sica and Falco's sarcinae had been smuggled aboard through the simple expedient of bribing a dock worker to include them amongst the legitimate supplies. To any casual inspection, they would appear to be nothing more than additional trade goods bound for upriver markets.

'Strange to be travelling without the full team,' Decimus observed, checking the security of his own gear whilst keeping his voice low enough to avoid the captain's attention.

'We've operated in smaller groups before,' replied Marcus. 'Remember Germania? We were scattered across half the province for three weeks before we managed to regroup.'

'That was different,' said Decimus. 'That was enemy action. This is Falco being Falco.'

Talorcan listened to this exchange with obvious interest. The previous evening's events had provided him with an excellent introduction to the sort of complications that seemed to follow the Occultum wherever they went.

'Does this happen often?' he asked.

'More often than Seneca would like, less often than it could,' Marcus answered diplomatically.

The conversation was interrupted by a commotion from the dock's landward approach as a small group of figures approached through the morning mist, their military bearing unmistakable even at a distance. At their head strode a Roman officer whilst behind him marched half a dozen legionnaires in full kit.

'Damn,' said Seneca quietly, recognising the urban

cohort's equipment and organisation. 'Someone's been asking questions.'

The patrol's leader proved to be a Decurion whose uniform was immaculate despite the early hour, his equipment bearing the sort of polish that suggested he spent considerable time ensuring his appearance met the highest standards of military presentation. Behind him walked a civilian whose condition told its own story, one arm supported by a sling, his face bearing a spectacular collection of bruises that painted his features in shades of purple and yellow.

'You there!' the Decurion called as his patrol approached the barge. 'Are you the men who chartered passage for this vessel?'

Seneca stepped forward, his face assuming a composed air of curious innocence.

'We are. Me and my men are travelling south on imperial business. Is there some problem?'

The Decurion's eyes swept over the group with, noting their military bearing.

'Indeed there is,' he replied. 'We're searching for a man involved in a serious assault last evening. Large fellow, scarred, speaks with the arrogance typical of gladiators. Witnesses place him with a group of soldiers matching your description.'

The injured civilian stepped forward, his good arm gesturing angrily whilst his words came thick with pain and outrage.

'That's them! I recognise these faces from the tavern. Where's the big one, the one who broke my arm? I demand justice!'

Seneca winced at the man's injuries. Falco's arena training remained evident even when he was too drunk to stand properly.

'I'm afraid you're mistaken, citizen,' he replied with courteous concern. 'We did encounter such a man last evening, but only briefly. He claimed to be some sort of gladiatorial champion. Loud fellow, rather full of himself. But we had no previous acquaintance with him and no idea where he went after we parted company.'

Marcus nodded his supporting agreement.

'Seemed the sort who'd make enemies easily enough, though. All that boasting about fighting lions and emperors throwing cloaks. Clearly not the sort of company respectable soldiers would choose to keep.'

'Emperors throwing cloaks?' the Decurion repeated with obvious scepticism.

'His words, not ours,' Decimus added helpfully. 'Said something about all the dead emperors rising from their graves to applaud his prowess. We assumed he was either drunk or mad. Possibly both.'

The injured man's face flushed with renewed anger.

'They're lying! These are his accomplices. They were all there when he attacked me!'

The Decurion held up his hand for silence, studying the group with calculating eyes.

'Nevertheless,' he said, 'I must insist on searching your vessel. If this man is hiding amongst your cargo, we'll find him.'

'Of course,' replied Seneca immediately. 'We have nothing to hide. Search wherever you wish.'

The captain, who had been watching this exchange with obvious unhappiness, gestured reluctantly towards his cargo hold.

'Be quick about it. The morning breeze is rising.'

The legionnaires spread out across the barge, their search systematic but respectful of the cargo's careful

47

arrangement. They checked behind amphorae, beneath sailcloth, inside coils of rope, anywhere a man might conceivably hide. The concealed military equipment drew no particular attention, appearing as it did to be simply more trade goods amongst the legitimate cargo.

After a thorough search, the soldiers regrouped near the gangplank as one of them approached their leader with the unwelcome news.

'Nothing, Decurio. No sign of the man we're looking for.'

The Decurion's expression suggested he had expected this outcome but remained dissatisfied with it. He turned back to Seneca.

'Very well. But understand this. If this man should reappear, you are required by law to take him into custody and deliver him to the nearest Roman outpost for questioning. The man he assaulted is the son of a very senior official, and this matter will not be overlooked.'

'Of course,' replied Seneca with earnest sincerity. 'Should we encounter him again, we'll certainly ensure he faces proper justice for his actions.'

'See that you do,' the Decurion said sternly. 'Roman law extends throughout the Empire, and no one, gladiator or otherwise, is above its reach.'

As the patrol departed with their wounded civilian companion casting resentful glances back at the barge, the captain ordered his crew to cast off. The morning breeze had indeed risen, filling the vessel's modest sail that would carry them south towards their appointment with whatever awaited them beyond the cataracts.

'Well handled,' Marcus observed quietly as Alexandria's harbour began to recede behind them.

'Falco causes me more stress than all the tribes of Britannia together,' replied Seneca, watching the city's walls grow smaller in the distance.

The barge settled into the comfortable rhythm of river travel, her crew adjusting sail and steering to take best advantage of the wind whilst her passengers found spots amongst the cargo where they could rest without interfering with the vessel's operation. The Nile stretched ahead of them, its brown waters carrying them towards the frontier and whatever lay beyond.

'I wonder where they are,' said Marcus, settling against a stack of grain sacks whilst watching the Egyptian countryside slide past.

'They'll reappear,' Seneca assured him, his voice carrying the confidence of long experience. 'Probably when we least expect them.'

Behind them, Alexandria continued its ancient routines, unaware that it had just played host to the beginning of an expedition that would test the limits of Roman ambition and courage. Ahead lay Syene, the frontier, and the vast unknown territories where answers to old mysteries waited to be discovered.

The morning passed peacefully as the barge made steady progress against the Nile's gentle current, and as her crew worked the sail and steering oars, the Egyptian countryside rolled past in its timeless rhythm, mud-brick villages, palm groves, and fields of grain that stretched towards the distant desert hills.

Seneca had begun to relax, enjoying the simple pleasure of river travel after the complications of their departure from Alexandria. The sun climbed towards its zenith, warming his face whilst a gentle breeze kept the heat bearable. Around him, his men had settled into the comfortable routine of soldiers in transit, checking equipment, dozing in whatever shade they could find, or simply watching the ancient land slip by.

Marcus sat against a sack of grain, half asleep in the afternoon sun when a familiar voice in the distance drew him from his comfortable slumber. He opened his eyes with a sigh and sat up to stare towards the distant riverbank, hardly able to believe what he saw.

'Seneca,' he said, shading his eyes against the sun's glare, 'look.'

Seneca looked across the brown waters where a dust cloud marked the progress of a cart moving parallel to their course. As he watched, the distant figure sitting in the back of the cart began waving enthusiastically, shouting something that carried across the water despite the distance.

'Can you make out what they're saying?' he asked.

Before Marcus could respond, Decimus let out a bark of incredulous laughter.

'By Jupiter's beard, it's them!'

As the barge continued its steady progress, the scene on the shore resolved itself with startling clarity. A simple cart bumped along the river road, guided by what appeared to be a local Egyptian leading a patient mule. But it was the cart's passengers that drew their astonished attention.

Sica sat on the driver's bench with characteristic composure, his dark features showing no sign of the previous evening's complications. Behind him, lounging against grain sacks with obvious contentment, Falco held up a large amphora and took a generous swallow before waving it in their direction like a battle standard.

'Ahoy, my brothers!' his voice boomed across the water,

carrying with remarkable clarity despite the distance. 'Behold how the gods provide for faithful soldiers!'

Decimus shook his head in disbelief.

'He's still drinking,' he said, not sure if he was impressed or angry. 'This doesn't bode well.'

Seneca felt his jaw tighten as he struggled to maintain his composure. Relief at seeing his men safe warred with frustration at Falco's apparent inability to recognise when discretion might be advisable. The sight of him celebrating their reunion with wine was both typical and maddening in equal measure.

'How did they even get a cart?' asked Talorcan, 'and why did Sica allow him to get more wine?'

From the shore, Falco's voice carried clearly across the water again as he gestured expansively with his amphora.

'Fear not, noble comrades! We have secured excellent transportation through my legendary powers of persuasion! This fine vehicle will convey us to our destination in comfort worthy of heroes!'

Seneca cupped his hands and called back across the water.

'Just head for the next dock! We'll pick you up there!'

'Excellent plan!' Falco shouted back, raising his amphora in salute. 'Though I should mention that someone will need to pay for the cart! We seem to have exhausted our financial resources during the procurement process!'

The admission was delivered with such cheerful unconcern that Seneca found himself torn between laughter and exasperation. Behind him, his men made no effort to hide their amusement at the situation, their chuckles and muttered comments providing a soundtrack of barely contained hilarity.

'Of course they have no money left,' said Marcus,

grinning despite himself. 'Why am I not surprised?'

'How much could a cart and mule cost?' said Decimus.

'More than Falco had, apparently,' replied Marcus.

Seneca turned away from the spectacle, seeking the captain who was watching the proceedings with obvious bewilderment.

'The next dock,' said Seneca with as much dignity as he could manage. 'We need to collect those two... travellers.'

The captain nodded slowly, his expression suggesting he had seen many strange things during his years on the river but few quite as peculiar as this.

'As you wish,' he said, with a sigh, 'though I hope your friends understand that I cannot carry livestock aboard my vessel.'

'I'll sort it out,' replied Seneca, though privately he wondered exactly what sort of arrangement Falco had made and how much it was going to cost to resolve.

From the shore, another cheerful shout reached them.

'Tell the captain not to worry about the wine! I'm bringing enough to share!'

Seneca closed his eyes and counted slowly to ten, a technique that had served him well through years of working with Falco. When he opened them again, the cart was still there, Falco was still drinking, and Sica was still attempting to manage whatever situation Falco had created through his unique approach to problem-solving.

'This,' he muttered to himself, 'is going to be a very long expedition.'

Chapter Seven

The Nile

The reunion at the small riverside dock provided considerable entertainment for the crew and passengers alike. Falco, now clutching two amphorae with obvious pride, had negotiated the transfer from cart to barge with the elaborate dignity of a man determined to prove he was entirely sober despite overwhelming evidence to the contrary.

'The mule was quite fond of me,' he announced as Sica guided him aboard. 'We had several philosophical discussions during our journey. Intelligent creature, really. Better conversationalist than most Senators.'

'I'm sure it was fascinated by your wisdom,' replied Seneca dryly, counting out silver to pay the bemused Egyptian who had provided the cart. The sum was considerably larger than he had anticipated, but given the fact he had brought his men to safety, he paid without complaint.

As the barge resumed its journey south, the captain casting frequent glances at their unconventional passengers, the Occultum settled once more into the comfortable rhythm of river travel. The Nile stretched ahead of them, its brown waters carrying them towards destinations that grew more exotic with each passing mile.

The following day brought them past the familiar sights of Lower Egypt, where organised agriculture and Roman administration had transformed the ancient land into a model of provincial efficiency. Fields of grain stretched to the horizon on both sides, their neat boundaries marked by irrigation channels that had regulated the river's bounty for countless generations.

'Look at that,' said Marcus, pointing towards a massive temple complex that dominated the eastern bank. The limestone walls rose in perfect proportion, their surfaces covered with hieroglyphic inscriptions that seemed to writhe and dance in the afternoon light.

'How old do you think it is?'

'Old enough to make Rome look like a frontier settlement,' replied Decimus, noting the precision of the stonework. 'Some of these temples were ancient when Caesar was still learning his letters.'

Falco, who had finally agreed to share his amphora with his comrades, squinted at the passing monument, trying desperately to appear more sober than he actually was.

'Beautiful stonework,' he pronounced carefully. 'Very... rectangular. Lots of pictures of birds and such. Probably tells the story of some Egyptian hero. Like me, but with more feathers.'

'Those aren't just pictures, you great oaf,' said Sica with exasperation. 'That's Egyptian writing. Each symbol has meaning, tells stories, records deeds.'

'Writing with pictures?' Falco considered this concept with the gravity it clearly deserved. 'Seems inefficient. Why not just use proper letters like civilised people?'

'Because they were writing when your ancestors were still learning which end of a spear was dangerous,' Talorcan observed, earning chuckles from the others.

As the days progressed, the scale and grandeur of Egypt's ancient monuments continued to astonish them. Temple followed temple, each one a testament to engineering skills and civilisations reaching back into the mists of time.

Massive stone sphinxes gazed across the water with expressions of eternal patience, whilst obelisks reached towards the sky like fingers pointing to the gods.

'Makes you think,' said Marcus quietly, watching a particularly magnificent temple complex slide past. 'Here we are, citizens of the greatest empire the world has ever known, and we're looking at buildings that were already ancient when Rome was founded.'

'More than ancient,' agreed Seneca. 'These people were building monuments to last forever when our ancestors were still living in mud huts. Imagine what they probably knew that we've forgotten.'

The statement hung in the air unanswered as the barge continued its stately progress southward, while around them, the evidence of Egypt's incredible antiquity mounted with each passing day.

As evening approached a few days into their journey, and the crew prepared to moor for the night, Falco, now sober at last, made an observation that surprised them with its insight.

'You know what's strange?' he said. 'All these temples, all this grandeur, and yet Egypt fell to Alexander without much of a fight. Then to us without much more. How does a civilisation that can build monuments like these become so... helpless?'

'Age,' Sica replied thoughtfully. 'Everything grows old eventually, even empires.'

The statement provoked uncomfortable silence. The idea that their own mighty empire might someday follow Egypt into decline was not one they cared to contemplate.

'Rome is different,' said Marcus finally, though his tone carried less conviction than his words. 'We adapt, we learn, we grow stronger through conquest. Look how we've made Egypt a part of ourselves whilst preserving what was best about it.'

'But have you preserved it?' asked Talorcan. 'Or are you just living amongst the ruins of something you don't really understand?'

Each day brought new wonders and deeper unease, as the monuments grew more exotic the further they travelled from Alexandria's Hellenistic influence. Here, the pure Egyptian style dominated, speaking of concepts and beliefs that seemed almost alien to Roman minds accustomed to practical engineering and rational organisation.

'Look at the size of those columns,' said Decimus, pointing towards a temple whose massive pillars dwarfed even the grandest Roman architecture. 'How did they even move stones that large?'

'More importantly,' Seneca added, 'why did they need them so large? What were they trying to prove?'

'Maybe they were compensating for something,' said Falco. 'You know how it is with powerful men, the bigger the monument, the smaller the actual power. Like those tiny emperors who build enormous palaces.'

'Or maybe,' suggested Decimus, 'they understood something about permanence that we don't. These buildings have lasted thousands of years. How many Roman monuments will still be standing just a few years from now?'

It was another uncomfortable question that none of them cared to answer.

Over the following days, they progressed deeper into Middle Egypt, where the Nile narrowed, and the desert pressed closer to the river's life-giving waters. Here, the contrast between ancient grandeur and present reality became even more pronounced and as the ancient monuments seemed to press closer, their massive presence creating an almost physical weight in the air, the Occultum found themselves speaking more quietly, as if the stones themselves demanded respect for their age and majesty.

'You know what troubles me most?' said Marcus as they watched another temple complex slide past in the golden light of late afternoon. 'We're Romans. We pride ourselves on being practical, on understanding how things work, but looking at these monuments, I have to admit - I have no idea how they built them. The engineering, the organisation, the sheer scale of the effort required...'

'It certainly makes you wonder,' agreed Decimus. 'Not just about the techniques, but the knowledge behind them. The mathematics, the astronomy, the understanding of materials and forces.'

'Perhaps that's why we're here,' said Talorcan. 'Not just to find some lost legion, but to rediscover what Egypt once knew. Maybe that's what this Panthera place represents, a chance to regain knowledge lost for generations.'

'Knowledge can be more dangerous than gold,' Sica warned quietly. 'Some things are lost for good reasons.'

As they reached the last part of their voyage, the character of the landscape changed significantly. The rich agricultural land that had characterised their journey gave way to something harsher, more obviously touched by the desert that stretched endlessly to the east and west. Palm groves became scarcer, villages further apart, and the ancient monuments seemed to crouch lower against the horizon as if seeking shelter from the increasing desolation.

'How much further to Syene?' asked Seneca

'Another day, perhaps two,' the captain replied, his weathered features showing the strain of navigating increasingly difficult waters. 'The river grows more dangerous here, rocks, rapids, and currents that can dash a boat to pieces if you're not careful.'

As if to emphasise his words, they passed the wreckage of another barge that had been driven onto the rocky eastern shore during a storm. The cargo had long since been stolen or scattered, but the broken hull served as a reminder that the Nile, for all its life-giving properties, remained a force of nature that demanded respect.

'Comforting,' muttered Falco. 'Nothing like the sight of shipwrecks to boost morale before entering unknown territory.'

'At least we know we're getting close to the frontier,' observed Seneca. 'These aren't trading waters anymore. From here on, everything becomes more dangerous.'

The truth of his words became evident as their journey continued and they began to encounter the cataracts that marked the transition from the civilised Nile to the wild river that flowed from the heart of Africa. Rocky outcroppings forced the water into narrow channels where it rushed with dangerous force, whilst the sound of rushing water provided a constant reminder of the power that lay just beneath the Nile's normally placid surface.

Eventually, the captain pointed towards a distant smudge on the eastern horizon. 'There lies Syene' he said with obvious relief, 'and the end of the journey for my poor boat.'

In the distance, they could make out the walls and towers of the frontier fortress that marked the southernmost extent of Roman Egypt. Beyond it, the river continued its course into lands that appeared on no Roman maps, territories where few civilised men had ventured and fewer still had returned to tell the tale.

As the barge approached the docks of Syene, the Occultum gathered their equipment and prepared to disembark. Behind them lay the ancient wonders of Egypt, monuments to a civilisation that had touched the gods and built for eternity. Ahead lay the unknown territories where their mission would truly begin.

The contrast was striking and somehow ominous. They were leaving behind the accumulated wisdom and grandeur of millennia to venture into lands where Roman law held no sway, and Roman engineering had built no roads. Whatever waited for them beyond the frontier would test not just their military skills, but their understanding of what it meant to be Roman in a world that predated Rome by thousands of years.

In the distance, beyond the town, they could see the walls of the legionary fortress where their mission would truly begin. But the image that lingered in their minds was not of Roman military efficiency, but of ancient temples reaching towards an eternal sky, built by a people who had understood something about permanence that modern Romans were still struggling to comprehend.

Chapter Eight

Syene

As their barge approached the dock, the Occultum could see that the normally quiet frontier post was alive with unprecedented activity.

Boats of every description crowded the waterfront, military transports unloading equipment, supply barges heavy with grain and oil, and smaller craft bringing food and wine in massive amphorae.

But it wasn't just river traffic that had transformed the sleepy border post. Desert caravans stretched in dusty lines beyond the harbour, their camels and donkeys laden with goods that had arrived via trade routes reaching deep into Africa. Nubian merchants haggled with Roman buyers over supplies, whilst Blemmye traders offered strings of ostrich feathers and leather goods worked with intricate patterns.

'Well,' observed Falco, shouldering his pack as they disembarked, 'this is busier than I expected.'

They pushed through the crowds of soldiers, merchants, and labourers, expecting to find someone waiting to receive them, but the officials who were trying their best to control the chaos seemed more concerned with managing the flow of traffic than welcoming new arrivals.

Taking matters into his own hands, Seneca led his team out of the town and across the hard ground towards the fortress. Eventually, they reached the gates and reported to the centurion in charge.

'Tribune Seneca,' he announced. 'Here as ordered by Senator Lepidus.'

The centurion barely glanced up from his tablet.

'Right, yes, very good. Find yourselves quarters somewhere and report to... someone. I'll get back to you when I can work out where you're supposed to be.'

'And where exactly are we supposed to find quarters?' replied Seneca.

'Anywhere you can,' the centurion replied distractedly, already turning his attention to the next crisis demanding his attention. 'The place is packed to the walls so try the abandoned temple complex down by the quarries if you're desperate.'

Left to their own devices, the Occultum found what shade they could against the fortress wall and settled down to wait whilst Seneca went in search of someone with actual authority. Around them, the controlled chaos of military preparation continued at pace, suggesting urgent deadlines were driving the operation.

'Do you think Lepidus is inside somewhere,' asked Talorcan, watching a train of pack mules loaded with supplies make their way through the gates.

'Either that, or he's already moved on,' said Marcus. 'This doesn't look like the sort of operation that waits for late arrivals.'

Sica studied the mix of people flowing through the fortress with professional interest. 'Look at the faces,' he said quietly. 'Half these men have never seen anything like this before. Whatever they're planning, it's bigger than anyone expected.'

It took Seneca the better part of an hour to locate someone with both authority and time to speak with him. The Optio he finally cornered was a sweating, flustered man, pushed beyond his normal limits by extraordinary circumstances.

'Tribune Seneca?' the Optio repeated, consulting a wax tablet covered with notes in several different hands. 'Yes, yes, you were expected days ago. Where have you been?'

'River travel takes time,' replied Seneca diplomatically, 'but we're here now. Where are we supposed to stay?'

'That's... complicated,' the Optio said, wiping sweat from his forehead with the back of his hand. 'Not here, that's for sure, perhaps it's better if I show you. Follow me.'

They climbed the stone steps that led to the fortress ramparts, passing guards who nodded recognition to the Optio whilst continuing their vigilant watch over the surrounding countryside. The walls of the fortress provided an excellent vantage point from which to observe the Nile's approach through the rocky landscape of the First Cataract, but it was what lay to the south that would explain everything.

'Out there,' said the Optio, pointing towards the ground that sloped away from the fortress towards the desert horizon.

Seneca looked in the direction indicated, and his breath caught in his throat.

To the south and east, where the desert stretched endlessly towards the unknown heart of Africa, a vast military encampment spread across the landscape like a city conjured from canvas and rope. Neat rows of leather tents stretched in every direction and cook fires sent thin columns of smoke into the clear air, whilst the distant sound of shouted orders and marching feet carried on the desert breeze.

'Sweet Jupiter,' Seneca whispered. It was a full legion. Four thousand men or more, with all their equipment, supplies, and support personnel. The scale was staggering, not just the number of tents, but the entire infrastructure required to support such a force at the edge of the world. He could see the orderly lines where the legion's headquarters would be located, the larger tents that marked Centurions' quarters, and the workshops and supply depots that formed a complete military city in the wilderness.

The expedition that would carry them into the unknown territories wasn't just a reconnaissance mission or an elite strike force, it was an army, gathered at the frontier and ready to march further south than Roman eagles had ever flown.

Chapter Nine

Syene

The walk from the fortress to the legionary camp took less than half an hour, the late afternoon sun beating down on them as they made their way across the rocky ground that separated Roman civilisation from the unknown wilderness beyond. As they drew closer, the scale of the encampment became even more impressive, a testament to the logistical mastery that had built an empire.

Neat rows of eight-man tents stretched in orderly lines, each century's area clearly marked by standards and equipment arrangements dictated by professional military organisation. Yet even at a distance, Seneca could see that something was different about this legion. The voices that carried on the desert air spoke with many different accents from across the empire, and the men moving between the tents displayed a variety of bearing and discipline that suggested diverse backgrounds.

They were met at the camp's perimeter by another duty Optio who consulted his wax tablet with the weary efficiency of someone who had processed hundreds of new arrivals in recent days.

'Tribune Seneca,' he repeated, checking their names against his list. 'Scout detachment, attached to Second Century, Third Cohort. Follow me.'

He led them through the camp's orderly tent lines, past cooking fires where men prepared their evening meals, and training areas where soldiers drilled with wooden swords under the watchful eyes of veteran instructors. The tent they were assigned stood in a section reserved for specialist units, scouts, engineers, interpreters, and other attached personnel whose skills were essential but didn't fit neatly into standard legion organisation.

'Home for the next few weeks,' the Optio announced, gesturing towards a leather tent that was noticeably larger than standard legionary accommodation. 'Built for a full contubernium, so you'll have plenty of room. Mess tent opens at noon, one meal a day. Other rations can be collected from the quartermaster but make them last. Latrines are fifty paces that way, water detail forms at dawn and dusk. Any questions?'

When there were none, he departed, leaving the Occultum to settle into their new quarters. The tent was indeed spacious, with room for ten men and after weeks of uncertainty and cramped river travel, it represented luxury.

'Not bad,' Falco observed, claiming a sleeping area near the tent's entrance. 'Though I do miss the excitement of being chased through Alexandria by angry vigiles.'

'Give it time,' replied Marcus dryly, unpacking his sarcina. 'I suspect this expedition will provide all the excitement we can handle.'

As his men settled in, Seneca set out to find Lepidus. The command area was easily identifiable by the larger tents, the increased activity, and the constant flow of messengers and officers that marked any military headquarters. But as he approached the main command tent, a familiar figure intercepted him before he could announce himself to the guards on duty.

'Seneca,' said Lepidus quietly, taking his arm and guiding him away from the bustling activity around the headquarters. 'Welcome to Syene. We need to talk.'

The Senator led him away from the command area towards a quieter section of the camp, his manner suggesting urgent need for discretion. When they were sufficiently isolated from curious ears, he turned to face Seneca.

'I was beginning to get worried,' he said. 'You are late.'

'We came as quickly as we could,' said Seneca. 'Is there a problem?'

'First things first,' said Lepidus. 'The legate of this legion knows nothing about the Occultum. As far as he is concerned, you're simply another scout detachment attached to provide reconnaissance capabilities.'

Seneca nodded understanding.

'And you want to keep it that way.'

'Absolutely. If he knew that six men under his command answered directly to imperial authority and operated outside normal military protocol...' Lepidus shook his head. 'It would complicate everything.'

'What is there to complicate? We are just going to find a unit of missing Romans.'

'Ah,' said Lepidus, 'that's the thing. There's more to it than that.'

Seneca's heart sank a little. He should have known there would be more, life in the Occultum was never that simple.

'Go on,' he said.

"There's something else you need to know,' said Lepidus, reaching into his toga to withdraw a small leather pouch. "The true reason Claudius has taken such personal interest in those missing men."

He opened the pouch carefully, revealing a necklace that caught the lamplight and threw it back in brilliant fragments. The workmanship was extraordinary with precious stones of impossible clarity creating patterns that seemed to shift and flow like living things.

'Do you remember the story about the dying man who the patrol found in the desert, the sole survivor from the

Rapax?'

'I do.'

'Well, this was clutched in the dying man's hands when the patrol found him. This is actually a copy, and a poor one at that but imagine the value of something similar, a hundred times the quality of this. The real necklace is extraordinary, and the craftsmanship suggests a level of sophistication that shouldn't exist in the territories beyond our southern borders."

Seneca studied the necklace with growing understanding.

"And Claudius thinks there's more where this came from."

"Much more," Lepidus confirmed. "The emperor has consulted with the finest jewellers and metalworkers in Rome, and they all agree, this piece represents techniques and materials that would require an established civilization to produce. Not some primitive tribe, but a people with resources, knowledge, and the infrastructure to support master craftsmen."

"Hence the full legion," Seneca observed.

"Precisely. If there's a civilization out there capable of producing such work, Claudius wants to know about it. The potential for trade, tribute, or conquest..." Lepidus let the implications hang in the air. "This necklace represents possibilities that could transform the southern frontier entirely."

"And the Occultum's role?"

"To find the source," Lepidus said simply, returning the necklace to its pouch. "The legion can provide security and establish Roman presence, but you'll be the ones who determine whether we're dealing with a handful of skilled artisans or something much more significant."

Seneca nodded slowly, understanding now why their

67

mission carried such weight in imperial circles.

"So this is not about finding any surviving members of the Rapax at all, a single piece of jewellery has convinced the emperor to risk four thousand men in unknown territory."

'Not exactly. The fate of the Rapax is important and could shape any further expeditions into the interior, but the gold is of personal interest to the emperor and if you find the source, keep that information to yourselves until you get back. Until then, you are just another military resource under the command of the Legatus.'

'Understood,' said Seneca with a sigh. 'We'll operate as scouts until circumstances require otherwise.'

'Good. Now let me bring you up to speed on what we've assembled here.'

As they walked through the camp, Lepidus provided a running commentary on the extraordinary force that had been gathered for the expedition and what Seneca saw confirmed his initial impressions, this was unlike any Roman legion he had ever encountered.

'They've been preparing for months,' Lepidus explained as they passed a training area where grizzled Centurions drilled men whose movements showed varying degrees of military experience. 'As word spread through the eastern provinces that volunteers were needed for a special expedition, men began arriving from every corner of the Empire.'

The diversity was immediately apparent. Seneca could see weathered veterans with decades of experience working alongside younger men whose expressions suggested recent recruitment from civilian life.

'Some are experienced legionnaires whose terms of service have expired but who re-enlisted for this mission,' Lepidus continued, pointing towards a group of men whose movements showed the automatic precision of professional soldiers. 'Veterans who couldn't resist one more campaign, especially one promising adventure and potential wealth beyond anything they'd seen before.'

They paused to watch a weapons training session where a former gladiator instructor demonstrated sword techniques to a mixed group of recruits. The instructor's movements were fluid and deadly, but his students ranged from competent to barely capable of holding their weapons without injuring themselves.

'Others are volunteers from the civilian population,' said Lepidus. 'Merchants ruined by bad investments, farmers whose crops failed, younger sons with no inheritance seeking fortune through military service. Some are running from debts, others from failed marriages or criminal charges. Whatever their background, they have been accepted into this legion with open arms.'

The training continued around them, but Seneca could see the challenges facing the instructors. Men who had never held weapons were learning basic formations alongside veterans who could execute complex manoeuvres in their sleep. The result was a somewhat fragmented military force that defied easy categorisation.

'And then there are the criminals,' added Lepidus. 'Men given the choice between execution and service in this expedition. Murderers, thieves, deserters from other units. Dangerous men, but dangerous in ways that might prove useful in the territories we're heading into.'

'A motley collection,' observed Seneca.

'Indeed. But they're training hard, and the veteran cadre is working miracles with the raw material. By the time we march south, they'll function as a legion. Perhaps not the finest in Roman history, but adequate for our purposes.'

'What about horses?' asked Seneca.

'They'll be provided before you leave,' replied Lepidus, 'and your role will be to range ahead of the main column providing intelligence about terrain, water sources, and potential threats.' Lepidus paused, studying the distant horizon. 'But if this expedition encounters something beyond the capabilities of a conventional legion, you'll handle it.'

'And the legate? When do we meet him?'

'Soon enough. He's a competent commander, but he is young and believes this is a straightforward military operation. March south, find survivors of the lost expedition, deal with whatever primitive tribes encountered, and return with glory for the Empire.

As they walked back towards the command area, Lepidus provided final instructions that would govern their conduct for the remainder of the expedition's preparation.

'Keep your heads down and operate as a normal scout unit until circumstances demand otherwise. Don't volunteer information about your previous missions or capabilities.

The sun was setting behind them, casting long shadows across the camp as the legion settled into its evening routine. More cooking fires began to spring up between the tents, and the sounds of men sharing meals and conversation provided a counterpoint to the constant activity of military preparation.

'How long until we march?' asked Seneca.

'Days, not weeks. The final supply convoys should arrive soon, and once the quartermasters confirm we have everything needed for extended operations, we'll move out.' Lepidus paused, studying the vast encampment that represented months of planning and preparation. 'Four thousand men, marching into territory that's never seen

Roman eagles. Whatever we find out there, we'll face it with overwhelming force.'

As Seneca made his way back to his tent, he reflected on what he had seen and learned. The legion preparing to march south was unlike anything in Roman military history, mixture of veterans and volunteers, professionals and criminals, all bound together by the promise of adventure and the hope of fortune in lands beyond the edge of the known world.

Whether such a diverse force would hold together under the pressures of campaign remained to be seen, but for now, they were his comrades in an undertaking that would test the limits of Roman ambition and courage.

Chapter Ten

Syene

The morning sun had barely cleared the eastern hills when Seneca emerged from his tent to find the camp already bustling with activity. The rhythmic sound of wooden swords clashing against shields echoed across the desert as centuries conducted their dawn training, whilst the steady tramp of marching feet marked cohorts drilling in formation on the packed earth that served as a parade ground.

Marcus and Falco joined him as he made his way towards the training areas. After years of operating as an elite unit, the sight of a full legion preparing for campaign was both familiar yet strangely foreign, accustomed as they were too small-unit operations where every man's capabilities were known and trusted.

'Impressive sight,' Marcus observed, watching a century execute a complex formation change with reasonable precision. 'Been a while since we've seen proper legion training.'

'Makes you remember why Roman armies conquered the world,' added Falco.' Nothing quite like it when it's done right.'

They paused at the edge of the first training area, where a veteran Optio was drilling recruits in basic sword work. His students attempted to mirror his actions with varying degrees of success.

'Watch the footwork!' the Optio barked, moving between the ranks to correct stances and grip positions. 'Your sword's only as good as the ground you're standing on. Lose your balance, lose your life!'

Some of the men responded well to instruction, their

movements showing the natural coordination that could be refined into genuine skill. Others struggled with even basic concepts, their attempts at swordplay more likely to injure themselves than any enemy they might face.

'Mixed bag,' said Falco quietly, noting the disparity in abilities amongst the trainees.

'More mixed than I'd like,' replied Seneca, watching a young recruit nearly drop his gladius whilst attempting a simple thrust. 'Some of these men have clearly never held a weapon before in their lives.'

They moved on to observe a more advanced training session where experienced legionnaires practiced complex manoeuvres under the watchful eye of a grizzled centurion, professional soldiers, their formations flowing like water whilst maintaining perfect discipline.

'Now that's more like it,' said Marcus with obvious approval. 'Those boys know their stuff.'

The contrast was striking. Where the first group had struggled with individual techniques, these veterans executed complicated tactical movements without apparent effort. Shield walls formed and dissolved on command, whilst individual combat flowed seamlessly into group tactics that could break enemy formations or hold against overwhelming odds.

'It's as if there are two different legions training in the same camp,' observed Marcus.

Their circuit brought them to an area where combat veterans were attempting to train men whose backgrounds clearly lay elsewhere. A former gladiator instructor demonstrated spear techniques to a group that included what appeared to be farmers and merchants.

'Steady pressure on the thrust,' the instructor called, 'your spear's got reach - use it! Keep the bastards at distance and stick them full of holes before they can close!'

One of his students executed the technique with natural violence that drew approving nods from the instructor. Another, clearly a former merchant judging by his careful attention to detail, approached the lesson with methodical precision that might serve him well if properly developed.

'At least they're trying,' Falco observed. 'Some of them might even survive their first real fight.'

'Greetings, Tribune,' said a grizzled centurion, offering Seneca a respectful salute. 'Centurion Lucius Cassius, Third Century, Second Cohort. Are you evaluating our training progress?'

'Just getting a feel for the men we'll be campaigning with,' said Seneca diplomatically. 'Quite a diverse group you've assembled here.'

'That's one way of putting it,' Cassius said with dry humour. 'We've been recruiting for months now, gathering men from every corner of the Empire. Some are exactly what you'd want for a mission like this. Others...' He gestured towards the struggling recruits. 'Others represent hope and desperation in equal measure.'

'What's the ratio?' Marcus asked bluntly. 'Experienced men to raw recruits?'

'About half and half. We've got a solid core of professional legionnaires from the garrison at Alexandria, men who know their business and can hold a line under pressure. Those men could march into Germania tomorrow and give a good account of themselves. Steady, reliable, professional. They'll be the backbone of whatever we accomplish out there.'

'And the others?' Falco asked, though his tone suggested he could guess the answer.

'Young men with no military experience but plenty of

enthusiasm,' Cassius replied. 'Volunteers from civilian life who've heard tales of African gold and decided to risk everything for a chance at fortune. Some will make decent soldiers given time and training. Others...' He shrugged expressively.

They watched a particularly inept recruit attempt to coordinate shield and sword work, his movements so poorly timed that he managed to strike his own shield with his gladius.

'Then there are the desperate ones,' he continued, 'but desperation makes men fight harder sometimes, especially when they know there's no retreat and no surrender. Some of our best soldiers started as criminals or slaves. Give them proper leadership and something to fight for, and they'll surprise you.'

The centurion's pragmatic assessment matched what they could see around them. Men with obviously criminal backgrounds trained alongside fresh-faced volunteers, whilst grizzled veterans attempted to pass on wisdom earned through years of bloody experience. The result was chaotic but not entirely without promise.

After thanking Cassius for his insights, the three members of the Occultum continued their tour of the camp. The scale of the operation became more apparent with each area they visited. This wasn't simply a military expedition, but a complete logistical undertaking that dwarfed anything they had experienced in their previous missions.

'Look at this,' said Marcus as they crested a small rise that provided a view back towards the fortress of Syene. 'It's like a second city.'

Spread between the legion's camp and the fortress walls, a temporary civilian settlement had sprung up to support the expedition's needs. Canvas-covered stalls housed merchants selling everything from weapons and armour to personal comforts and luxury items that soldiers might want for extended campaign. Cooking tents filled the air with the smells of roasting meat and exotic spices, whilst armourers worked at portable forges to repair equipment and craft custom pieces.

But it was the corrals that truly demonstrated the expedition's ambition. Hundreds of horses stood in carefully organised pens, their breeds ranging from sturdy Roman cavalry mounts to the smaller, hardier animals favoured by desert peoples. In other fenced off areas, camels complained loudly as they were loaded with supplies, their ungainly forms perfectly adapted to the harsh conditions they would soon encounter.

'Ugly bastards,' Falco observed. 'Give me a horse any day.'

Perhaps most impressive was the gathering of indigenous personnel who would accompany the expedition into territories where no Roman unit had travelled and returned alive. Nubian guides sat in small groups, their dark skin marked with tribal scarification while Egyptian interpreters conversed in rapid Arabic with Berber traders whose caravans had brought them from the western oases.

'Look at the variety,' said Marcus, studying the collection of local expertise. 'Hunters, trackers, and guides who probably know water sources we've never heard of. Those animal handlers are probably capable of keeping camels and horses alive in conditions that would kill European stock.'

'And cooks who know how to prepare local foods,' Falco added practically. 'Nothing worse than starving in the middle of plenty because you don't know what's safe to eat.'

'This is what a real expedition looks like,' said Seneca as they completed their circuit and began walking back towards their own quarters. 'Not six men skulking through enemy territory, but a proper Roman army with all the support necessary for extended operations.'

'It's impressive,' replied Marcus. 'But I keep thinking about that dying man who reached Syene. He was part of an expedition too, yet something out there destroyed it so completely that only one man survived to tell the tale.'

'Maybe they just got unlucky,' Falco suggested. 'Disease, hostile tribes, navigation errors. Any of those could destroy an expedition, especially one operating without proper support.'

As they approached their tent, the sounds of military preparation continued around them. Men trained with desperate intensity, knowing that their lives might depend on skills learned in these final days before departure.

'At least we won't be going alone this time,' said Marcus with a sigh, settling onto his sleeping mat and beginning the daily ritual of equipment maintenance. 'Whatever we face out there, we'll have four thousand Romans at our backs.'

'Assuming they don't break and run at the first sign of real trouble,' replied Falco. 'Half-trained aren't exactly the most reliable troops for difficult campaigns.'

'They'll hold if the veterans hold,' said Seneca with the confidence of long experience. 'And the veterans will hold because they're professionals. It's what they do.'

Outside their tent, the great machine of imperial logistics continued its relentless work. Soon, very soon, they would march south into territories that existed only as blank spaces on Roman maps and whatever awaited them there, they would face it with the full might of a Roman legion behind them.

Chapter Eleven

Syene

The pre-dawn darkness carried the familiar sounds of a legion preparing for formal inspection, the muted conversations of men checking equipment one final time, the soft clink of mail being adjusted, the whispered curses of soldiers discovering last-minute problems with their kit. Seneca emerged from his tent to find the camp already stirring with activity as four thousand men prepared to present themselves for their commander's scrutiny.

'Full parade,' Marcus observed, buckling on his sword belt. 'It's been a while since we've stood in ranks for a proper inspection.'

'Wonder if we'll remember how,' Falco muttered. 'Years of operating independently can make a man forget the finer points of military protocol.'

The Occultum made their way through the pre-dawn gloom towards the assembly area where the legion was forming up. Centuries fell into place within their cohorts, whilst cohorts aligned themselves according to the ancient traditions that had built an empire.

As the other scouts attached to the Second Cohort, they took their position at the left end of the formation, where specialist units traditionally stood during formal ceremonies. Around them, other attached personnel found their designated places, engineers, interpreters, medical staff, and the various specialists whose skills would prove essential in the days and months ahead.

'Impressive sight,' Decimus observed quietly as the formation took shape around them. In the growing light of dawn, the scale of the gathering became apparent - rank upon rank of armed men stretching across the parade ground in perfect alignment, their equipment gleaming despite the early hour.

The diversity that had been so apparent during training became less obvious when viewed as a formed legion. Whatever their individual backgrounds, the men had been drilled into the familiar patterns of Roman military organisation. Veterans stood alongside recruits, criminals next to volunteers, but all bore the same equipment and displayed the same disciplined bearing.

The sound of a horn echoed through the morning air as the Primus Pilus stepped forward to issue the first command, his voice carrying easily across the formation.

'Aquila... *Advance!*'

The legion's standards appeared at the head of the formation, carried by men chosen for both their reliability and their courage. The golden eagle that gave the legion its identity caught the morning light as it took its place before the assembled ranks, flanked by the smaller standards that marked individual centuries and cohorts.

Behind the standards came the legion's senior officers, their approach marked by the distinctive sound of cavalry hooves on sun-baked ground. Even at a distance, their bearing proclaimed authority and long experience in the art of command.

Gaius Cornelius Flavus, the Legatus Legionis, proved younger than many had expected. His posture bore the measured caution of a man newly entrusted with command, and he rode with deliberate precision, his mount stepping high and careful, guided by a hand still adjusting to the reins of authority.

From the front of the formation, the voice of the Primus Pilus thundered again across the parade ground.

'Ad signa… *state!*'

Four thousand legionaries snapped to rigid attention, the clatter of armour and shield bosses punctuated by the deep blast of a cornu. The legion's standards rose high as the Aquilifer held the legion's sacred eagle aloft, but as the sunlight reflected off the metal, Gladii remained sheathed; Roman tradition favoured discipline over display, and a drawn sword was a tool, not a flourish.

The legate began his slow pass along, flanked by standard-bearers and his lictors, his horse picking its way between the cohorts. He offered no words, only the silent judgement of a commander committing faces, postures, and discipline to memory, the first measure of the men he would lead into uncertain lands.

As he neared their position, Seneca studied the young officer. His features were un-weathered, suggesting patrician blood rather than the hard-earned chiselling of campaign life. His armour was imperial-issue, ornate and of fine make, Lorica Segmentata chased with silver, greaves polished to mirror brightness, all marking him as a man of status.

From somewhere behind Seneca, a voice murmured, barely audible:

'Tied to Claudius, they say. Nephew, maybe. Sent to earn his spurs before he's given a province.'

Seneca made no reply, but the information was useful to know. Such expeditions were never only about war. A lost legion, rumoured riches, and the allure of conquest was the kind of theatre the Senate adored. The whole thing was a stage for ambition, not just strategy and overall, it was an impressive sight… but as his gaze turned to the man riding just behind the legate, Seneca's blood turned cold. The man carried no vine staff, for that symbol of Centurions belonged to his past, this was the *Praefectus Castrorum*, the camp prefect: once a Centurion, now risen to third in command of the legion beneath only the legate and the senior military tribune and every line on his face spoke of campaigns survived and legions drilled into shape, a man forged by service rather than status.

'Sweet Jupiter,' Marcus whispered, having followed Seneca's gaze to the approaching officers. 'Is that who I think it is?'

'*Scipio*,' hissed Seneca, 'He was the camp prefect of Legio XVI Gallica in Germania.'

The name sent a chill through the members of the Occultum who remembered their encounter. Scipio had been the man assigned to eliminate them when political complications had made their continued existence inconvenient.

'What's he doing here?' asked Falco, his hand unconsciously moving towards his sword hilt.

'Commanding this legion's Centurions, apparently,' replied Decimus grimly. 'The question is whether he knows we're here, and what he plans to do about it if he does.'

The officers drew closer but paid little heed to the scouts as they passed. But when Scipio's gaze passed over the Occultum, there was the slightest of changes in his expression. Recognition perhaps, but subtle and silent.

'He saw us,' said Marcus under his breath.

'Aye,' replied Seneca, eyes fixed on the departing figure. 'He did.'

The formal ceremony continued with the traditional pronouncements and benedictions that marked such occasions.

Priests offered sacrifices for the expedition's success, whilst Flavus delivered a speech about duty, glory, and the honour of extending Roman civilisation into lands where barbarians had never seen the eagles.

The speech was competent but uninspiring, delivered with the careful precision of someone who had rehearsed the words but lacked the natural authority to make them compelling. Around them, Seneca could sense the mixed reactions of men who were more concerned with survival than abstract concepts of imperial glory.

When the ceremony concluded and the legion was dismissed to make final preparations, the Occultum returned to their quarters. The encounter with Scipio had introduced a new and unwelcome complication to an already difficult mission, and they needed time to consider the implications.

'What do you make of it?' Marcus asked, as they settled inside their tent to talk.

'I think we have a problem,' replied Seneca bluntly. 'Scipio isn't the kind of man who forgets a grudge and this expedition is the perfect opportunity to settle old scores.

'The bastard already tried to kill us once,' Falco muttered. 'If he tries again, we'll deal with him once and for all.'

Seneca shook his head, his tone more cautious.

'That's exactly what concerns me. Scipio's a clever man. If he moves against us, it won't be with open blades, he'll probably do it cleanly, with justification.' He looked around the circle, letting his words settle. 'Whatever his reasons for being here, one thing is certain, the success of this mission, and our role in it, just became a great deal more complicated.'

Chapter Twelve

Syene

The following days passed in a blur of final preparations, the temporary camp transforming into a well-oiled military machine ready for extended campaign. Despite the lingering tension of Scipio's presence, the Occultum found themselves settling into the familiar rhythms of legion life with surprising ease. Years of independent operation had not dulled their ability to function within the larger structure of Roman military organisation.

Each morning brought fresh challenges as quartermasters wrestled with the logistics of moving four thousand men into unmapped territory. Supply trains stretched beyond the horizon, loaded with everything from replacement weapons to medical supplies, whilst native guides argued amongst themselves about the best routes south. The air rang constantly with shouted orders as the great machine of imperial conquest prepared for motion.

Seneca attended the daily briefings with other commanders, where maps were studied and routes debated with methodical precision. The discussions were pragmatic rather than inspiring, water sources, supply caches, potential threats, and contingency plans for difficulties beyond their current planning.

'The seasonal river runs dry after the summer floods,' one of the Nubian guides explained through an interpreter, his scarred hands tracing routes on the crude map. 'Eight days south, maybe nine if the camels are heavily loaded. Good water when it flows, but the tribes there...' He shook his head meaningfully. 'They do not welcome strangers bearing weapons.'

The young legatus leaned forward, his questions revealing a systematic approach despite his lack of battlefield experience.

'What would they accept as tribute for safe passage?'

'Steel, mainly. Roman weaponry is worth more than gold to them. But they also value coloured cloth, wine, sometimes Roman coins if they shine enough to make pretty ornaments for their women.'

After years of operating with minimal intelligence and constantly changing objectives, the methodical planning felt almost luxurious to Seneca. Here was the might of Rome brought to bear on a single problem, resources and expertise gathered from across the Empire to ensure success.

The afternoons were spent observing the legion's developing character whilst maintaining their cover as ordinary scouts and what Seneca saw was encouraging. The diverse collection of veterans, volunteers, and criminals was slowly melding into something resembling a functional military unit.

The evenings brought different preparations. Men wrote letters home that might be their last, repaired equipment with obsessive care, and engaged in conversations that preceded dangerous undertakings. Gambling increased, as did visits to the camp's unofficial brothels, whilst the more religious members made elaborate offerings to their chosen gods.

Despite their concerns about Scipio's presence, the intervening days passed without incident. The camp prefect was visible throughout the preparation process, ensuring the legion's logistical arrangements met professional standards, but he made no direct contact with them.

'He's watching us,' Marcus observed quietly during one

of their equipment checks. 'Never openly, but sometimes I catch him looking in our direction.'

'He's waiting for the right moment,' replied Seneca, testing the edge of his pugio. 'He's smart enough to know that any move against us needs to be carefully planned. A false accusation would only strengthen our position. I think he'll wait until we're deep in hostile territory, far from witnesses or authority figures who might question his actions.'

The night before their departure finally arrived and the Occultum spent their last evening quietly, keeping to themselves as had become their habit. They had faced impossible odds before, but always as an independent unit. This time they would be part of something larger, bound by orders that might conflict with their usual methods.

Outside their tent, men talked quietly amongst themselves after trying unsuccessfully to sleep. Equipment was checked yet again, personal effects secured, and silent prayers offered to whatever gods might be listening, but just as they settled into an inevitable but somewhat exciting acceptance, the tranquillity of their final night was shattered by the thunder of approaching hoofbeats, growing louder as riders approached the camp's perimeter.

Seneca emerged from his tent to find the camp stirring with curiosity and alarm. Cavalry arrivals at night usually meant urgent news, and urgent news was rarely good when any military force was about to depart on a campaign.

'How many do you reckon?' asked Marcus, joining him in the darkness.

'A full turma, maybe more,' replied Seneca, listening to the approaching thunder.

'Where is the Legatus,' shouted the commander,

reigning in his horse. 'I require immediate audience by command of Claudius himself!'

'Imperial business,' Falco muttered, having joined Seneca outside their tent. 'That's never good when it arrives in the middle of the night.'

Around them, the camp stirred with controlled excitement. Men emerged from tents to observe the newcomers, whilst officers gathered near the command area where the tribune would be received.

The cavalry moved through the camp, their horses' hooves striking packed earth with measured rhythm. Even in darkness, their bearing proclaimed elite status, these were not ordinary auxiliaries but horsemen whose training marked them as imperial guards or special messengers.

The tribune himself was barely visible, but his bearing suggested youth combined with the confidence that came from powerful connections. He dismounted near the command area and was immediately escorted toward Flavus's quarters.

'Praetorian cavalry,' Decimus observed, studying the passing riders. 'Look at their kit. Whatever message they're carrying comes from the highest levels of authority.'

'Whatever it means,' said Seneca eventually, 'there's nothing we can do about it. Let's try to get some sleep.'

The following morning, Seneca was already outside as Marcus emerged from the tent.

'Any word about last night?' he asked.

'Nothing official,' replied Seneca. 'But several senior centurions were called to the command tent before dawn. I'm sure we'll find out soon enough. In the meantime, let's get some hot food. Today's the day we pick up our horses.'

An hour or so later, Seneca and his men joined the

stream of soldiers moving toward the paddocks. As scouts, they had been assigned quality mounts capable of carrying armed men across difficult terrain but as they neared, a familiar voice called out.

'Seneca, I need to speak to you.'

Lepidus approached through the organised chaos of departure preparations.

'Lepidus,' replied Seneca carefully. 'I trust you slept well after last night's excitement.'

'I didn't sleep at all,' said Lepidus bluntly. 'We need to talk.'

He led them toward a scattered collection of rocks that offered crude seating away from the camp's activity.

'What I'm about to tell you,' he said quietly, 'changes everything. I've just found out that the delegation that arrived overnight came directly from the Governor of Egypt. There's been an uprising in the western districts near Paraetonium. Local tribes have overrun three garrison posts and are threatening the trade routes to Cyrenaica.'

The name carried weight. Paraetonium controlled the coastal road between Alexandria and the western provinces, a vital link that kept grain flowing to Rome and maintained imperial authority across North Africa.

'The Governor needs immediate reinforcements,' Lepidus continued. 'His own troops are spread too thin, and he can't risk the uprising spreading to other districts. If Paraetonium falls, the entire western frontier could collapse.'

Seneca felt a cold certainty settling in his stomach. Military expeditions were always subject to political realities, but the timing of this crisis seemed almost deliberately malicious.

'So we're being recalled,' said Marcus flatly.

87

'Not exactly,' said Lepidus. 'The expedition proceeds as planned, but the experienced soldiers, the men who know their business, are to leave for Alexandria immediately. The Governor's request takes precedence.'

The implications crashed over them like a tide and Seneca could see the same realization dawning on each of his men's faces as they processed what this meant for their survival in the territories ahead.

'You're sending us into unknown territory with recruits and criminals,' said Decimus quietly. 'Men who've had weeks of training instead of years of experience.'

'The newer soldiers will continue south under the original command structure,' Lepidus confirmed. 'They're not completely untrained, the centurions have done remarkable work in the time available.'

'Remarkable work with civilians and criminals,' Talorcan observed. 'Against whatever killed two hundred experienced legionaries of the Twenty-First Rapax.'

'How many men?' Seneca asked, though he suspected the answer would be worse than he feared.

'Approximately four hundred. Perhaps fewer once the most unreliable elements are weeded out.'

Four hundred. Less than a tenth of the force they had planned to take into the unknown territories. Men whose military experience could be measured in weeks rather than campaigns, facing dangers that had destroyed seasoned veterans.

'This is madness,' said Marcus bluntly. 'Those recruits will break at the first sign of real trouble. Half of them have never seen actual combat, and the other half will desert the moment things get difficult.'

'Nevertheless, those are our orders,' replied Lepidus.

'The mission continues with available resources.'

Sica, who had been listening in characteristic silence, finally spoke.

'When do the experienced troops depart?'

'As soon as they can. The Governor's messenger emphasized the urgency of the situation near Paraetonium, and every day of delay risks further deterioration of imperial authority in the western districts.'

Marcus shook his head slowly, the implications clear in his expression.

'We'll be nursemaids to a collection of amateurs. Fighting whatever's out there whilst simultaneously trying to keep our own men from falling apart.'

'The alternative is to abandon the mission entirely,' said Lepidus firmly, 'return to Rome and explain to the emperor why we ignored direct orders yet again because the task seemed too difficult.'

The senator's words carried the weight of finality for they all understood the political realities that governed their existence. Failure to complete this mission, regardless of circumstance, was not a luxury they could afford.

'Is there anything you can do?' asked Seneca, though he already knew the answer.

'Nothing. The Governor's authority over military resources in Egypt is absolute when provincial security is threatened. I can't countermand his orders without facing the wrath of Claudius.' Lepidus studied their faces, seeing his own resignation reflected in their expressions. 'I'm sorry, but you'll have to do the best you can with what's available. It's not ideal, but you've succeeded under impossible circumstances before.'

'This is different,' replied Marcus grimly. 'Before, we only had to look after each other. Now we'll be depending on men we barely know, whose loyalty and competence remain untested.'

'Then you'll have to test them quickly,' said Lepidus. 'Because in three days, you march south with whatever force remains. The die is cast, gentlemen. From here on in, you have to make do with what you've got.'

Chapter Thirteen

Syene

A few days later, Seneca sat astride his horse atop a rocky outcrop south of the camp, watching the last cohort of experienced legionaries marching north at forced pace toward Alexandria. The sight of their departing standards felt like watching the tide retreat, leaving them stranded on an increasingly hostile shore.

'Look at them go,' Falco observed, shading his eyes against the morning sun. 'Double time in this heat. They'll be dead on their feet before they reach the first way station.'

To one side, the Nile stretched northward like a brown ribbon connecting their position to the familiar world of Roman authority. A small fleet of river vessels was also making its way downstream, their sails bright against the water as they carried Lepidus and the other senior officials back to Alexandria. Even at this distance, Seneca could make out the distinctive awning that marked the senator's barge, already several miles downstream and growing smaller with each passing moment.

'And there goes our last connection to imperial authority,' said Decimus quietly. 'Once those ships disappear around the bend, we're truly on our own.'

'We've been on our own before,' said Sica, 'and I for one prefer it that way.'

'Not like this,' replied Talorcan, gesturing toward the scene behind them. 'Never like this.'

The Occultum turned in their saddles to observe what remained of the great expedition that had been planned with such care and precision. Instead of the magnificent force that had gathered at Syene, a ragged column of barely four hundred men was already moving south.

The contrast was devastating. Where professional legionaries had once marched in perfect formation, volunteers and criminals now struggled to maintain even basic order. Pack animals wandered between the loose ranks, their loads shifting dangerously as inexperienced handlers failed to secure them properly, and the few guides who remained moved with obvious unease at the head of this makeshift army.

'Sweet Jupiter,' muttered Marcus, studying the chaotic procession. 'It looks more like a refugee exodus than a military expedition.'

The young legatus rode near the front of the column, his bearing still confident despite the dramatic reduction in his command. Behind him, the few remaining centurions attempted to maintain some semblance of military discipline amongst men whose training could be measured in weeks rather than campaigns and shouted orders echoed across the desert as they tried to prevent the formation from dissolving into complete disorder.

'At least they're moving in roughly the same direction,' muttered Falco. 'That's something, isn't it?'

'For now,' replied Marcus. 'Wait until they encounter their first real enemy.'

As they watched, a commotion broke out near the rear of the column as a group of pack camels broke away from their handlers and wandered off toward the river, their loads of precious supplies swaying dangerously. The men assigned to retrieve them were running about in obvious panic, their shouts adding to the general confusion.

'Should we help?' asked Talorcan.

'Let them sort it out themselves,' said Seneca firmly.

'They need to learn how to handle these problems without us. We won't always be there to rescue them from their own incompetence.'

They watched as the handlers eventually managed to corral the wayward animals, though not before several supply bundles had fallen and split open, scattering their contents across the rocky ground. Other soldiers rushed to gather the spilled goods whilst the guides looked on with expressions of barely concealed disgust.

'How long do you think they'll last?' Decimus asked quietly.

'Depends on what we encounter,' replied Seneca, 'heat, thirst, difficult terrain, some of them might survive long enough to become actual soldiers, but if we meet organized resistance...'

He left the sentence unfinished, but they all understood. Untrained men facing experienced enemies rarely survived their first encounter.

'The guides don't look happy,' Sica observed, noting the tense conversations taking place amongst the Nubian trackers.

'Can you blame them?' replied Falco. 'They agreed to lead a proper Roman legion into the interior. Now they're stuck with this. If I were them, I'd be considering my options too.'

The possibility of their guides abandoning the expedition was one they couldn't afford to contemplate. Without local knowledge of water sources, safe routes, and tribal territories, even the most experienced Roman force would be doomed in the vast wilderness that stretched beyond the Nile's life-giving valley.

The column was now well past their position, its tail end disappearing behind a ridge as the expedition continued its march into unknown territory. The dust cloud it raised hung in the still air like a funeral shroud, marking the passage of what might be the most ill-prepared Roman expedition in the Empire's history.

'Well,' said Falco with forced cheerfulness, 'at least it can't get any worse.'

'Don't say that,' Marcus warned. 'The gods take such statements as challenges.'

A distant shout from the direction of the column suggested that something else had indeed gone wrong, and the sounds of confusion and inefficiency carried clearly across the desert, a constant reminder of the challenges ahead.

'Come on,' said Seneca with a sigh, turning his horse toward the departing expedition. 'Time to see what we can salvage from this disaster.'

As they spurred their horses toward the retreating column, each member of the Occultum was privately calculating their chances of survival. Four hundred inexperienced men, led by guides whose loyalty remained questionable, marching into territory that had already swallowed a much better-prepared expedition without trace.

But they were the Occultum. They would proceed into the unknown, do their best with the resources available, and trust to their gods and their own skills to see them through whatever trials awaited. It's what they did.

Chapter Fourteen

The Deserts South of Syene

After five days of march, the initial chaos of departure had given way to the sort of organized confusion that marked any large body of men learning to function together under difficult conditions. Problems that had seemed insurmountable during the first day were now handled with increasing efficiency as soldiers and officers adapted to their circumstances.

The pack animals no longer wandered freely through the ranks. Handlers who had struggled with unfamiliar camels and mules during those first chaotic hours now at least kept their charges moving in the right direction, and supply distribution, which had initially taken hours of shouting and confusion, now proceeded with something approaching military efficiency

Most importantly, the men themselves were beginning to look like soldiers rather than a collection of desperate volunteers. The daily routine of march, camp, and guard duty was imposing its own discipline on recruits who had never experienced proper military life and centurions who had initially despaired of their raw material were discovering that some of these men possessed natural aptitude for warfare that proper training might develop into genuine competence.

'They're learning,' Marcus observed as he and Seneca watched the morning's departure from a rocky prominence that overlooked the route. 'Still rough around the edges, but they're starting to function as a unit.'

They spurred their horses to catch up with head of the column where the Nubian guides maintained their steady pace alongside the mounted scouts. The local trackers had consistently refused offers of horses, preferring to travel on foot across terrain that would have challenged even experienced cavalry mounts.

'Horses are for flat ground and easy riding,' one of the guides had explained through an interpreter. 'Here, feet are better. More sure, quieter, less water needed.'

The heat had been their constant companion since leaving the Nile's moderating influence and by midmorning, the sun transformed the landscape into a furnace that sapped strength and clouded judgment with relentless intensity. Men who had boasted of their tolerance for warm weather during the comfortable days at Syene now understood the difference between Mediterranean heat and the pitiless intensity of the African interior.

Yet the expedition adapted and water discipline, initially ignored by soldiers accustomed to unlimited supplies, became second nature as men learned to ration their precious liquid.

The guides set a punishing pace and seemed to possess an instinctive understanding of how far the column could travel in such conditions before exhaustion began claiming lives. When they called halts, men collapsed gratefully into whatever shade they could find, but they were always ready to resume the march when the order came.

'How much further to the desert proper?' Seneca asked Khaemwaset, the senior guide with extensive experience in the deep interior.

The Nubian pointed toward the horizon, where the rocky hills they had been traversing, gradually gave way to lower, more rounded terrain. 'Two days, maybe three. Then the sand begins, and the real journey starts.'

'How bad is it?'

Khaemwaset's expression grew serious as he considered his answer.

'Bad. Four days crossing to the first oasis. The sand is deep, walking is hard, and the sun…' He gestured expressively. 'The sun wants to kill everything that moves.'

That evening, they camped beside a tributary of the Nile that would be their last reliable water source before entering the desert proper. The stream was modest compared to the great river they had followed from Alexandria, but its clear water represented life itself in the harsh landscape that awaited them.

The entire expedition threw itself into the task of water collection with organised efficiency. Every container was filled to capacity whilst soldiers and pack animals drank their fill of the precious liquid. Men who had complained about the weight of their equipment now understood why experienced campaigners emphasized water storage above all other considerations.

The guides moved through the camp, checking water containers and advising on conservation techniques that might mean the difference between life and death in the days ahead. Their knowledge, earned through years of survival in one of the world's most hostile environments, was now the expedition's most valuable asset.

'Drink little but often,' Khaemwaset advised. 'Big drinks make you sick in the heat. Small sips keep you strong.'

As night fell, the temperature dropped enough to provide relief from the day's oppressive heat, but the guides warned that such comfort would soon become memory. The desert they would enter at dawn was a place where the sun ruled absolutely, where shade was non-existent and water more precious than gold.

'Tomorrow we find out what these men are really made of,' Decimus observed as they checked their equipment one final time.

'Tomorrow we find out what we're all made of,' Seneca corrected. 'The desert doesn't care about experience or training. It just wants to kill you, and it's very good at its job.'

Around them, the expedition settled into what might be their last comfortable night for some time. The guides spoke quietly amongst themselves in their own language, their conversation presumably covering route selection and water management strategies that would determine whether four hundred Romans lived or died in the harsh days ahead. They had guided expeditions before, but never one with so many inexperienced men and so little margin for error.

But for now, they had water, shade, and one last night of relative comfort before entering a place where the very landscape was their enemy.

Halfway through the following day, the desert announced itself with the subtlety of a sword thrust. One moment they were walking on solid ground dotted with sparse vegetation, the next their feet were sinking into sand that seemed to grasp at their ankles with every step. The change was so abrupt that several men stumbled, their bodies unprepared for the treacherous footing that would define the next stage of their journey.

Within an hour, the true nature of their ordeal became apparent. The sun, which had been merely oppressive during their march through rocky terrain, transformed into something approaching malevolence. It struck down from a cloudless sky with physical force, turning armour into instruments of torture and making each breath feel like swallowing heated metal.

The guides had warned them, but warnings could not prepare men for the reality of deep desert travel. The sand reflected heat upward whilst the sun hammered down from above, creating a furnace that attacked from every direction. Sweat evaporated before it could cool skin, leaving only salt crystals that stung eyes and made clothing chafe against flesh with every movement.

'Water discipline,' the centurions called repeatedly as they moved between the ranks. 'Small sips only. Make it last.'

But desperation overwhelmed training as men who had never experienced such thirst abandoned careful rationing for the immediate relief of deep drinks. Water that should have lasted the entire day was consumed in the first few hours, leaving soldiers to face the remainder of the march with empty skins and growing panic.

The Occultum walked alongside the struggling column, their horses moving with a sluggish gait.

'Look at them,' said Marcus quietly, gesturing toward the main body where men were beginning to stagger with increasing frequency. 'Half of them won't make it to the first oasis at this rate.'

'The guides warned them,' replied Decimus, though his tone carried more concern than criticism. 'Can't say they weren't told what to expect.'

But knowing what to expect and actually experiencing it were different things entirely. Men who had endured the heat of Mediterranean summers discovered that the desert operated according to different rules, where the sun became an active enemy seeking to drain every drop of moisture from human bodies.

Falco, despite his natural resilience and years of

campaign experience, began showing signs of distress by midday. His usual boisterous commentary faded to occasional muttered complaints, whilst his normally erect posture gradually slumped as exhaustion claimed its toll.

'Are you all right?' asked Sica, moving closer to his struggling comrade.

'Never better,' replied Falco with forced cheer, though sweat streamed down his face. 'Just enjoying this lovely desert air. Very... warming.'

But his attempts at humour couldn't disguise the pallor beneath his sun-darkened skin or the way his hands shook slightly as he reached for his water skin. The desert was claiming him as surely as it was claiming the inexperienced recruits, proof that even veteran soldiers weren't immune to its effects.

By late afternoon, the column's formation had dissolved into a loose mob of struggling men following the guides more by instinct than conscious decision. Soldiers who had started the day with military bearing now stumbled forward like sleepwalkers, their eyes fixed on the ground ahead as they concentrated on just placing one foot in front of the other.

'We need to stop,' Talorcan observed, noting how men were beginning to fall behind despite the centurions' increasingly desperate exhortations.

'The guides set the pace,' replied Seneca, though he shared his comrade's concern. 'They know what they're doing.'

The Nubians maintained their relentless stride across the burning sand, their movements still fluid despite hours of punishing travel. They called occasional halts for rest, but these brief respites provided little relief from the sun's assault. Men fell gratefully to the hot sand, but the heat continued its work even during these precious moments of rest.

Falco was among those who struggled most during the final hours before reaching their designated camping site.

'Almost there,' said Sica, though the oasis they were seeking remained several days away.

'Good,' Falco mumbled, his usual eloquence reduced to single-word responses. 'Hot... very hot.'

The campsite, when they finally reached it, proved to be little more than a depression in the sand where scattered palm trees provided minimal shade. Men collapsed wherever they could find space, their immediate concern being survival rather than military organization.

The guides moved through the sprawling camp, identifying cases of heat exhaustion and providing practical advice that might prevent deaths during the night ahead. Their knowledge, passed down through generations of desert travel, was now the expedition's lifeline.

'Small sips,' Khaemwaset repeated as he moved between groups of suffering soldiers. 'Wet cloth on head and neck. Body learns to fight the heat, but slowly, slowly.'

Falco was among those receiving the most attention from the experienced guides. They took one look at his condition and immediately began implementing the sort of desert medicine that had kept men alive in these conditions for centuries.

'You drink too much, too fast,' one of them diagnosed, studying Falco's symptoms. 'Body cannot use so much water at once. Makes you sick instead of strong.'

'I'll remember that for next time,' replied Falco weakly, accepting the wet cloth they placed on his forehead with obvious gratitude.

But as the sun set and temperatures began dropping with shocking speed, the desert revealed another face of its hostility. The same landscape that had been an oven during the day transformed into a freezer that caught the expedition unprepared for such dramatic change and the Occultum set up their small campaign tent, creating a shelter that would protect them from the cold.

'Feels like ice after the heat,' Falco observed, his condition improving slightly as his body temperature began stabilizing. 'This place can't make up its mind whether it wants to cook us or freeze us.'

'It wants to kill us,' replied Sica pragmatically, checking his comrade's skin colour. 'The method doesn't matter as long as it achieves the objective.'

Around them, the sounds of an expedition learning harsh lessons echoed through the cold night air. Men who had stripped off armour and clothing to escape the heat now shivered uncontrollably as they sought warmth from whatever sources they could find. Fires sprang up throughout the camp as soldiers burned whatever they could find in desperate attempts to stay warm.

'They're learning the hard way,' Marcus observed, listening to the sounds of misery from beyond their tent walls.

'Better they learn now than die later,' replied Seneca. 'The desert doesn't give second chances to the unprepared.'

Dawn brought its own set of problems. As the sun began its daily assault, a disturbing discovery emerged from the morning roll call. Seven soldiers were missing from their assigned positions, along with a horse and several precious water skins.

Their tracks were clearly visible in the sand, heading back along the route they had travelled the previous day. The footprints told a story of men who had abandoned hope during the coldest hours of night and chosen to attempt a return to civilization rather than face continued torment in the unknown territories ahead.

During the morning briefing, the young legatus was torn between military necessity and anger at the desertion.

'We should send a patrol after them,' he said to Seneca and the senior centurions who had gathered around him. 'We need to make an example of them to deter anyone else.'

'They'll die anyway,' Khaemwaset interjected bluntly when the situation was explained to him. 'Desert doesn't forgive mistakes. Men who run in fear make many mistakes.'

'But we can't just let them desert without punishment.'

"Send men after them,' said the guide, 'you lose more people. Desert takes everyone who doesn't respect its power.'

The brutal logic was inescapable, but the guides' advice carried the weight of absolute authority in this environment, and ignoring their counsel would doom the entire expedition.

'We proceed as planned,' said Flavus finally. 'Let the gods deal with them as they wish.'

As the column formed up for another day's march into the burning emptiness ahead, each man carried the knowledge that the desert had already begun claiming its tribute. Seven Romans were probably walking to their deaths somewhere behind them, whilst just under four hundred more faced the prospect of joining them if they failed to meet the harsh demands of survival in one of the world's most unforgiving environments.

The sun climbed higher, promising another day of torment, but the expedition moved forward because it had no other choice, each step taking them deeper into territory where human endurance would be tested to its absolute limits.

Chapter Fifteen

The Desert

Another two days passed, each worse than the previous and when the fourth day dawned like a curse from the gods themselves, the sun rose blood-red through a haze of heat that promised no mercy for the struggling expedition below.

Another eighteen men had vanished during the night, making over a hundred in total during the journey. Some had deserted, their footprints leading back toward the false hope of retreat while others had simply wandered off into the darkness, their minds addled by heat and thirst until they could no longer distinguish between reality and the mirages that tormented them during daylight hours. Three more lay wrapped in torn cloaks, their bodies bearing witness to the desert's absolute judgment of human frailty.

The guides moved through the camp with expressions of growing concern, their weathered faces showing the strain of leading so many inexperienced men through terrain that forgave no mistakes. Even their legendary endurance was being tested by the responsibility of keeping alive soldiers who seemed determined to kill themselves through ignorance and panic.

'Water ceremony,' Khaemwaset announced as the surviving men formed into a loose approximation of military formation. The ritual had become the day's most critical moment, the time when the water was rationed from what remained in the containers strapped to the horses' backs.

But today the ceremony erupted into violence before the guides could begin their careful distribution as a recruit lunged forward, desperation overcoming what remained of his military training as he grabbed for a water skin belonging to the soldier beside him.

'*Mine!*' he screamed, his voice cracked and hoarse from the dry air. '*I need it more! I'm dying!*'

The owner of the skin fought back with equal desperation, both men rolling in the sand as they clawed for possession of liquid more precious than gold. Other soldiers watched with strange detachment, their own exhaustion and thirst so complete that even this violent struggle for survival failed to stir them from their stupor. Men who would normally have intervened or joined the fray simply stared with hollow eyes, too drained to care about anything beyond their own immediate suffering.

'*Enough!*'

Scipio's voice cut through the chaos like a blade as he strode into the melee, his scarred face showing no emotion as he assessed the breakdown of discipline.

'Step away from that man,' he ordered, directing his words toward the initial perpetrator who still clutched the stolen water skin against his chest.

'He has more than his share,' the young man protested, his eyes wild with thirst and fear. 'Look at him, he's stronger than me. He doesn't need it as much.'

'I said step away.'

The soldier looked around desperately, seeking support from comrades who avoided his gaze, understanding that survival now depended on absolute adherence to what remained of military law.

'I was just…'

Before he could finish his sentence, Scipio's sword emerged from its scabbard and found the man's throat, ending both his protest and his life with professional efficiency.

The body dropped to the sand, blood mixing with

precious water from the punctured waterskin to create mud that would be dry within minutes. Scipio cleaned his blade on the dead man's tunic before returning it to its scabbard, his movements deliberate and unhurried.

'Anyone else feel entitled to another man's water ration?' he asked, his voice carrying clearly across the silent formation.

No one responded. The lesson was clear, written in blood and spilled water that represented hope itself in this merciless landscape. Theft of water was death, and death would be swift and public.

'Resume the distribution,' Scipio ordered, stepping over the corpse as if it were merely another obstacle to be navigated.

The guides continued their careful rationing, but the violence had poisoned the atmosphere further. Men eyed each other with suspicion that went beyond military caution, calculating who might be weak enough to steal from and who might be strong enough to steal from them. The bonds that held military units together were dissolving in the heat like everything else.

The march resumed, feet moving more from habit than conscious decision and men who had begun the desert crossing as soldiers now walked like refugees, their equipment jury-rigged to provide minimal protection from the sun's assault. Armour had become unbearable torture devices, with much discarded along the route despite the centurions' increasingly desperate attempts to maintain proper equipment standards.

Falco rode slumped over his horse's neck, his condition deteriorating again despite his comrades' careful attention. The brutal heat had drained him to the point where speech required more energy than he could spare, leaving him to endure in silence.

'He needs real shade and unlimited water soon,' Sica observed quietly, 'or we'll lose him.'

By midday, the expedition had ceased to function as a military force in any meaningful sense. Men staggered forward in loose groups that bore no relationship to their original centuries, following the guides more by instinct than orders. Officers who attempted to maintain formation found themselves shouting at soldiers too exhausted to comprehend commands, let alone obey them.

The sun reached its zenith with malevolent intensity, transforming the landscape into a furnace that seemed designed specifically to torture human beings and sand burned through the soles of caligae whilst metal equipment became too hot to touch, forcing men to wrap cloth around anything they needed to handle.

'Can't...go...on,' gasped a young recruit who had collapsed beside the makeshift path they were following. His water skin lay empty beside him, its contents consumed hours earlier despite repeated warnings.

'Get up,' ordered a centurion whose own condition was barely better than the man he was trying to motivate. 'The oasis isn't far now.'

But it was a lie, and everyone knew it. The oasis remained a hope rather than a certainty, its location known to the guides but invisible to everyone else in the expedition. Men were beginning to doubt its existence entirely, wondering if they were following mirages created by minds as addled as their own.

More soldiers began falling behind, their bodies finally surrendering to the accumulated torture of four days in hell. Some were helped by comrades who could barely support themselves, whilst others were left to accept whatever fate the desert offered. Men who had endured impossible conditions were reaching the absolute limits of human endurance, their bodies and minds shutting down under pressures that no amount of training could prepare them for.

The guides exchanged worried conversations in their own language. They had done everything possible to keep the expedition alive, but the desert was claiming its toll regardless of their expertise. Realising he had to do something, Khaemwaset approached Flavus with a desperate but necessary suggestion.

'Give all water now,' he said, his words cutting through the haze of heat and exhaustion. 'All of it. Men and animals.'

The young commander stared at him in disbelief.

'All of it? That's madness. If we're wrong about the distance…'

'If you don't, many die in next few hours,' Khaemwaset interrupted bluntly. 'Look at them. Without water now, half your men never see sunset.'

Flavus looked around at his collapsing force, seeing the truth in the guide's assessment. Soldiers were dropping where they stood, their bodies finally surrendering to the accumulated torture.

'And if the oasis isn't where you think it is?'

'Then we all die together instead of watching them die one by one.' The guide's eyes held absolute certainty. 'Oasis is close. Very close. But these men need strength to reach it.'

The decision hung in the burning air for a long moment before Flavus nodded grimly.

'Do it. Distribute everything we have left.'

The next hour became a desperate gamble with death itself as centurions moved through the ranks with the remaining water supplies, giving men and animals whatever liquid remained. Some soldiers were too far gone to drink properly, requiring careful assistance to get precious fluid into their systems.

When the distribution was complete, empty water skins hung like funeral shrouds from pack saddles and equipment belts. They had committed themselves utterly to reaching the oasis, with no reserves left for any miscalculation.

The march resumed, with each step an act of faith in Khaemwaset's promise, every breath a gamble against the desert's inexorable hunger and men stumbled forward knowing that there would be no second chances, no reserves to sustain them if their guide had miscalculated even slightly.

As the hours passed and the sun continued its merciless assault, doubt began to gnaw at even the strongest minds. The ridge Khaemwaset had spoken of remained tantalizingly distant, shimmering in the heat haze like a cruel mirage. Some men began to mutter prayers to gods who seemed deaf to their suffering, whilst others simply focused on placing one foot in front of the other until their bodies finally surrendered.

Falco slumped further over his horse's neck, his condition deteriorating rapidly despite the emergency water ration. Around him, soldiers were beginning to fall with increasing frequency, their bodies finally overwhelmed by heat, exhaustion, and the terrible knowledge that salvation lay just beyond their reach, if it existed at all.

The column stretched into a ragged line of dying men, each one driven forward only by the animal instinct for survival and the fading hope that their Nubian guide knew what he was doing. Officers had long since abandoned any attempt to maintain formation, focusing instead on keeping as many men moving as possible toward their uncertain destination.

Then, just when despair seemed ready to claim them all, Khaemwaset stopped abruptly at the crest of a low ridge. He shaded his eyes with one hand whilst pointing ahead with the other, his weathered face showing the first expression of relief they had seen in days.

'There,' he said simply.

Beyond the ridge, shimmering in the distance like something from a dream, lay a cluster of palm trees surrounding what appeared to be open water. The oasis was real, visible, and achievable for men who could summon the strength for one final effort.

The word spread through the disintegrating column like wildfire, water, shade, survival, hope. Men who had been ready to collapse found reserves of energy they didn't know they possessed, whilst those who had fallen behind during the day's march somehow found the strength to catch up.

The final approach to the oasis became a controlled stampede as the survivors stumbled and ran toward salvation. Military formation dissolved entirely as soldiers focused only on reaching the promise of water and shade that lay tantalizingly close.

But they had made it. Against odds that had seemed impossible during the darkest moments of the crossing, enough of the expedition had survived to continue their mission into the unknown territories beyond. The desert had claimed its tribute in blood and suffering, but it had not claimed them all.

The oasis awaited, offering the promise of rest, recovery, and perhaps the chance to forge this collection of survivors into something resembling a military force again. But that was tomorrow's challenge. Today, survival was enough.

Chapter Sixteen

The Oasis

Three days in the shade of date palms had begun to restore something approaching humanity to the expedition's survivors. The oasis proved to be more substantial than it had appeared from the ridge, a collection of natural springs feeding into several pools, surrounded by enough vegetation to provide both shelter and sustenance for a force their size.

Men who had arrived as walking corpses were slowly regaining their strength on a mix of dates, fresh water, and uninterrupted rest. The guides had declared a mandatory recovery period, their experience telling them that pushing the weakened men further would only result in more deaths.

The Occultum had established their own small camp away from the main body where Falco was recovering well from his ordeal, his natural resilience reasserting itself now that he had access to unlimited water and proper shade. His colour was returning, along with his appetite and his irrepressible commentary on their circumstances.

'Paradise,' he declared, lounging beneath a palm tree, popping another date into his mouth. 'After four days in hell, this place feels like the garden of the gods themselves.'

The evening routine had become comfortable and familiar. Equipment maintenance, meal preparation, and the sort of quiet conversations that marked soldiers at rest all over the known world. It wouldn't last long but for now, Seneca found himself able to relax for the first time since departing Alexandria.

'I'm going to get some water,' he said, getting to his feet and heading towards one of the smaller pools.

A few minutes later, he crouched near the spring where it emerged from the ground and filled his flask before standing up and securing the stopper, but before he could finish, a sound behind him sent him spinning around, and he found himself standing face to face with Scipio.

The camp prefect stood perhaps ten paces away, his hands empty and visible. His scarred features showed no immediate hostility, but his presence in this isolated spot clearly wasn't accidental.

The silence stretched between them, heavy with the weight of their shared history and mutual distrust. Water lapped quietly against the pool's edges whilst somewhere in the distance, the sounds of the recovering expedition provided a backdrop to their confrontation.

'Tribune Seneca,' said Scipio eventually.

His voice carried neither warmth nor obvious threat, the tone of someone acknowledging a fellow soldier without suggesting personal friendship. It was professionally correct whilst maintaining careful distance.

'Scipio,' replied Seneca, equally emotionless.

Another silence fell between them, each man assessing the other's intentions and capabilities. Seneca's hand remained within easy reach of his sword hilt, whilst Scipio's posture suggested similar readiness despite his apparently relaxed stance.

'We need to talk,' said Scipio finally.

'Do we?'

'Yes. About Germania and Rome. About what happened there, and what needs to happen here.'

Seneca studied the older man's face, looking for signs of deception or hostile intent. What he saw was fatigue, professional concern, and something that might have been grudging respect.

'I'm listening.'

Scipio moved closer, but slowly and obviously, his movements designed to avoid triggering defensive reactions. When he was close enough for quiet conversation, he stopped and met Seneca's gaze directly.

'What happened in Germania was politics,' he said bluntly. 'Orders from above, in a situation beyond my control. I did what I was commanded to do, just as you did what you were commanded to do.'

'You tried to have us killed.'

'I followed orders that would have resulted in your deaths, yes. There's a difference, though perhaps not one that matters to you.'

The admission was surprisingly direct, lacking the sort of justification or excuse that might have made it easier to dismiss. Scipio was acknowledging the reality of their past conflict without attempting to minimize its significance.

'And now?' Seneca asked.

'Now we're both Roman officers serving under impossible conditions with insufficient resources and too many ways to fail.' Scipio gestured toward the main camp where the exhausted soldiers were slowly recovering from their ordeal. 'I've been watching your unit since we left Syene. Professional competence, loyalty to each other, and the ability to still function under overwhelming pressure. It's everything we need in this situation.'

'Flattery, Scipio? You disappoint me.'

'Assessment,' replied Scipio. 'The men respect you, even the criminals. They may not understand exactly what you are, but they know you're something special and that kind of influence could be crucial if things get worse.'

Seneca considered this, noting the careful way Scipio was presenting his argument. No appeals to friendship or shared values, just practical recognition of military necessities.

'What exactly are you proposing?'

'Cooperation. Not friendship, not forgetting the past, just professional collaboration for the duration of this mission. You continue doing whatever it is you do, and I'll handle legion administration and discipline. We stay out of each other's way except when circumstances require us to work together.'

'And if those circumstances never arise?'

'Then we complete this mission and return to our respective duties without further contact. Clean, simple, professional.'

The offer had a certain appeal, Seneca had to admit. Scipio's competence was undeniable, his handling of the water thief had been brutal but necessary, and his management of the legion's logistics had been exemplary throughout their ordeal. Having him as an active enemy would complicate an already difficult situation. But trust was another matter entirely.

'I'll need to discuss this with my men,' he said finally.

'Of course. But while you're considering it, remember that we're heading into territory that killed over two hundred experienced legionaries. Whatever's waiting out there, we'll face it with men who've barely learned which end of a sword is dangerous. We can't afford internal conflicts when external threats are probably going to test us beyond our limits.'

The logic was unassailable, even if the source remained questionable. Seneca found himself nodding acknowledgment despite his continued reservations about Scipio's ultimate intentions.

'I understand your position.'

'Good, And I understand yours. You have no reason to

trust me, and every reason to watch for treachery. I accept that. Just remember that killing you all in a camp full of witnesses would be remarkably stupid even for someone with hostile intentions.'

'Unless you planned to kill us individually when heads were turned elsewhere.'

'Unless that, yes,' Scipio agreed with disturbing honesty. 'But if I wanted you dead for personal reasons, there would have been easier opportunities during the desert crossing. Accidents happen in such conditions, and men die from natural causes all the time.'

The frank admission of how easily they could have been eliminated sent a chill through Seneca. It was true, the desert crossing would have provided countless opportunities for subtle assassination that could never be proven.

'I'll consider your proposal,' said Seneca finally. 'But until I've discussed it with my unit, I expect you to maintain the same distance you've kept since Syene.'

'Agreed… and Tribune?'

'Yes?'

'Whatever you decide, remember that success requires all of us. Personal grievances are luxuries we can't afford when survival is at stake.' With that, he turned and walked back toward the main camp, leaving Seneca alone with his thoughts and the sound of water lapping against stone. The encounter had raised as many questions as it had answered, but one thing was clear, the expedition's internal politics were about to become as complex as its external challenges. Whether that complexity would prove beneficial or disastrous remained to be seen.

The evening settled over the oasis with blessed coolness,

and Seneca found himself sitting beside Marcus near one of the smaller pools, away from the main group. The sound of gently lapping water provided a peaceful backdrop to their quiet conversation, whilst date palms rustled overhead in the gentle breeze.

'Hard to believe we made it through,' said Marcus, flexing his injured fingers in the lamplight. 'There were moments in that desert when I thought we'd all end up as bleached bones, just another expedition that vanished into the sand.'

'Those men held together better than I expected,' replied Seneca, watching Falco regale a group of soldiers with yet another arena story. 'Raw recruits and criminals, but they learned fast.'

'They had to, really' Marcus observed grimly. 'Learn or die, it's as simple as that. The desert doesn't give second chances to the unprepared.' He paused, testing his shoulder where the old wound still ached. 'I've seen veteran legions break under less pressure than what we put those boys through.'

'Desperation is a powerful teacher,' Seneca agreed. 'Strip away everything a man thinks he knows about himself, and you discover what he's really made of. Most of them surprised themselves, I think.'

They sat in comfortable silence for a while, each lost in his own thoughts about the brutal crossing they had endured so far. Around them, the sound of quiet conversations mixed with the gentle splash of soldiers washing in one of the lower pools, creating an atmosphere of hard-won tranquillity.

Marcus picked up a handful of sand, letting it run through his fingers as he contemplated their journey. When he spoke next, his voice carried a different quality, more personal.

'Seneca,' he said, 'can I ask you something? About Veteranus.'

Seneca glanced at his friend, noting the careful way Marcus had phrased the question.

'What about him?'

'Do you know where he really is? I mean, not just that he's sorting out personal business, but where he is exactly? Ever since we got back from Britannia I've noticed he has been... *different*, I suppose.'

Seneca was quiet for a long moment, studying his friend's weathered features in the flickering light. These were men who had bled together, who had saved each other's lives more times than either could count and if anyone deserved the truth, it was Marcus. But some secrets carried weight beyond personal trust.

'Why do you ask?' he said eventually.

'Because I'm worried about him,' replied Marcus honestly. 'I know Veteranus keeps his own counsel, always has. But lately... there's something eating at him. Something more than just the usual darkness he carries around. And now he's gone off somewhere without even a conversation. Something's doesn't feel right.'

Seneca nodded slowly. He had noticed the same things Marcus was describing, the way Veteranus had become even more distant on their journey from Britannia to Rome, more prone to long silences and brooding contemplation.

'You're right to be concerned,' he said finally. 'And you deserve to know the truth, but what I'm about to tell you goes no further than this conversation. Understood?'

Marcus straightened slightly, recognizing the gravity in his commander's tone.

'Of course. You have my word.'

Seneca took a deep breath, choosing his words with care.

'Veteranus has a son,' he said bluntly, his voice barely above a whisper. 'A boy he's never met. He didn't even know he existed until a year or two ago.'

Marcus's eyes widened in genuine shock, his hand stopping mid-motion as he processed this revelation.

'A son? But how... Veteranus never mentioned... I mean, he's never talked about having any family at all. Never even hinted at a past before he joined us.'

'Because he didn't know,' Seneca continued, glancing around to ensure they weren't overheard. 'Lepidus knew about the child for years but deliberately kept it from him. You have to understand, Marcus, that when we first recruited Veteranus years ago, he was nothing more than a wild animal. Savage, unpredictable, and driven by rage and pain that went deeper than anything we could heal. When Lepidus found out about the child, he thought the knowledge would either destroy Veteranus completely or turn him into something even more dangerous.'

'Sweet Jupiter,' Marcus breathed. 'A child he never knew about. But who was the mother? What happened to her?'

'All I know is that when Lepidus found out, he had her sent to southern Italy and married her off to a farmer down there. Apparently both she and the child are safe and happy, but the knowledge has been eating away at Veteranus for months.'

'And Lepidus said nothing?'

'What could he say? Veteranus was barely human back in those days, more beast than man, and liable to kill anyone who looked at him wrong. The knowledge that he had fathered a child would have broken what little sanity he had left.'

Marcus shook his head slowly, trying to imagine the weight of such a secret.

'So what changed?' he asked. 'How did he find out?'

Seneca's expression grew more complex, the weight of difficult decisions showing in his weathered features.

'Lepidus had been funding the boy's upbringing,' he explained. 'But when you were all missing in Britannia, Lepidus needed Veteranus back and told him about his son to get him to cooperate with the rescue mission. It was... brutal, but effective. Veteranus would have torn half of Britannia apart with his bare hands to earn the right to meet his child.'

The silence that followed was profound and Marcus stared into the dark water, clearly struggling to reconcile this information with what he knew of their violent comrade.

'Can you imagine?' continued Seneca, 'all these years, Veteranus has been fighting and killing and surviving, thinking he was alone in the world and never knowing he had a son growing up without him. And now that knowledge has come to light, it's almost as if it has given him a reason to live.'

'Gods' blood,' Marcus whispered. 'No wonder he's been so different. The weight of that knowledge... suddenly finding out you have a child you've never held, never spoken to...'

'It's been eating him alive,' Seneca confirmed. 'You've seen how he gets during quiet moments, when he thinks no one is watching. That distant look, like he's trying to picture something he can't quite grasp. He's been imagining what his son looks like, what kind of person he's becoming.'

Marcus was quiet for a long moment, processing the emotional magnitude of the situation.

'And now?'

'Now Lepidus is fulfilling his promise to him,' said Seneca. 'Veteranus is probably on his way there now, meeting

119

his son for the first time.'

'What's the boy been told?'

'That his father was a soldier who served with distinction but couldn't care for him due to his duties. Not entirely false, just... incomplete. The family was instructed to prepare him for this meeting when the time came.'

Marcus leaned back against a palm tree, overwhelmed by the implications.

'How do you even begin such a conversation? 'Hello, I'm your father, the one who's been absent your entire life because I was too broken to be trusted with your existence?'

'I don't know,' Seneca admitted, 'but Veteranus has earned the right to try. Whatever mistakes he's made, whatever darkness he carries, he deserves the chance to know his child.'

They sat in contemplative silence, watching the gentle movement of water in the pool whilst around them the camp settled deeper into its peaceful evening routine. Finally, Marcus spoke again.

'Will he come back? To the unit, I mean. Or will fatherhood change him too much?'

'I don't know,' Seneca said honestly. 'Part of me hopes it does change him. We have some bad history between us, him and I, but the man deserves something in his life besides violence and death. But the Occultum... we're his family too, in our own way. I think he'll return, but perhaps as someone different. Someone with more to live for than just duty and revenge.'

'And if he doesn't return?'

'Then we will wish him well and continue our work. The Occultum has survived losses before.'

Another comfortable silence fell between them, broken only by the gentle sounds of the oasis at rest.

'You understand why this stays between us,' Seneca added, his tone carrying a gentle warning. 'If Veteranus thought his personal life was common knowledge then who knows how he would react.'

Marcus met his commander's gaze directly.

'Of course,' he said simply, 'and I hope it goes well for him. Whatever else Veteranus has done, whatever darkness he carries, I believe every man deserves the chance to know his child.'

'So do I, Marcus,' replied Seneca quietly. 'So do I.'

Chapter Seventeen

The Settlement

The second stage of the desert crossing proved that survival was indeed the greatest teacher and the men who emerged from the oasis bore little resemblance to the untested recruits who had departed Alexandria months earlier. Death and desertion had culled the weak in body and spirit, leaving behind a core of survivors who had learned the harsh lessons necessary for existence in the world's most unforgiving environment.

Water discipline, which had been a lethal problem during the first crossing, now became second nature, and men who had once gulped precious liquid in desperate excess now rationed their supplies with careful precision. The sight of empty skins no longer triggered panic, replaced instead by grim determination and hardened resilience.

The guides set an equally punishing pace, but this time the column maintained better cohesion as it moved across the burning landscape. Centurions who had watched their men fall apart during the previous crossing now commanded soldiers who moved with discipline rather than panic. Equipment was properly secured, formations maintained reasonable integrity, and the sort of basic military competence that should have been present from the beginning finally asserted itself.

But the desert continued to claim its tribute. Heat exhaustion, dehydration, and simple physical collapse removed men from the ranks with terrifying regularity while others succumbed to the psychological pressure of endless torment. The losses were significant but not catastrophic and they had retained enough strength to continue functioning as a military force whilst shedding the elements least likely to contribute to their ultimate success.

The settlement that finally greeted them on the far side of the desert appeared like a gift from the gods themselves. Built around a ravine where an ancient well provided reliable water, it had served for centuries as a waypoint for caravans and travellers crossing the deep desert. A few dozen mud-brick buildings clustered around the precious water source, whilst date palms provided blessed shade for structures that had sheltered countless expeditions over the generations.

'Old place,' Khaemwaset explained as they approached the settlement's modest walls. 'Very old. Grandfathers of grandfathers stopped here, paid for water, rested animals. Custom as old as the desert itself.'

The Romans made camp just outside the settlement, and the locals, well accustomed to dealing with large groups of exhausted strangers, emerged to greet them with practiced efficiency.

The population proved to be about a hundred souls, men, women, and children whose ancestors had built their lives around serving the needs of desert travellers. They moved amongst the weary soldiers with the calm competence of people who understood exactly what such groups required.

'They know their business,' Marcus observed as they began providing food and water for the expedition without being asked. 'No panic, no confusion, just professional hospitality. They've clearly done this many times before.'

For a week, the expedition once again rested and recovered in the settlement's protective embrace and men who had been pushed to their physical limits ,slowly regained strength on a diet of dates, goat meat, and unlimited access to fresh water. Equipment was repaired, injuries tended, and the sort of maintenance performed that kept armies functioning in hostile territory.

'We're in better shape than I expected,' Decimus observed as they conducted their evening equipment check. 'The desert hurt us, but it didn't break us.'

'It broke the ones who needed breaking,' replied Falco, his recovery from the crossing now complete. 'What's left is tougher than what we started with.'

'The question is whether it's tough enough for whatever's waiting ahead,' said Seneca. 'The desert was just the beginning. The real challenges lie in the lands where the Twenty-First Rapax disappeared.'

As their week of recovery neared its end, preparations for departure began again with renewed efficiency. The expedition that would continue south bore little resemblance to the collection of amateurs who had left Alexandria. Hard experience had forged them into something approaching a proper military force, albeit one significantly reduced in numbers.

The day before they were to leave, Khaemwaset arranged a meeting between the settlement's headman and Flavus to discuss the traditional payment for water and hospitality.
The meeting took place in a modest hut, with Khaemwaset serving as interpreter between the Roman commander and the tribal leader whose people had maintained this oasis for generations.

'He says the price is traditional,' Khaemwaset translated as the headman spoke in measured tones. 'The group is very large, much larger than any others but in good faith to our

Roman friends, he requires just ten of your camels, a very cheap price for all the water and fresh meat.'

Flavus listened to this pronouncement with growing disbelief, his face reddening as the full implications of the demand became clear.

'*Preposterous!*' he exploded, rising from his seat with obvious indignation. 'We are Romans! We don't pay tribute to desert savages for the privilege of purchasing water that flows freely from the ground and a few scabby goats!'

'My lord,' Khaemwaset began, his tone carrying urgent warning, 'this is not tribute. This is custom, tradition. The settlement survives by…'

'I don't care what their traditions are,' Flavus interrupted. 'We've already paid them generously in silver for supplies and accommodation. If they think they can extort additional payment from a Roman legion, they're gravely mistaken.'

The headman listened to this exchange with impressive composure, his weathered features showing no reaction to the Roman commander's obvious anger and when Khaemwaset reluctantly translated the refusal, he simply nodded acknowledgment and rose to leave.

'That's it?' Flavus asked, surprised by the lack of argument or negotiation.

'He says he understands,' Khaemwaset replied, though his expression suggested deep concern. 'Roman custom is different from desert custom.'

After the headman departed, Khaemwaset remained behind to plead with the legatus one final time.

'My lord, please reconsider. This settlement depends on traditional payments from travellers. Without them, the people starve, and more importantly for us, refusing to honour old customs...' He shook his head gravely. 'Word spreads quickly in the desert. Other settlements may not welcome us if they hear we ignored proper protocol.'

'Are you threatening me, guide?'

'No my lord, just explaining consequences. Desert people have long memories for insults and longer memories for those who respect their ways.'

But Flavus remained unmoved by these arguments, his decision final. The meeting concluded with obvious tension, leaving Khaemwaset to walk further into the settlement to make whatever peace he could with the settlement's leadership.

The following morning brought the familiar sounds of an expedition preparing for departure. Equipment was loaded, animals prepared, and the Roman column formed up for the next stage of their journey into unknown territory.

The Occultum had heard about the previous day's diplomatic crisis and as they prepared their horses and equipment, the implications of Flavus refusal weighed heavily on their minds.

'Short-sighted,' Marcus observed as he secured his pack. 'These people have survived out here for generations. Their customs exist for good reasons.'

'The legatus sees it as weakness,' replied Talorcan. 'Giving in to demands from primitives who should be grateful for Roman silver. He doesn't understand that refusing traditional payment is worse than robbery, It's an insult to their ancestors, their way of life, and everything they hold sacred.'

As the column began moving out of the settlement, Seneca noticed Sica making a subtle gesture toward his comrades, a signal they had used countless times to indicate a brief detour. Without comment, the Syrian peeled away from their small group and made his way back to the settlement's main gate where the headman stood watching their departure.

The conversation between the Syrian and the tribal leader was brief and conducted entirely in gestures before Sica reached into his kit and withdrew one of his prized possessions, a curved Syrian dagger bearing the sort of intricate patterns that marked it as both weapon and work of art.

He presented the blade with the formal courtesy due to a respected equal, offering it handle-first in the manner of someone giving a gift rather than paying tribute. The headman accepted it with a solemn nod, his weathered fingers testing the weapon's balance with obvious appreciation for its quality.

No words were spoken, but understanding passed between them. The traditional obligation had been acknowledged, if not fully satisfied and honour had been preserved on both sides through the simple act of mutual respect.

Sica rejoined his comrades without comment, though he could feel the headman's eyes following his progress as he caught up with the departing column. Behind them, the settlement's inhabitants watched in silence as the Romans disappeared into the heat shimmer, their expressions unreadable.

'What was that all about?' asked Marcus quietly as they rode together.

'Necessity,' replied Sica. 'Some debts shouldn't be left unpaid.'

'Flavus won't appreciate unauthorized diplomacy behind his back.'

'Flavus doesn't need to know,' replied Sica, and both men urged their horses forward to catch up with the rest of their comrades.

Two days beyond the settlement, the expedition's fortunes seemed to be turning. The ground beneath their feet had transformed from the punishing sand of the deep desert to harder, more forgiving terrain that allowed for easier marching. Scattered acacia trees provided occasional shade, whilst the distant outline of mountains promised an end to the endless flatness that had dominated their journey thus far.

The column moved with renewed confidence, and men who had survived the desert's worst trials now walked with something approaching military bearing. The transformation was remarkable. Men who had stumbled through the desert like walking corpses now maintained proper formation and responded to orders with reasonable promptness. The brutal selection process of the crossing had left them with soldiers who understood the value of discipline and cooperation. Water remained precious but was no longer the desperate concern it had been during the crossing and game trails and scattered vegetation suggested they were entering territory where life might actually be sustainable.

As evening approached, they established a camp in a grove of scattered trees that provided both shelter and defensive positions and for the first time since leaving the Nile, the mood in camp approached something resembling optimism as men who had been focused solely on survival now contemplated the possibility of success.

The evening's highlight came when several of the guides returned from a hunting expedition carrying two gazelles they had taken with their skilled archery. The animals weren't large, but in the context of their recent hardships, they represented a feast of magnificent proportions.

'Fresh meat,' Falco announced with obvious delight as

the carcasses were prepared for cooking. 'Sweet Jupiter, I'd forgotten what real food tasted like.'

'What are you going on about?' asked Sica. 'We ate goat in the settlement.'

'Goat isn't real meat,' declared Falco. 'Not for a stallion such as me.' This body needs nurturing and fed with the best that money can buy.' He flexed his muscles to reinforce his argument as Sica sighed and turned away.

The guides demonstrated their expertise once again, showing the Romans how to make the most of their prizes. Every scrap of meat, bone and organs were prepared for a rich soup that would provide nourishment for the entire force.

As darkness fell and the fires sprang up throughout the camp, the expedition experienced something it had almost forgotten, genuine contentment. Men gathered around the fires sharing stories and jokes, their voices carrying the sort of easy camaraderie that marked efficient military units.

'This is more like it,' Falco declared, savouring a bowl of the gazelle soup with obvious relish. 'Proper food, decent ground to sleep on, and nobody trying to kill us. Paradise compared to what we've been through.'

'Don't get too comfortable,' Seneca warned, though his own mood had lightened considerably. 'We're still deep in unknown territory, and we haven't forgotten what happened to the Twenty-First.'

'Let me enjoy this moment,' replied Falco. 'Tomorrow can bring whatever disasters it wants, but tonight we're eating like kings and sleeping on ground that won't try to cook us alive.'

Even Sica seemed more relaxed than usual, his normally vigilant demeanour softened by the combination of good food and relative security. Around them, the sounds of a contented military camp provided a comforting backdrop to their conversation.

'The men needed this,' Decimus observed, listening to the laughter and conversation from the main body. 'Morale was rock bottom after the desert crossing. A night like this might remind them why they're here.'

'Speaking of which,' said Talorcan, 'do we actually remember why we're here? Finding survivors of an expedition that disappeared years ago seems increasingly unlikely the further we travel.'

'We're here because the emperor ordered it,' replied Seneca pragmatically. 'Whether we find survivors or just determine what happened to them, we complete the mission and return to report our findings.'

The evening passed peacefully, with guards posted according to proper military protocol and men settled into their sleeping arrangements with something approaching confidence, secure in the knowledge that they had overcome the worst challenges so far and emerged stronger for the experience.

Dawn came slowly, and the camp stirred into life. The morning routines proceeded normally until a guard's shout of alarm shattered the peaceful atmosphere.

'*Centurio! Come quickly!*'

The cry carried such urgency that men throughout the camp immediately reached for weapons, their hard-won survival instincts overriding the previous night's contentment. Many ran toward the source of the alarm whilst others formed defensive groups without waiting for orders.

What they found sent a chill through the entire expedition. One of the night sentries lay sprawled beside his post, his throat opened in a precise cut. The man's weapons remained in their scabbards, suggesting he had been killed without warning or struggle.

'Search the entire perimeter!' commanded Scipio, his voice tight with anger and growing alarm. 'Check every post, account for every man!'

The systematic search that followed revealed the full scope of the disaster. Nine more bodies were discovered at various points around the camp's perimeter, each killed in the same efficient manner. Ten men had died during the night without anyone raising any alarm or alerting their comrades to the presence of enemies.

'How is this possible?' Flavus demanded, his fury evident as he surveyed the evidence of complete security failure. 'How does anyone manage to kill ten trained men without detection?'

The surviving guards were assembled for immediate questioning. These were men who had survived the desert crossing and proven their competence under extreme conditions, yet they had been rendered completely ineffective by an enemy they had never seen.

'We heard nothing, Centurio,' stammered the Optio responsible for guard duties. 'No sounds of struggle, no calls for help, nothing. It was as if the night itself killed them.'

The explanation satisfied no one, least of all Flavus whose anger sought a target for the humiliation of being attacked without warning in their own camp.

'Incompetence!' he declared. 'Criminal incompetence that cost ten Romans their lives! Every surviving guard from last night will receive ten lashes for failure of duty!'

The punishment was harsh but understandable given the circumstances. Ten good soldiers were dead because their comrades had failed to maintain proper vigilance, and such failures demanded consequences that would prevent repetition.

As the morning progressed and the full implications of the night's attack became clear, speculation ran wild through the ranks. Who had killed their comrades? How had the attackers penetrated their defences so completely? And were they still being watched by enemies who could strike again at will?

Seneca and Sica conducted their own investigation, examining the bodies and the surrounding area for clues that might explain the night's events. What they found was disturbing, the cuts were precise and professional, made by someone with extensive knowledge of human anatomy and the skills necessary to kill quickly and silently.

'I don't understand,' said Seneca. 'They had the skill to kill ten sentries without being detected but did not continue the infiltration or steal any supplies. Why just kill ten men and then disappear?'

As they returned to their own camp area, Sica spotted something that made his blood run cold. There, driven into the ground just outside their tent, was the curved Syrian dagger he had presented to the settlement's headman a few days earlier.

He retrieved the weapon quickly, checking to ensure no one else had noticed its presence. The blade was clean, showing no signs of the night's violence, but its message was unmistakably clear.

'What is it?' Seneca asked, noting his comrade's sudden tension.

'Nothing,' replied Sica, sliding the dagger back into his kit with careful casualness. But privately, he understood exactly what had happened during the night. The settlement's headman had appreciated his gesture of respect, but traditional obligations demanded more than symbolic payment. The price had been ten camels, but as the Romans had refused to pay properly, the settlement had collected its own tribute. Ten lives for ten camels. It was, in the harsh arithmetic of survival, a fair exchange. The settlement's people had taken what was owed to them according to customs older than Rome itself.

By noon, the expedition moved out with renewed vigilance, every man now understanding that they travelled through territory where enemies could strike without warning and disappear like shadows in the night. The lesson had been written in blood, and its message was clear. In this harsh environment, Roman authority meant nothing to people who followed older, harsher laws.

Chapter Eighteen

The Edge of the Jungle

The character of the land changed dramatically as they moved further from the desert's harsh embrace. Rolling hills replaced flat terrain, whilst scattered trees gradually thickened into something approaching proper forest. The punishing heat that had defined their existence for weeks gave way to a different kind of discomfort, the oppressive humidity of dense vegetation that made every breath feel like drowning in warm water.

The path they followed grew increasingly narrow, forcing the column into single file as ancient trees pressed in on both sides, their canopy blocking much of the sunlight and creating a perpetual twilight that made distance judgment difficult.

'This doesn't feel right,' Flavus observed to Khaemwaset as they navigated another winding section of trail. 'Are you certain this is the correct route?'

The guide nodded in response, his eyes following landmarks only visible to him and his brethren.

'Correct path,' he said. 'Very old path, used by traders and travellers for many generations. Soon we reach river, then destination is close.'

The promise of the end of their journey proved a false hope when they finally emerged from the forest to find themselves standing at the edge of a ravine that dropped away into misty depths. Far below, the sound of rushing water confirmed the presence of the river Khaemwaset had promised, but reaching it seemed impossible given the precipitous nature of the walls that enclosed it.

What drew every eye, however, was the structure that spanned the chasm. A rickety rope bridge, ancient and precarious looking, stretching across the ravine to disappear into the forest on the far side. The construction was clearly native work, with woven vines and wooden planks that looked barely capable of supporting a single man, let alone an entire expedition.

'You expect us to cross that?' Flavus asked incredulously, studying the swaying bridge with obvious alarm.

'Only way across,' Khaemwaset confirmed. 'Bridge very old, but strong. Has carried many travellers safely.'

Seneca and Marcus rode up alongside the leaders and stared at the problem.

'It would take days to get the entire force across,' said Marcus quietly, 'and that's assuming it doesn't collapse under the weight.'

'We'll reinforce it,' decided Flavus. 'Assemble the men.'

What followed was a demonstration of Roman engineering at its most practical as fresh ropes from their supplies were stretched across the ramshackle bridge, and suitable trees felled to be shaped into logs of appropriate dimensions. Teams of men lowered themselves into the ravine to anchor stabilising lines on either side whilst others constructed a series of wooden platforms that could be lashed to the new rope framework, and within a few days, the native bridge was transformed.

But as the bridge neared completion, another problem became apparent. The jungle beyond the ravine was clearly denser than anything they had yet encountered, with vegetation so thick that their pack animals would struggle to navigate the narrow paths. The camels, in particular, would be useless in such terrain, so another work party was organized to create a semi-permanent camp on their side of the ravine, positioned to control access to the bridge whilst providing secure accommodation for the animals and supplies they couldn't take further.

More trees were felled and shaped into palisade stakes, creating a defensive perimeter large enough to contain the camels and horses. Guard towers were placed at strategic points providing observation over the surrounding approaches, whilst internal structures offered protection from weather and potential attacks.

When the work was complete, they had created a small but secure fortress that could serve as their lifeline to the outside world and Scipio selected an experienced Optio and ten reliable men to garrison the position, with orders to maintain the depot until the expedition's return.

'You're our anchor,' he explained to the Optio as he briefed him on his responsibilities. 'Whatever happens beyond that bridge, this position stays secure until we return. Without it, none of us are getting home.'

The garrison understood their critical role. They would protect not just the spare supplies and animals, but the expedition's only known route back to civilization. It was a responsibility that carried the weight of every man's survival. But as preparations for crossing began in earnest, Khaemwaset delivered news that cast doubt over their entire enterprise.

'We go no further,' he announced firmly. 'Beyond bridge is bad place. Evil spirits, ancient curses. My people will not enter such territory.'

Flavus stared at him in disbelief.

'What do you mean, you won't go further?' he asked. 'We need guides! You can't abandon us now!'

But Khaemwaset remained unmoved. The guides had

brought the expedition as far as their courage and customs allowed, but they would not cross into territory they considered cursed by forces beyond human understanding.

'Bad magic beyond river,' Khaemwaset repeated with final authority. 'Old places where bad things happen and should not be disturbed. We have fulfilled our agreement. From here, you go on alone.'

Faced with the complete refusal of their guides, the legatus summoned Seneca for urgent consultation. The situation was explained with growing desperation as the expedition's leadership realized they were about to lose the local knowledge that had kept them alive so far.

'Your unit will have to take over navigation,' said Flavus bluntly. 'Scipio says you're our most experienced scouts and without the guides, you're our only hope of finding our way through whatever lies ahead.'

Seneca accepted the responsibility with characteristic stoicism, though privately he understood the magnitude of what they faced. Leading an expedition through unknown territory with only crude maps and no local guides was the sort of challenge that killed men.

'We'll do what we can,' he said simply, and turned away to report back to his men.

Chapter Nineteen

The Jungle

The transformation from desert soldiers to jungle expedition began the moment they left their horses and camels at the bridge depot. Each man now carried a sarcina loaded with supplies that would have to sustain them through unknown territory, grain, olive oil, salt pork, and precious water skins that represented life itself in this humid wilderness. The weight was crushing in the oppressive heat, but there was no alternative. Every ounce of equipment had been carefully calculated to provide maximum survival capability whilst remaining portable by men already weakened by their desert ordeal.

Seneca led the Occultum to the front of the column, where they took up the thankless task of cutting a path through vegetation so dense it seemed designed by hostile gods to stop human progress. The jungle pressed against them like a living wall, vines thick as a man's arm intertwining with thorny shrubs and trees whose trunks disappeared into a canopy so thick that precious little sunlight reached the forest floor.

Marcus swung his gladius in methodical strokes, hacking through a curtain of hanging vines that blocked their advance. The blade, designed for stabbing enemies on European battlefields, served adequately as a jungle knife, though the unfamiliar work sent jolts of pain through his still-healing arm.

'Like cutting through rope,' he muttered, pausing to wipe sweat from his eyes. 'Rope that grows back the moment you turn away.'

Behind him, Falco wielded his own sword with characteristic enthusiasm, attacking the undergrowth as if it were a personal enemy.

'At least it's not trying to kill us directly,' he observed, severing a particularly stubborn vine. 'Though give it time. I'm sure this green hell has plenty of ways to murder Romans.'

The work was exhausting in the humid air, the sweat pouring from their bodies despite the filtered sunlight, and their clothing quickly became soaked through with moisture that had nowhere to evaporate in the still air beneath the canopy.

Every hundred paces or so, Sica would draw his dagger and carve a distinctive mark into the bark of any distinctive tree, a simple pattern that would guide them home if they needed to retreat through this green maze.

'Good thinking,' said Seneca during one of these episodes. 'Though I hope we won't need them.'

'Hope is fine,' Sica replied, continuing his careful carving. 'Planning is better.'

The jungle was alive in ways that defied Roman understanding. Birds with plumage of impossible brilliance flashed through the undergrowth, emerald parrots whose harsh cries echoed through the humid air, and larger birds whose calls provided a constant soundtrack to their laborious progress. Monkeys chattered in the canopy above, occasionally throwing fruit or debris at the sweating Romans below with what seemed like deliberate malice.

'Barbarian monkeys,' Falco declared after a particularly well-aimed piece of fruit struck his head. 'No respect for superior civilizations.'

The diversity of life was staggering. Butterflies the size of a man's hand floated past in clouds of orange and black, whilst beetles as large as mice scuttled across their path with armoured efficiency. Flowers bloomed in spectacular profusion, their perfumes competing with the earthier scents of decomposition and new growth that characterized the jungle floor.

But it was the sounds that proved most unsettling. The constant drip of moisture from the canopy above created a rhythm like light rain, whilst the rustle of unseen creatures moving through the undergrowth kept everyone on edge. Occasionally, larger sounds would echo through the forest, the crack of a falling branch, the splash of something entering water, or calls from creatures whose nature could only be guessed at.

'What was that?' Talorcan asked as a deep, rumbling call echoed from somewhere ahead.

'Something large,' replied Decimus grimly. 'Something we probably don't want to meet.'

The column's progress was agonizingly slow. Where they might have covered twenty miles in a day on open ground, the jungle reduced them to perhaps three or four miles of actual advance, forcing the entire expedition into a vulnerable snake of men that stretched back through the undergrowth for hundreds of paces.

Behind the Occultum, the sounds of just over three hundred men struggling through the jungle created a constant commotion as centurions shouted orders, and soldiers cursed as they caught on thorns or stumbled over roots.

'So much for stealth,' Marcus observed as a particularly loud curse echoed from somewhere behind them.

'We gave up stealth when we brought all these men into the jungle,' replied Seneca. 'We just have to hope that whatever's out there isn't immediately hostile.'

The decision of where to make camp each night proved critical. The jungle offered no natural clearings, forcing them to create their own space by cutting away enough vegetation to accommodate their numbers. The work was backbreaking after a full day of trail cutting, but absolutely necessary for survival, and when darkness fell, it did so with shocking completeness. The canopy that had filtered sunlight during the day now blocked out the stars, creating a darkness so absolute that men couldn't see their own hands in front of their faces. Only the glow of their fires provided islands of light in an ocean of impenetrable black.

They built many fires, more than military efficiency would normally dictate and every twenty paces or so around their perimeter, flames leaped toward the canopy, creating a barrier of light that might discourage whatever nocturnal predators the jungle concealed. The soldiers gathered in small groups near each fire, their faces illuminated by dancing flames whilst facing the darkness that seemed to press against them with physical weight.

The jungle's night chorus was overwhelming, a symphony of frogs that croaked and bellowed in countless different voices, crickets whose calls rose and fell in waves, and dozens of other insects whose sounds created a wall of noise that made sleep difficult. But it was the other sounds that kept men awake, clutching weapons and starting at every shadow.

Something large was moving through the forest beyond their fires. They could hear it, the crack of branches, the rustle of displaced vegetation, and occasionally what sounded almost like footsteps. Whatever it was seemed to be circling their camp, just beyond the reach of their firelight, taking its time to assess these strange intruders.

'Big cats,' suggested one of the men during a whispered conversation around the command fire. 'The guides mentioned there were leopards in this region.'

'Could be,' Seneca agreed, though his tone carried doubt. 'But it sounds bigger than any cat I've ever heard.'

'Elephant?' Falco suggested hopefully. 'They're plant eaters aren't they? They might just be curious.'

A sound that was definitely not elephantine echoed from the darkness, a low, rumbling call that suggested predatory interest rather than herbivorous curiosity. Whatever was out there was assessing them as potential prey, and the knowledge sent chills through men who had faced Germanic warriors and British druids without flinching.

Decimus sat with his back against a tree trunk and his sword across his knees. The blade remained ready whilst his eyes strained to penetrate shadows that danced just beyond the firelight.

'I can't see anything,' he whispered to Talorcan, who had drawn the same watch. 'But I can feel something watching us.'

'I know,' replied Talorcan quietly. 'I've been feeling it since sunset. Whatever's out there, it's patient. Waiting for something.'

The night passed with agonizing slowness, marked by the changing of guards and the constant maintenance of fires that represented their only protection against unknown dangers.

Dawn came gradually, filtered through layers of vegetation until it was difficult to distinguish morning from the perpetual twilight of the forest floor. But with daylight came a temporary cessation of the more sinister night sounds, replaced by the resumption of the jungle's daytime chorus, and as the expedition stirred to life to begin preparing for another day's march, Seneca made his way to the command area where

Flavus was consulting their crude map with obvious frustration.

'Tribune,' the young commander said, looking up from the nearly useless piece of parchment. 'I need to know how much further we have to go. The men are already showing signs of strain, and we've barely begun.'

'What can you tell me about the route ahead?' Seneca asked, studying the map that showed little more than their approximate position and a few geographical features marked in rough sketches.

'According to what the guides said before they abandoned us,' replied Flavus, 'we continue directly south until we reach an impassable river. They called it the River of Death, though they refused to explain why. Once we reach it, we're supposed to head downstream until we arrive at... something. They said we would know when we got there.'

Seneca stared at him in disbelief.

'That's all? Continue south to a river we can't cross, then follow it downstream until we recognize something we've never seen before?'

'That's all they would tell us and every time I pressed for more details, they became agitated and started talking about evil spirits and ancient curses. According to them, the river marks the boundary of the territory where the Twenty-First Rapax disappeared.'

The information was maddeningly vague, but it was all they had. Seneca studied the map once more, noting the rough distance markings that suggested the river was still many days away through jungle terrain.

'We'll continue cutting the trail,' he said finally, 'and try to pick up the pace if possible. The sooner we reach this mysterious river, the sooner we can assess whatever we're really facing,' and with that sobering assessment, he returned to the

Occultum, who were already preparing to resume their role as pathfinders for the struggling expedition.

Chapter Twenty

The Jungle

Within a few days, the expedition began to resemble a column of walking wounded more than a Roman military force. The jungle's countless torments had accumulated into a different type of crisis that threatened to destroy them more completely than any enemy army.

The mosquitoes proved to be their most persistent tormentors. Clouds of the tiny vampires rose from every pool of stagnant water, every patch of rotting vegetation, every shadow where moisture lingered and attacked with relentless hunger, seeking any exposed flesh to feast upon. Men who had started the jungle march in regulation military dress now wrapped themselves like Egyptian mummies, using spare tunics, torn cloaks, and strips of cloth to cover every inch of skin except their eyes.

But even total coverage couldn't stop the insects entirely. They found ways through the smallest gaps, around loose bindings and under the edges of improvised face coverings. Soon, every man's exposed skin was a mass of inflamed bites that itched with maddening intensity.

But the real problems began when men started scratching. In the humid heat, the smallest break in the skin became a gateway for infection and scratches that would have healed in days under normal conditions festered and spread, becoming angry red wounds that wept pus and refused to close.

'Don't scratch,' became the constant refrain from the medics. 'Whatever you do, don't scratch.'

But telling exhausted, miserable men not to scratch wounds that tormented them every waking moment was like ordering the sun not to rise. Human nature proved stronger than military discipline, and the infections spread through the ranks like wildfire.

But just as bad as the mosquitoes was the water situation. The humid air made men feel constantly thirsty, their bodies craving liquid to replace what poured from them as sweat. Discipline that had been learned through brutal desert experience began to break down again as soldiers consumed their carefully rationed supplies at dangerous rates.

'Save your water!' the centurions called repeatedly. 'Small sips only!'

But the jungle played tricks with men's minds. The constant sound of dripping moisture, the sight of pools and streams that seemed to offer unlimited refreshment, the oppressive humidity that made every breath feel insufficient, all combined to create a psychological thirst that overwhelmed rational water management.

When they did find sources of water, desperation overcame caution and veteran soldiers who knew better watched in horror as newer recruits threw themselves down beside muddy streams, drinking directly from sources that any experienced campaigner could see were contaminated.

'Boil it first!' Marcus shouted at a group of men who were gulping brown water from a stagnant pool. 'Strain it through a cloth, then boil it!'

'Takes too long,' one of them replied between desperate swallows. 'I'm dying of thirst now, so I'll take the risk.'

'You'll be dying of worse things if you keep drinking that,' replied Marcus, but his words fell on ears deafened by desperation.

The consequences appeared within hours as dysentery struck the column like a plague, turning strong men into helpless invalids who could barely walk without soiling themselves. The sounds of retching and the stench of liquid excrement became constant companions as the expedition struggled forward through the jungle's oppressive embrace.

Men who had been proud Roman soldiers were reduced to crawling behind bushes every few hundred paces, their bodies wracked with cramps and explosive diarrhoea that left them weak and dehydrated. Others vomited everything they tried to consume, their systems rejecting both food and water until they became empty vessels held upright only by stubborn will.

A few days later, they knew they could go no further and when they reached a relatively clean stream flowing over rocky ground, Flavus called a halt.

'We stop here,' he announced. 'Get the medics working, establish a proper camp, and pray to whatever gods might be listening that we can save enough men to continue.'

The Occultum established their own small camp upstream from the main body. Their condition was noticeably better than the general population, still battered by the jungle's assault, but functional rather than debilitated.

Seneca watched Sica carefully strain the stream water through multiple layers of cloth before boiling it over their small fire. The many missions they had shared across three continents had taught all of them the skills necessary to at least survive where others fell short.

Around the fires that evening, as the medics worked desperately to save lives in the background, the Occultum walked quietly amongst the men, sharing their knowledge wherever possible.

'The water,' said Sica, holding up a cup of the carefully

prepared liquid. 'Never drink anything you haven't boiled, no matter how clean it looks. The invisible enemies are the deadliest.'

'And strain it first,' Talorcan added, demonstrating with a piece of cloth that had already filtered dozens of cups. 'Everything that floats, everything that moves, everything that might carry disease, remove it before you heat it. And with the mosquitoes,' he continued, adjusting the cloth wrapped around his face. 'Cover everything you can, seal every gap. Better to sweat than to scratch, better to itch than to fester, and if you can, clean your hands before touching any wound. Use wine or vinegar if you have it, boiled water if you don't. Infection kills more soldiers than enemy weapons.'

Seneca listened to his men share survival techniques learned through campaigns across the empire but as the sounds of dying men echoed from the main camp, he wondered if knowledge alone would be enough to see them through this green hell.

The medics did what they could, their limited supplies stretched beyond all reasonable limits. They had salves for infected wounds, but not enough for the dozens of men whose scratches had become suppurating sores. They had herbs that might ease dysentery's grip, but insufficient quantities for the many men whose systems had been devastated by contaminated water.

'We're losing them faster than we can treat them,' the senior medicus reported to Flavus on the third day of their enforced halt. 'The infections are spreading, the dysentery is getting worse, and we simply don't have the resources to handle this many sick men.'

The young commander stared at the rows of improvised shelters where his soldiers lay dying, his face showing the strain of watching his command disintegrate through causes no military training had prepared him for.

'How many?' he asked quietly.

'Twenty-three dead since yesterday. Another forty who won't see the week out unless something changes. Perhaps sixty more who are too weak to march but might recover given time and proper treatment.'

The numbers were brutal. Disease and infection were claiming them at a rate that would leave Flavus with perhaps three hundred effective soldiers by the time they could resume their march, if they could resume their march at all.

The burials began on the fourth day of their halt and several men who had survived the desert crossing, who had endured the bridge building and the initial jungle march, now lay wrapped in their own cloaks beneath hastily carved wooden markers. The jungle seemed to watch patiently, as if waiting to spread their sprawling tendrils over the disturbed earth to erase all evidence of Roman presence.

'Seventy graves in total,' Seneca reported to Flavus on the morning they finally prepared to continue. 'Seventy good soldiers who died because they couldn't adapt fast enough to conditions none of us were prepared for.'

'And the others?'

'A dozen men too sick to travel but should recover given time. We'll leave them with supplies and hope they can follow our trail back to the depot, but...'

'But we both know they won't,' Flavus finished. 'They'll die here, in this fever-ridden swamp, because I didn't have the knowledge to keep them alive.'

Seneca looked at the young officer with something approaching sympathy. Command in impossible conditions aged men quickly, and the weight of losing nearly a hundred soldiers to disease and infection was clearly crushing him.

'You couldn't have known how brutal the jungle would be,' he said. 'The men who died were learning the same lessons we all had to learn. They just ran out of time before they mastered them.'

The expedition that continued south was harder, more experienced, and significantly smaller than what had entered the jungle weeks earlier. They pressed on because they were Romans, because duty demanded it, and because retreat would cost them as many lives as advance. But each man now understood that fulfilling their mission was only half the challenge. Getting home alive would test them beyond anything they had yet endured.

To their immense relief, the jungle began to thin after another few day's march. The oppressive canopy that had blocked out the sky gradually gave way to scattered trees, then isolated groves, until finally they emerged onto something that seemed impossible after weeks in the green hell, vast open plains that stretched to the horizon under an endless blue sky.

The transformation was so dramatic that men actually stopped and stared, blinking in sunlight they had almost forgotten existed. After the claustrophobic press of vegetation and the constant twilight of the forest floor, the sight of open grassland felt like emerging from a tomb into the land of the living.

'Sweet Jupiter,' Falco breathed, pulling the cloth wrappings from his face to feel the wind against his skin. 'I was beginning to think the whole world had turned into that cursed forest.'

But it was the wildlife that truly lifted their spirits. The plains teemed with life in spectacular abundance, herds of gazelle that moved across the grassland like flowing water, strange striped horses that watched them with curious rather than fearful eyes, and countless other creatures whose names they didn't know but whose meat they could certainly appreciate.

'Look at them,' said Marcus with wonder, pointing toward a herd of gazelle that grazed peacefully perhaps two hundred paces away. 'They're not even afraid of us.'

The animals' lack of fear proved a godsend for the expedition's survival. These creatures had clearly never encountered humans before, and certainly not humans with weapons designed for killing at distance so when the best archers among the Romans took position and began selecting targets, the gazelle stood curiously watching until the arrows found their marks.

'Like shooting targets in the Campus Martius,' one of the archers observed with satisfaction as he retrieved his arrow from a cleanly killed gazelle. 'Except these targets are going to feed us for days.'

Within hours of emerging onto the plains, they had more fresh meat than they had seen since leaving Alexandria. The men prepared the food with enthusiasm they hadn't shown in weeks, and morale, which had plummeted during the jungle ordeal, began rising like smoke from their cooking fires.

The streams that crossed the plains ran clear and clean, fed by distant mountains rather than the stagnant pools of the jungle. Men could drink without fear, filling their water skins from sources that sparkled in the sunlight and tasted like the mountain springs of home.

A few nights later, the Occultum established their usual camp on slightly elevated ground that provided good observation over the surrounding plains. For the first time since entering the jungle, they could see for miles in every direction, no hidden dangers lurking behind walls of vegetation, and no oppressive canopy blocking their view of potential threats.

'Much better,' Seneca agreed, noting how the improved conditions were affecting his men. Even Sica seemed more relaxed, though his habitual vigilance remained intact. 'The men needed this. A few days of decent food and clean water might restore enough strength to face whatever's waiting at this so-called River of Death.'

As evening approached, the expedition settled down into the usual night activities. Guards were posted according to proper protocol, but for the first time in weeks they could see their entire perimeter clearly. The sounds that rose from the plains were those of grazing animals and normal wildlife rather than the mysterious threats that had haunted their jungle nights.

Falco was regaling a group of soldiers with one of his usual stories, his voice carrying clearly across the camp without the need to compete with the jungle's oppressive chorus, while other men sat around fires, their spirits lifted by full bellies and the luxury of being able to see the stars overhead.

The first attack came without warning on the third night on the open plains when a scream of absolute pain and terror shattered the peaceful atmosphere and men throughout the camp jolted awake with weapons already in their hands.

The initial scream was immediately joined by desperate calls for help, but the words were cut off by sounds that turned blood to ice water. Something was dragging the screaming man away from the camp, and whatever it was moved with terrifying power through the grass beyond their firelight.

The victim's screams continued for perhaps twenty heartbeats, pleas for help that grew more distant and more desperate before ending abruptly in a terrifying silence that signalled the end of his suffering.

Several soldiers started running toward the perimeter with weapons ready, but Scipio's voice cut through their movement like a blade.

'*Hold your positions!*' he roared with absolute authority. 'No one leaves the light of the fires!'

'But Quintus...' one of them protested.

'Quintus is already dead,' said Scipio. 'And if you go charging into that darkness, you'll join him. Return to your posts immediately.'

The camp prefect's military bearing brooked no argument, but the decision was clearly resented, and many of the men stood at the edge of their firelight, weapons ready, listening to the deathly sounds from the darkness. The knowledge that they were abandoning a comrade, dead or alive, was almost too hard to bear.

The remainder of the night passed without sleep for anyone. Guards doubled their vigilance whilst off-duty soldiers sat around fires that were built higher and brighter than usual. Every sound from the darkness sent hands to weapons, for every movement of grass in the night breeze could have been approaching death.

'What do you think it was?' Talorcan whispered to his comrades as they maintained their own watch.

'Definitely a big cat,' Sica replied quietly. 'Probably a lion. Something that is strong enough to drag off a full-grown man.'

Dawn revealed the truth in all its grim detail. Following the clear trail through the flattened grass, they found what remained of Quintus perhaps three hundred paces from the camp's perimeter. Vultures were already at work on the corpse, their efficient scavenging having reduced a Roman soldier to scattered bones in the space of a few hours.

'Mother of the gods,' someone whispered, staring at the gruesome remains.

The bones had been cracked open for their marrow, the skull crushed like an eggshell, and every scrap of meat stripped away. Whatever had taken Quintus hadn't been alone.

A few hours later, they resumed their march with increased vigilance, arrows nocked and eyes constantly scanning the grassland for signs of movement. The herds of game animals that had seemed so obligingly peaceful now served as early warning systems, and when the gazelle and zebra became restless or moved away from certain areas, the Romans knew to be especially alert.

Finally, two days later, they reached the banks of a wide, muddy river, moving like a brown ribbon cutting across the endless grassland. The water looked calm enough, the current manageable, and the far shore was clearly visible perhaps a few hundred paces away but for soldiers who had bridged German rivers and crossed British estuaries, it was just one more manageable challenge.

The following morning, the column prepared to cross, but Sica was concerned. He had been observing one of the men who bore a freshly butchered leg of deer draped over his sarcina, and something about the blood seeping from the fresh meat troubled him. He left the Occultum and walked over to the soldier.

'Hand it over,' he demanded, gesturing toward the

haunch of venison.

'What? Why?' the soldier protested. 'It's good meat. We killed it a few hours ago.'

'Just give it to me,' Sica insisted, and after the soldier reluctantly complied, he hurried to the riverbank where men were just starting to wade in. 'Stop!' he called out. 'Get back to the bank!'

The soldiers returned in confusion as Sica marched past Flavus without a word and hurled the bloody leg of meat far out into the river. For a few moments there was nothing, but as Flavus turned to challenge him, the surface erupted as a huge crocodile surged up to grab the meat. Within moments a second beast joined the first and the river came alive with dozens of the massive reptiles, all converging on the scent of blood. The sight was extraordinary and terrifying as crocodiles bigger than anyone had ever seen before broke the surface with explosive violence.

Everyone stared at the seething river in stunned silence. The placid water had transformed into a feeding frenzy of armoured death, each reptile easily large enough to take down a horse, let alone a man.

Flavus stared at the impossible sight, his face pale as the reality dawned on him. The crocodiles were like nothing any Roman had ever encountered, even on the Nile. They were massive, numerous, and clearly accustomed to feeding on anything that entered their domain. This was clearly the river the guides had warned them about.

'Change of plans,' he said quietly, realising how close they had come to disaster. 'We follow the river downstream.'

As the expedition prepared to move along the riverbank, every man now understood why this waterway had earned its ominous name. The River of Death was no metaphor, it was a literal description of what awaited anyone foolish enough to enter its crocodile-infested waters.

Chapter Twenty-One

The River

The journey south along the riverbank proved to be by far the easiest leg of their expedition thus far. The abundant game that had blessed them on the plains continued along the water's edge, with herds of antelope and gazelle providing easy hunting for the remaining archers. The river itself offered an unlimited supply of fresh water, carefully taken from feeder streams well away from the deeper pools where shadows might conceal lurking death.

For the first time since leaving Syene, the mood in the column approached genuine optimism bordering on excitement. Their bellies full, their water skins topped up and even the occasional glimpses of massive lions watching them from the grassland couldn't dampen their spirits. They knew they were close and whatever waited for them at the end of their journey, few believed it could be as bad as the deprivations they had suffered over the previous few weeks.

The trees gradually closed in again as they followed the river's meandering course, but it was nothing like the suffocating hell of the deep jungle they had endured. These were more open woodlands, with enough space between the trunks for the column to maintain reasonable formation and sufficient canopy gaps to let in blessed sunlight.

Herds of elephants proved to be a constant source of wonder and nervous entertainment. The massive beasts moved through the landscape like living mountains, their trumpeting calls echoing across the water as they came down to drink. The Romans gave them respectful distance, awed by creatures that dwarfed anything they had encountered in their Mediterranean world.

'Look at the size of them,' Falco whispered as they watched a family group bathing in a quiet backwater. 'Like something from the old myths. Walking mountains with tusks like ivory spears.'

The lions remained a constant concern, though they seemed content to observe rather than attack. Glimpses of tawny forms moving through the tall grass kept weapons close at hand and guards alert, but the big cats appeared to prefer the abundant game to Roman soldiers who now travelled in disciplined groups.

Another week passed without serious incident, each day bringing steady progress along the increasingly winding river. The water grew faster, the further they travelled, tumbling over rocks and creating currents too dangerous to cross, but their path was clear - follow the river downstream until they found whatever destination the guides had cryptically promised they would recognize.

After establishing another evening camp in a grove of acacia trees that provided both shelter and defensive positions, Seneca decided to take the Occultum forward to scout the route for the following day's march as the river had become noticeably swifter, with white water rapids a warning of changing terrain ahead.

They moved carefully through the gathering dusk, following the water's edge as it wound between increasingly rocky outcroppings. The sound of rushing water grew louder with each step, suggesting falls or major rapids somewhere ahead. But it was the quality of the light that first caught Seneca's attention, a strange, golden glow that seemed to emanate from beyond the next bend in the river.

'You see that?' Marcus asked quietly, pointing toward

the unusual illumination that painted the rocks ahead with warm, flickering light.

'I see it,' replied Seneca, though he couldn't explain what might be causing such a phenomenon. 'Stay alert. We don't know what we're walking into.'

They rounded the rocky outcropping that had blocked their view, and suddenly the river curved sharply to reveal the source of the mysterious light. The waterway cascaded over a series of magnificent falls, the late afternoon light refracting in the billions of water particles hanging in the air. But as they emerged onto a precipice overlooking the falls below, it wasn't the natural beauty that stopped them in their tracks, it was the astonishing vista that opened up before them.

'*Sweet merciful Jupiter,*' Decimus whispered, his voice thick with awe. 'I've seen Roman cities, Germanic strongholds and British hillforts. I've seen the cities of Greece, Alexandria's palaces and Egyptian temples, but this... this is beyond anything I could have imagined.'

They stood in absolute silence for long moments, their minds struggling to process the magnitude of what lay before them.

In front of them stretched a huge depression in the ground, several miles across and filled with lush vegetation that extended from one side of the crater to the other. The river cascaded magnificently over a series of falls to their right, crashing far below with a deafening roar before settling down and meandering peacefully across the crater floor to form a lake halfway across, the home of thousands of pink flamingos, moving as one as if in a coordinated dance of elegance.

It was an astonishing sight, but even all that splendour was dwarfed into insignificance by what they could see built into the far cliff face, the immense ruins of a city carved directly into the living rock itself where massive terraces climbed the cliff face in perfect symmetry, connected by staircases that looked like ribbons of white stone from their distant vantage point.

    The structures were clearly ancient. This was a city that had been old before Romulus and Remus were even born, perhaps even old when the pyramids of Egypt were still being planned by ambitious pharaohs. The vine covered stones seemed to emanate the weight of millennia, weathered by countless seasons yet still standing in magnificent yet weathered defiance of time itself.

    The realization struck each man simultaneously, a certainty that required no confirmation or debate. They were staring at their final destination, the place that had existed only as a name whispered by a dying man in the Egyptian desert. They were staring at Panthera.

Chapter Twenty-Two

The Valley

Dawn came with a flurry of activity. The expedition had spent the night in final preparations as what remained of their force, barely three hundred men after the brutal journey through desert and jungle, now prepared to descend into a world that might hold the answers they sought.

Seneca stood at the edge of the precipice, studying the narrow path that wound down the cliff face like a ribbon of pale stone. The route was clearly ancient, but age had taken its toll and sections had crumbled away, leaving gaps that would need careful negotiation.

'We'll descend in single file,' he called to the assembled men, his voice carrying clearly above the distant roar of the falls. 'Test every step before you commit your weight. One mistake up here kills not just you, but potentially the man below you.'

Flavus joined the lead elements just behind the Occultum, his armour fresh and intact having been carried by one of his staff most of the way. Around him, his surviving soldiers wore whatever protection they had managed to preserve through the weeks of brutal campaigning. Some still possessed proper mail shirts, whilst others made do with reinforced leather tunics salvaged from fallen comrades.

'Remember,' Scipio called out from further down the line, 'whatever we encounter down there, we face it as Romans. Disciplined, professional and unafraid.'

When everyone was ready, the descent began into an otherworldly cathedral of stone and mist. Above them, the ancient cliff face stretched toward a sky where enormous birds rode the thermal currents with effortless grace, eagles and vultures whose wingspans dwarfed anything they had seen in the Mediterranean world. The massive raptors circled endlessly, their keen eyes tracking the column of men who dared to invade their domain.

The rock face itself teemed with life in ways that defied expectation. The perpetual mist from the waterfall had created a unique ecosystem where creatures flourished in the humid microclimate. Brilliant green lizards skittered across the stone, their scales catching the light like living jewels. Spiders with legs spanning a man's hand spun webs that glittered with captured moisture, whilst multi-coloured frogs no larger than a thumb created a symphony of chirps and trills that echoed off the cliff walls.

'Don't touch anything,' Sica warned as they negotiated a particularly treacherous section where the path narrowed. 'Bright colours in the wild usually mean poison. Those frogs could probably kill a horse with a single touch.'

Tiny snakes, some no thicker than a man's finger, basked on sun-warmed ledges or coiled in crevices that offered protection from the elements. Their scales displayed patterns of such intricate beauty that they seemed more like decorative art than living creatures, sapphire blues melding into emerald green and garnet reds, creating geometries that would be beautiful in any piece of jewellery.

The sound of the waterfall grew louder as they approached, and the very air began to vibrate with the power of countless tons of water plummeting from the heights above.

'Stay close!' Seneca called over the increasing roar. 'The path curves behind the falls here. We'll be walking through spray and mist so every step will be uncertain!'

The transition from open cliff face to the hidden passage

behind the waterfall felt like entering another world entirely. The thunderous noise became all-encompassing, a physical force that seemed to drive thoughts from men's minds through sheer overwhelming power. The air turned thick with moisture that soaked through clothing and made every breath feel like drowning.

Around them, the walls gleamed with perpetual wetness. Strange formations of stone had been sculpted by millennia of spray into shapes that suggested faces, animals, and forms that belonged in dreams rather than reality, making the walls seem alive in the dancing light, shifting and flowing like the memories of ancient gods.

'Magnificent,' Talorcan shouted, his voice barely audible above the waterfall's roar. 'Like walking through the heart of creation itself.'

The ethereal beauty of their passage was broken by a sharp cry of alarm from somewhere in the column behind them. One of the men had disturbed a small snake coiled in a shadowed crevice, causing it to strike with lightning speed, and whilst its fangs scraped harmlessly off the man's armour, the shock of the attack caused him to jerk backward instinctively.

His foot slipped on stone made treacherous by the perpetual moisture, and suddenly he was windmilling his arms as he fell toward the valley floor far below. The sound of his voice was quickly swallowed by the waterfall's thunder, leaving only the knowledge that another Roman would not see the completion of their mission.

'*Keep moving!*' Scipio commanded harshly. 'Don't look down, don't think about it. One foot in front of the other!'

The column pressed on, each man now acutely aware of how precarious their situation remained. The path continued its winding descent behind the cascade, offering glimpses of the valley beyond through breaks in the tumbling water, but an hour or so later, disaster struck again when a veteran of many years was navigating the wettest section of the path and his hobnailed caligae failed to find purchase on stone polished smooth by eons of spray.

The slip happened quickly. One moment he was moving carefully along the ledge, the next he was sliding helplessly toward the edge as his feet went out from under him and his desperate grab for a handhold succeeded only in dislodging loose stones that clattered into the abyss.

But this time, instead of falling to his death on the distant valley floor, the current of the waterfall itself claimed him, the massive torrent sweeping the struggling soldier away like an inconsequential piece of debris.

'Two men,' said Marcus grimly as they paused to reorganize after the second loss. 'Two good soldiers lost to this cursed path.'

The remainder of the descent passed in tense silence as each man focused entirely on the placement of his feet and the security of his handholds. The beauty that surrounded them, the dancing lights in the spray, the incredible diversity of life clinging to the cliff face, even the sense of descending through layers of creation itself, took on an ominous quality now that they understood how easily this otherworldly realm could claim their lives, but when they finally emerged onto a broad shelf of stone that marked the transition from cliff face to valley floor, the survivors of the descent found themselves in what could only be described as paradise.

The air was warm but not oppressive, filled with the perfume of flowers they had never seen before. Colourful butterflies drifted past in clouds of gold and scarlet, whilst the sight of streams branching off into the distance transformed this hidden valley into a garden worthy of the gods themselves.

Seneca called a halt away from the constant roar of the waterfall, allowing the exhausted men to rest whilst he surveyed the landscape that stretched before them. The ancient city carved into the far cliff face dominated the view, its impossible architecture more magnificent from this lower vantage point. But between them and their destination lay miles of forestry still concealing any hidden dangers.

Once rested, the column continued with the Occultum on point, checking the path before them and after the treacherous descent behind the waterfall, the soft earth beneath their feet felt like the embrace of familiar ground, and the expedition spread out from their tight single-file formation into something approaching proper military order.

The terrain was surprisingly accommodating, well-drained soil with paths worn smooth by generations of use, winding between groves of fruit trees whose species they couldn't identify, and flowers bloomed in impossible profusion, their perfumes mixing with the earthier smells of rich soil and flowing water.

The valley teemed with life in ways that kept everyone on edge. Brightly coloured birds exploded from cover without warning, their harsh cries echoing through the undergrowth as they fled the approaching humans while small deer-like creatures bounded away through the tall grass. Overhead, families of monkeys followed their progress with obvious curiosity, chattering amongst themselves in what sounded almost like commentary on these strange invaders.

The main column followed perhaps three hundred paces behind Seneca and his men, maintaining a loose formation, finding themselves in a landscape so lush and abundant that it seemed almost supernatural.

Sica and Talorcan flanked the advance party on either side, their role, to watch for threats approaching from the sides whilst the main scout group focused on the route ahead.

As they moved carefully through a grove of trees whose fruit hung heavy and golden in the dappled sunlight, Decimus noticed a clearing where the vegetation patterns seemed different from the surrounding landscape. Something about the way the grass grew, the spacing of the trees, suggested human intervention rather than natural development.

'Hold,' he called quietly, 'I think I have something.'

The advance party converged on his position carefully, weapons ready but not obviously threatening. What they found was clearly the remains of an old campsite, fire-blackened stones arranged in a rough circles along with patches of ground where vegetation had never properly reestablished itself.

But it was old, clearly abandoned for years rather than months. Dead branches lay where they had fallen, undisturbed by any recent activity whilst small trees sprouted from what had once been carefully maintained open ground.

'Roman?' Marcus asked, studying the arrangement of stones that had once supported cooking fires.

'Hard to tell,' replied Decimus, kicking at the scattered remains of what might have been a lean-to shelter. 'Could be anyone who knew how to make a proper camp.'

Sica looked around the camp carefully, pausing when he saw the slightest glint of something that seemed unnatural in the circumstances, its surface dulled by exposure but unmistakably metallic. He bent down and carefully brushed away the debris, before picking up the object.

'Seneca,' he called quietly, 'look at this.'

Seneca walked over and looked at the object, immediately recognising the design, a broken and badly tarnished Roman equipment buckle.

'This must be it,' said Seneca quietly. 'The place where the Twenty-First made camp when they reached the valley.'

They began searching the area with systematic thoroughness, their eyes scanning every inch of ground for additional evidence. Other pieces soon emerged from their concealment, fragments of leather that might once have been part of armour or equipment, corroded metal that could have been weapon components, and most tellingly, several more buckles and fittings that bore the unmistakable marks of Roman military manufacture.

Moving through the outer edge of the abandoned campsite, Talorcan's attention was drawn to an unusual mound covered with what appeared to be a thick growth of moss and creeping vines.

The formation was roughly circular, perhaps eight feet across and raised slightly above the surrounding ground level. Its organic covering was so complete that it might have been a natural feature, but something about its shape and positioning relative to the campsite suggested otherwise.

As he approached the mound, his foot struck something solid beneath the organic covering, and the moss began to slip away, revealing what lay beneath. For a moment, his mind struggled to process what his eyes were showing him, and then the full horror of the discovery crashed over him like a physical blow.

'What is it?' Seneca called, noting his comrade's obvious distress.

'You need to see,' said Talorcan.

The other members of the Occultum converged on the site to stare at the macabre discovery, finally realising they were looking at the remains of the Twenty-First Rapax.

As the men pulled away the vegetation, the mound revealed a charnel house that defied the peaceful beauty of their surroundings, dozens of human skeletons, perhaps more, arranged in careful layers like cordwood. The bones had been picked absolutely clean by countless insects, and gleamed white in the filtered sunlight that penetrated the grove's canopy.

Word of the discovery spread quickly through the column, and soon a crowd of soldiers had gathered around the macabre site. Men who had witnessed the brutality of frontier warfare, who had seen the aftermath of Germanic raids and British tribal conflicts, stared in horrified fascination at this methodical arrangement of human remains.

'Mother of the gods,' someone whispered, making the sign against evil as he studied the nearest skull. 'How many men are in there?'

'Enough,' replied Marcus grimly, noting how the bone pile extended deeper into the mound than their initial excavation had revealed. 'More than enough to account for a substantial military force.'

Seneca studied the arrangement with concern. Something about the careful organization of the remains troubled him beyond the obvious horror of discovering so many dead Romans. The bones were too neat, too deliberately placed to represent the aftermath of a conventional battle.

'This doesn't make sense,' he said finally, voicing the concern that had been growing in his mind. 'If these men were killed in a fight, if they died defending themselves or trying to escape, why are they all piled up like this? Bodies fall where they're struck down. You don't arrange them in careful stacks unless...'

He left the sentence unfinished, unwilling to voice the

implications that were beginning to form in his thoughts. Around him, soldiers shifted uneasily as they contemplated what sort of enemy would take the time to collect and organize their victims' remains.

Sica had been kneeling beside the bone pile, examining individual specimens with his usual careful attention He lifted a thigh bone, turning it over in his hands whilst his trained eye noted details that others might miss.

The bone was completely clean, as were all the others visible in the pile. But it was the marks on the bone that told the true story. Sica ran his finger along a series of parallel scratches that scored the femur's surface, noting their depth and pattern with growing certainty about what they represented.

'Falco,' he called, his voice carrying an unusual tension. 'Come look at this.'

'What is it?' Falco asked, approaching the kneeling Syrian with obvious reluctance. The sight of so many human remains had shaken even his normally robust spirits.

Sica held up the thigh bone, pointing to the series of marks that decorated its surface. 'These scratches,' he said quietly, 'they're not random. Look at the pattern, the depth, the way they're distributed along the bone.'

Falco studied the markings with growing unease, though their significance remained unclear to him.

'What am I supposed to be seeing?'

'Cut marks,' Sica replied. 'Made by blades, probably flint knives or sharpened stone tools. But not made during battle, not inflicted as wounds. These cuts were made after death, and they served a very specific purpose.'

He demonstrated by running his finger along the scored lines, showing how they followed the natural attachment points where muscle groups would have been anchored to the bone.

'They're butcher marks,' he continued, his words falling into the horrified silence that had descended over the gathered soldiers. 'Someone took their time with these bodies, methodically removing every scrap of meat from every bone. This wasn't combat, it wasn't even execution… this was food preparation.'

The implications of his words crashed over the group like a physical blow. Several men stepped back from the bone pile as if proximity might somehow contaminate them, whilst others made signs against evil with trembling hands.

'Are you saying…' Falco began, though he seemed unable to complete the thought.

'I'm saying these men weren't just killed,' Sica replied, rising to his feet with the thigh bone still in his hand. 'They were eaten. Every last one of them.

He gestured toward the careful arrangement of the remains, his Syrian pragmatism allowing him to analyse the horror with clinical detachment.

The word 'cannibals' hung unspoken in the air, though every man present understood exactly what Sica was describing. The Twenty-First Rapax hadn't just been defeated in battle, they had been hunted, captured, and consumed by enemies who viewed Roman soldiers as nothing more than a convenient food source.

Scipio, who had arrived at the site as word of the discovery spread, listened to Sica's analysis with grim acceptance before realising that they too were probably in immediate danger.

'Form up,' he commanded, ' and get back to your units. If they did this to the Twenty-First, they'll try to do it to us.'

But before anyone could move to implement his orders,

a soft whistling sound cut through the air, and one of the optios standing near Scipio suddenly arched his back, his eyes widening in shock as an arrow sprouted from his throat like some grotesque flower. Blood frothed from his mouth as he tried to speak, and he toppled backward into the pile of ancient bones.

Chapter Twenty-Three

The Valley

The peaceful afternoon air suddenly filled with the whistle of arrows as more shafts sliced through the air and found gaps in Roman armour. From the direction of the waterfall, a line of warriors emerged from concealment, unlike any enemy the expedition had previously encountered. These were not the organized Germanic warriors many had faced in previous campaigns, nor the disciplined British tribes who fought with the experience of tribal warfare, these were primitives in the truest sense, men whose technology and warfare had remained unchanged for countless generations.

Their skin was as dark as polished bronze, marked with intricate scarification that created patterns of raised flesh across their chests and faces. Feathers and bones adorned their hair, whilst necklaces of teeth, some clearly human, hung around their necks like trophies of previous victories. They wore minimal clothing, mostly animal skins worked into simple loincloths, their bodies painted with ochre and ash.

Their weapons were crude but effective, bows carved from single pieces of wood and strung with sinew, spears tipped with fire-hardened points or carefully knapped obsidian, and war clubs studded with sharp stones that could crush bone and tear flesh with equal efficiency. Yet among these primitive implements, Seneca caught glimpses of something far more sickening, the gleam of iron spear points, the distinctive outline of Roman gladii, and even fragments of lorica Segmentata worn as trophy armour.

'They're carrying our weapons,' he called to Scipio as another flight of arrows forced the Romans to huddle behind improvised cover. 'Equipment from the Twenty-First!'

The implications were chilling, but there was no time to contemplate them as the tribal warriors closed the distance with terrifying speed.

Despite the surprise and horror of their situation, Scipio's professional instincts kicked in immediately and his voice cut through the chaos.

'Form a line,' he roared, his weathered face showing no trace of the fear that gripped lesser men. *'Present shields!'*

The response surprised even Seneca with its efficiency. The months of hardship, the desert crossing, the jungle ordeal, the constant pressure of survival in hostile territory, had all forged the men into something harder than what they had been when they left Alexandria, and they responded to Scipio's command like veteran legionaries.

Within moments, the line of shields locked together, forming a solid wall of defence, but no sooner had it set than the tribal charge crashed home, like a wave breaking against rock. War clubs thudded against iron-edged shields, while crude spears thrust towards any gap in the Roman line.

But courage without discipline was insufficient against the methodical brutality of Roman warfare and the legionaries behind their shields struck out with practised precision, their gladii finding the gaps between ribs, and the exposed throats of enemies who fought with passion rather than technique.

'Steady!' Scipio called as the melee reached its peak intensity. 'Let them break themselves against us!'

The tribesmen fought with no fear, but their individual bravery couldn't overcome the collective strength of Roman military doctrine and one by one, they fell before the disciplined tactics of soldiers who had learned to fight as a single organism rather than a collection of individuals.

Within minutes, the surprise assault was over, and the surviving warriors melted back into the tall grass as quickly as they had emerged, leaving behind a scattered collection of bodies that marked the high tide of their assault. The Romans maintained their formation for several more minutes, shields ready and weapons prepared for renewed attack, but the immediate threat had passed.

'*Stand down the line,*' Scipio called eventually. 'Check casualties and secure the perimeter. This isn't over.'

As the soldiers began the grim task of assessing their losses and tending their wounded, Seneca walked among the fallen enemies, keen to extract whatever information he could.

The dead warriors were indeed primitive and close up, their weapons revealed themselves to be even cruder than initial observation had indicated. Spear points that had seemed sharp and deadly were actually poorly knapped stone, dulled by use and imperfectly hafted to shafts that were little more than shaped sticks.

The body of one warrior in particular drew his attention, his war club a simple piece of hardwood studded with river stones that had been lashed in place with strips of hide whilst his only armour was a vest made from animal hide that wouldn't stop a determined thrust from a Roman dagger.

'Look at this,' said Seneca to Scipio, who had joined him in examining their fallen enemies. 'These men are barely human. They certainly haven't experienced anything close to what we call civilisation. Crude weapons, minimal armour, and no tactical sophistication beyond basic ambush techniques.'

Scipio nodded agreement, his own assessment reaching the same conclusion.

'Brave enough, I'll grant them that. But hardly the sort of enemy who could defeat two hundred trained legionaries in open combat.'

'Exactly,' replied Seneca, his voice carrying growing concern. 'The Twenty-First Rapax weren't farmers or merchants, they were experienced soldiers with proper equipment and military training. How could primitives like this have overcome them?'

The question hung in the air, unanswered and deeply troubling. If these were the people responsible for the bone pile they had discovered, how had they managed to overcome an entire Roman expedition?

As they discussed the possibilities, Talorcan's voice suddenly cut through the trees, sounding the alarm.

'More warriors,' he shouted, 'up there on the cliff face!'

Every man turned to follow his gaze, and there, on the precipitous path they had descended earlier that morning, they saw something that sent ice through the veins of every man present. The narrow trail was alive with movement as hundreds more warriors descended to join the fight.

'Sweet Jupiter,' Falco breathed, estimating the numbers streaming down the cliff face. 'There must be hundreds of them.'

Seneca stared at the approaching force with growing understanding. The primitives they had just fought weren't the real enemy, they were nothing more than expendable advance guards sent to test Roman capabilities and draw them into the open. The bone pile hadn't been created by these few men with crude weapons, it had been created by these disciplined warriors now descending to finish what their scouts had begun.

The real killers of the Twenty-First Rapax were coming, and they vastly outnumbered the surviving Romans who found themselves trapped on the valley floor with nowhere to run.

The sight of hundreds of disciplined warriors pouring down the cliff face like a dark tide transformed Scipio from camp prefect into the veteran commander who had earned his rank through decades of impossible battles, and his voice boomed across the valley floor.

'*Close formation! three centuries, standard deployment!*' he roared, '*Move! Move! Move!*'

The response was immediate and three compact formations took shape across the valley floor in the classic manipular arrangement that had conquered the known world. Centurions moved between the ranks with urgent efficiency, adjusting spacing and ensuring proper equipment readiness.

'Steady, lads!' called one as he checked the alignment of his century. 'Remember your training! Trust your shields, trust your brothers, and let these barbarians break themselves against Roman steel!'

The first warriors reached the valley floor as the formations completed their deployment, their descent having taken less time than anyone had thought possible. These were not the crude primitives they had defeated earlier, these fighters moved with the coordinated precision of experienced warriors, but before they could properly assess their new enemies, Scipio's voice thundered across the field with the command every legionary knew was coming.

'*Testudo!*'

The response was instantaneous and beautiful in its deadly efficiency as three hundred shields snapped upward and outward in perfect synchronization, creating impenetrable walls of bronze and iron that gleamed in the afternoon sun. The men in the front and outer ranks locked their shields edge to edge, while those behind raised theirs overhead, forming a roof that could deflect arrows, spears, and even stones dropped from above, creating three armoured boxes that resembled the shells of massive tortoises.

Within seconds, the Romans had transformed from vulnerable individual soldiers into living fortresses that could advance across any terrain while maintaining near-perfect protection from enemy attack.

The first wave of warriors launched themselves against the defensive formation, their screams of enthusiasm deafening to those beneath the shields. Obsidian-tipped spears scraped harmlessly across bronze shield bosses, whilst war axes designed to split skulls merely dented the overlapping protection.

From within the testudo formations, gladii emerged like venomous serpents, striking through carefully managed gaps between shields. The short stabbing swords that had conquered Gaul and Germania now proved their worth against African warriors, finding the spaces between ribs with methodical precision. Men fell screaming as Roman steel punched through flesh and organs, their blood pooling on ground that had been peaceful grassland just days before.

'Five paces forward,' Scipio commanded, his voice penetrating the din of combat. 'On my command... *now!*'

The three testudo formations began moving forward together. Each step was measured and coordinated, shields maintained in perfect alignment whilst the deadly gladii continued their deadly work of killing. Warriors who threw themselves against the shield walls found only death, whilst those who tried to find gaps in the formations discovered that Roman discipline left no openings to exploit.

The heat within the testudo formations was unbearable as men pressed shoulder to shoulder in suffocating proximity. The weight of shields held overhead for extended periods sent cramps through arms and shoulders, whilst the constant tension of maintaining formation against repeated attacks drained strength with relentless efficiency. But the training and hardships had paid off and the formations held.

Marcus found himself in the front rank of the leftmost formation, his shield pressed against those of his comrades whilst his gladius worked with automatic precision. Thrust, withdraw, reset, thrust again, the motions as natural as breathing through years of training and combat. Around him, men grunted with effort and pain, their faces red with exertion and streaked with the sweat that came from fighting for their lives in the suffocating heat.

'Hold the lines!' Scipio called from somewhere behind them. 'Remember your spacing! Trust your training!'

On the edge of the formation to Marcus's right, one of the men began to falter as exhaustion overwhelmed his strength and as his shield started to droop, creating a gap in the wall, a warrior with a bone-handled spear saw the opening and lunged forward, his obsidian point seeking the vulnerable flesh beneath the weakening protection.

'Gaius!' Marcus shouted, but the warning came too late, and the spear point found its mark over the falling shield, punching through mail rings and deep into the soldier's chest. The soldier screamed and fell backward, his life's blood fountaining from the wound whilst his shield fell completely away from the formation.

But before the gap could widen further, the soldier behind Gaius stepped over his body, dropping his shield to fill the breach, whilst his gladius sought vengeance for his fallen comrade. The attacking warrior found himself suddenly facing not one weakened enemy but a fresh opponent who drove his blade deep into the barbarian's throat with professional efficiency.

'*Close up!*' his Centurion shouted as other soldiers adjusted their positions to maintain formation integrity. 'Lock the line! Keep those shields tight!'

The pattern repeated itself across all three formations as individual Romans fell to exhaustion, enemy weapons, or simple bad luck, but each testudo absorbed casualties like a living organism, maintaining its deadly effectiveness even as the men within it paid the price of survival in blood and pain.

For the warriors attacking the formations, the experience must have been like fighting against some supernatural force. No matter how many of them fell to Roman gladii, no matter how fiercely they pressed their attacks, the shield walls remained impenetrable, and warriors brave enough to face lions and elephants found themselves helpless against enemies they couldn't reach. The very ground became treacherous with bodies and spilled blood, and gradually, the ferocity of the attacks ebbed.

'They're withdrawing!' someone called from within the central formation as the intensity of attacks began to diminish.

Indeed, the warriors were beginning to fall back from the slowly advancing Romans. These were not mindless barbarians throwing themselves uselessly against impossible odds, they were intelligent fighters who recognized when a particular approach had failed and by the time darkness began to settle over the valley, they had melted back into the surrounding vegetation leaving behind a field strewn with their dead.

'Break formation!' Scipio commanded eventually, 'but maintain a line. We need to check these bastards have really gone.'

Although the relief of emerging from the suffocating formations was immediate and profound, bodies ached from the unnatural positions whilst minds struggled to process the violence they had just witnessed. Some men sat heavily on the blood-soaked ground, too exhausted to care about the carnage surrounding them while others quietly carried out the routines of equipment maintenance, their actions automatic whilst their thoughts remained trapped in the killing frenzy they had just survived.

As soon as they received confirmation the warriors were truly gone, water became an immediate priority as soldiers tried to replace what they had lost through hours of sweating in their wood and iron ovens. The few water skins that remained were passed from hand to hand with careful discipline, each man taking only what he needed whilst ensuring his comrades received their share. They would be refilled soon enough from one of the many streams but for now, they needed to stay alert and defend their current position.

Scipio established guard posts around their perimeter allowing many of the exhausted men to find rest amongst the corpses of their enemies, and as night settled over the valley and cook fires were lit under carefully controlled conditions, Flavus summoned his senior officers for a briefing.

'Casualty report,' he began without preamble, his young face showing the strain of experiencing his first pitched battle.

'Seventeen dead, twenty-three wounded,' replied Scipio. 'It could have been much worse, but we can't sustain many more fights like that.'

'The men performed better than I expected,' said Flavus. 'Whatever else this expedition has done, it's turned them into proper legionaries.'

'They had to become proper legionaries,' replied Scipio grimly. 'The only other option was death.'

For the next few minutes, the conversation turned to

how they could get out of the predicament they were in, including returning to the top of the crater to recover and reorganise. Seneca listened to them patiently before interjecting with his own opinion.

'We can't go back,' he said. 'The path up the cliff is too narrow, too exposed. They'd pick us off one by one as we tried to climb in single file, and it would be slaughter. Besides, don't forget that they came from that direction, and I suspect there could be even more waiting for us up there.'

'I agree,' said Scipio. 'But we can't stay here either. This position is indefensible in the long term. They can attack us from any direction, wear us down with repeated assaults until our supplies and energy are exhausted. And we know what happens to those they take prisoner.'

'That leaves only one option,' said Seneca. 'We continue forward. Push deeper into the valley toward that ancient city and hope we find somewhere we can defend.'

The silence that followed his words was heavy with the implications of their choice and as the harsh reality of their situation settled over the group, a new sound began to echo across the valley from the surrounding forests. Low and rhythmic, it started as barely more than a whisper but gradually grew in volume and complexity until it filled the night air with its primitive message, jungle drums sending messages across vast distances.

The scattered warriors they had defeated were not retreating, they were regrouping, calling their scattered forces together for what would undoubtedly be a much larger and more coordinated assault.

Chapter Twenty-Four

The Valley

Dawn brought no relief from the drums that had echoed through the night, their rhythmic pounding now joined by the sounds of movement and unnatural calls in the surrounding forest. Scipio's scouts reported large numbers of warriors converging on their position from multiple directions, whilst smoke from numerous fires suggested the enemy was preparing for extended operations rather than another quick assault.

'We move now,' Flavus decided after consulting with his senior officers. 'Every moment we delay here gives them more time to organize and surround us completely.'

The Romans broke camp and headed towards the ancient ruins that remained their only hope. If they could reach those massive stone walls, they might be able to hold out long enough to... what? No one spoke of long-term survival anymore. They simply focused on the immediate goal of staying alive for another hour, another day.

The retreat began as an orderly withdrawal, three centuries moving in coordinated fashion across the valley floor whilst maintaining defensive formations. But as they advanced deeper into the crater, the terrain itself began working against them. What had appeared from a distance to be solid ground revealed itself as an extensive wetland, fed by underground springs and the runoff from the mighty waterfall.

The water started as ankle-deep inconvenience, slowing their progress whilst making formation-keeping difficult on the treacherous footing. But within half a mile, it had deepened to knee-height, then waist-deep, forcing the heavily armoured

Romans to struggle through murky brown liquid that concealed whatever dangers lay beneath the surface.

'Stay together!' Seneca called as the Occultum led the way through the swamp, but even as he spoke, the first scream echoed across the wetland as something massive erupted from the placid water beside the leftmost century. A crocodile longer than three men burst from concealment with explosive violence, its jaws clamping down on the leg of its victim with the sound of breaking bone.

'*Crocodiles!*' Marcus shouted, though the warning was hardly necessary as more of the massive reptiles began emerging from their hiding places throughout the swamp.

Within moments, the water around them erupted into chaos as dozens of the prehistoric predators, drawn by the disturbance and the scent of warm-blooded prey, launched themselves at the struggling Romans.

Another man disappeared beneath the surface in a welter of blood and thrashing water, his screams cut short as the crocodile performed its death roll while nearby, another soldier drove his gladius repeatedly into the skull of a smaller reptile that had clamped onto his shield arm, the iron point finally finding the brain through an eye socket.

'*Keep going,*' roared Scipio. '*It's our only chance.*'

The battle in the swamp was unlike anything in Roman military doctrine. Soldiers trained to fight on solid ground now struggled to maintain footing whilst stabbing downward at targets that could submerge and reappear anywhere. The crocodiles showed no fear of steel or shouting, their ancient brains recognizing only the opportunity for an easy meal.

Three more men fell to the reptilian assault before the carnage eased, but as they pushed away from the bloody waters, one of the men jerked backward with a sharp cry of surprise, a thin dart, barely longer than a man's finger, protruding from his neck like some exotic ornament.

'What in Jupiter's name,' he began, pulling the projectile free with trembling fingers, but before he could complete the thought, his voice began to change, becoming strained and raspy as if something was constricting his throat.

His eyes widened with growing panic as he struggled to draw breath, his hands clawing at his neck whilst his face began to turn an alarming shade of blue. Within moments, his legs gave way beneath him, and he toppled forward into the brown water with a splash that sent ripples across the surface.

'Poison darts!' Marcus shouted, realizing what they were facing. 'Did anyone see where it came from?'

'There!' Decimus called, spotting movement in the branches overhead. 'Thirty paces, behind that massive trunk!'

The Roman archers responded quickly, their arrows arcing upward toward targets that flickered in and out of the leafy canopy. Some shafts struck home with satisfying thuds, sending bodies tumbling from their perches to crash into the water below, but for every warrior who fell, another seemed to take his place, the ancient trees that had stood for centuries now serving as natural fortresses.

More darts found targets and men fell on all sides, but the survivors knew they could do nothing to save their comrades.

'Press forward!' Scipio commanded, *'shields up!'*

The Romans raised their shields whilst continuing their advance through the treacherous water. It was guerrilla warfare at its most effective, invisible enemies striking from perfect concealment before melting away to attack again from unexpected directions.

'Keep moving!' Flavus ordered as the men started to flag

through exhaustion. 'Don't stop for anything! Our only chance is to reach solid ground!'

The march through the swamp became a nightmare of endurance and terror. Men struggled through water that seemed determined to drag them down whilst fighting enemies they couldn't see until it was too late, and by the time they finally staggered from the deadly swamp onto the solid ground at the base of the ancient ruins, their numbers had been catastrophically reduced. Of the three hundred men who had entered the wetland, barely a hundred emerged. Crocodiles, poison darts, and simple exhaustion had claimed the rest, leaving behind a force too small to constitute a proper fighting unit of any strength.

As the survivors collapsed onto the relative safety of solid ground, many looked up at the city looming above them, the ruins defying easy description. Massive blocks of granite, each weighing tons, had been fitted together with precision that would have impressed Roman engineers, rising directly from the cliff face in a series of terraces that climbed toward the sky like stairs built for giants.

Carvings covered every available surface, figures of men and animals rendered with artistic skill that suggested a civilisation far more sophisticated than anything they had expected to find in the African interior and the very stones seemed to emanate age and power, as if the builders had intended their work to last until the end of time itself.

But there was no time for admiration. Already, the sounds of pursuit echoed from the swamp behind them as their enemies appeared in the distance in a fleet of dugout canoes.

Flavus looked around in desperation, before realising the scattered masonry at the base of the ruins offered the only defensive positions available, broken columns and fallen blocks that could provide cover for men making their last stand.

The surviving Romans spread out among the ancient stones, each man finding what cover he could whilst checking his remaining equipment. Arrows were counted, sword edges tested, and final preparations made for the battle that would determine whether any of them would live to see another sunrise.

The Occultum was intact but exhausted, and Marcus carried a flesh wound on his forearm where a thrashing crocodile's claw had found a gap in his armour.

'Let me look at that,' Falco offered, noting how Marcus favoured his injured arm.

'Later,' replied Marcus curtly, waving away the assistance. 'There'll be time for that if we survive the next hour.'

Around them, the battered survivors readied themselves for what they knew would be their last stand. Some whispered prayers to distant gods, while others simply studied the weapons in their hands, grimly aware that no divine favour would be enough.

From the swamp beyond their position, the enemy began to emerge like predators approaching helpless prey, paddling canoes in numbers seeming to multiply with each passing moment.

'Two hundred at least,' Scipio estimated grimly, studying the approaching enemy through narrowed eyes. 'Maybe three. They're taking their time because they know we have nowhere to run.'

The noise grew louder as the warriors left their canoes to form up on solid ground and as the sound built it seemed to make the swamp vibrate with primitive power. The noise was overwhelming, and the Romans knew they were heavily outnumbered, but as the reality of their predicament sunk in, a new sound cut through the din with crystalline clarity. A horn, blown from somewhere high above the Romans' position, its notes carrying an authority that caused every head to turn upward toward the source.

On one of the ruined terraces, silhouetted against the ancient stones, stood a line of figures unlike any they had yet encountered. These were tall men, elegant warriors whose bearing spoke of natural nobility. But what drew every eye was not the men themselves but their companions, each warrior held a great cat on a chain, leopards whose spotted coats gleamed in the afternoon sun.

At the center of this line stood a figure who commanded attention through his sheer presence alone. Taller than his companions and magnificently muscled, his skin was marked with intricate scarification that created patterns of incredible complexity across his chest and arms. Ornaments of gold and precious stones adorned his neck and arms, whilst his hair was dressed with feathers from birds whose species the Romans could not identify.

But it was what he held that caused every man below to catch his breath in wonder and terror. In each hand, controlled by chains of what appeared to be pure gold, he held a black panther, their yellow eyes surveying the scene below with the sort of calculating intelligence that made them perfect predators.

The massed warriors at the edge of the swamp looked up at this apparition with expressions that mixed fear and reverence in equal measure. Their chanting faltered, then died away entirely as they recognized whatever authority these newcomers represented.

A second horn blast echoed across the valley, and the tall warriors released their leopards simultaneously, watching them bound effortlessly down the stepped pyramid towards the men below.

The Romans pressed themselves against whatever cover they could find, certain that they were about to be torn apart by a coordinated assault of trained predators, but as the great cats reached the base of the ruins, something unexpected happened, the leopards leaped over the cowering Romans without pause, their powerful bodies sailing through the air to land among the massed warriors who had come to slaughter the survivors.

The warrior ranks, so confident moments before, dissolved into screaming chaos as the great cats did what they had been bred and trained to do and men who had shown no fear of Roman steel found themselves helpless against claws and fangs that could tear through flesh and bone with effortless ease. Within moments, the carefully organized assault became a panicked rout as the primitive tribesmen fled back toward their canoes, leaving behind comrades who would never rise again.

In minutes, it was over. The leopards methodically finished their work amongst the fallen, their jaws dripping with blood whilst their handlers descended from the ruins to reclaim them, moving through the Roman positions without fear or hostility, their attention focused entirely on their deadly companions who returned to their chains with the docility of well-trained hounds.

Seneca watched in stunned silence as the magnificent chieftain continued to look down from his elevated position, his panthers still standing beside him like extensions of his own deadly will.

Here was someone whose very presence commanded respect, whose authority over both beasts and men spoke of power beyond anything the Romans had expected to encounter, and as the handlers finished collecting their leopards and began moving back toward the upper terraces, the chieftain finally spoke.

'*Come.*'

As he turned away, everyone stared at the chieftain's back in astonishment. It had only been one word, but it changed everything.

He had spoken Latin!

Chapter Twenty-Five

The Stone City

'Form up,' called Scipio to his surviving men. 'Weapons lowered. Follow my lead.'

The climb through the ruins proved to be as magnificent as it was treacherous. Ancient steps carved directly from the living rock wound upward through multiple terraces, each level revealing new wonders of engineering and artistry. Massive stone blocks fitted together without mortar created walls that had withstood millennia of weather, whilst intricate carvings covered every available surface with scenes of hunts, battles, and strange ceremonies.

'Look at the stonework,' Marcus murmured as they passed between columns depicting scenes of men and great cats working in harmony. 'This makes Roman engineering look like it was the result of a child playing with building blocks.'

The ascent continued through level after level of architectural marvels, each terrace revealing new evidence of the builders' ambition and skill. Water channels carved directly into the stone carried fresh springs from somewhere high in the cliff face, creating small waterfalls and pools that provided both practical necessity and aesthetic beauty.

But it was the entrance to the city proper that truly demonstrated the power and sophistication of their hosts. Massive wooden doors, each easily twenty feet in height, stood open to receive them. The timber was dark with age but showed no signs of decay, whilst iron bands as thick as a man's arm reinforced the structure against any conceivable assault. On either side of the entrance, stone panthers crouched in eternal vigilance, their emerald eyes seeming to track the movements of anyone who approached.

The entrance passage beyond the doors was vast enough to accommodate a full Roman cohort in formation, its walls reaching up into shadows that flickered with the light of torches mounted in bronze brackets. The workmanship was extraordinary, every stone precisely cut and fitted, every torch holder crafted with artistic as well as functional purpose. This was not merely a fortification, but a ceremonial space designed to awe and intimidate visitors in equal measure. Awaiting them just inside the doors, were two men adorned in ceremonial robes and as the romans entered, they turned around and led the way into the torchlit gloom.

The Romans followed and once inside, the sound of the great doors closing behind them echoed through the passage like thunder, followed immediately by the scraping of massive timber beams being moved into position. Falco turned to see at least ten more warriors working together to lift reinforcing planks that would make the entrance impregnable to any conceivable assault from outside.

'Well,' he observed quietly, 'I suppose we're committed now.'

The journey deeper into the complex became a guided tour through wonders that challenged every assumption about barbarian capabilities with corridors wide enough for entire centuries, and side passages disappearing into darkness that suggested the city extended far deeper into the cliff face than was visible from outside.

Their guides moved through winding passages that would have left the Romans hopelessly lost within minutes, oil lamps and torches providing pools of light along the way.

Finally, their guides led them into a chamber spacious enough to accommodate their numbers comfortably. To one side, a carefully carved channel in the wall carried fresh water from some hidden spring to settle in a large stone basin that reflected torchlight like a mirror.

Dozens of ceramic jugs lined the floor around the basin and the sight of unlimited clean water after the horrors of the swamp crossing proved irresistible to men who had been rationing every drop for days. The Romans rushed forward with desperate urgency, discipline temporarily forgotten as many threw themselves down beside the basin to drink directly from the crystal-clear water while others filled the ceramic jugs and drained them in long gulps.

Seneca found himself drinking more water than he had consumed in the previous three days combined, the cool liquid washing away the taste of fear and exhaustion that had dominated his existence since entering the valley. Around him, his men were similarly occupied, their attention focused entirely on replenishing what they had lost during their ordeal.

It was the sound that brought them crashing back to reality, the unmistakable noise of heavy doors slamming shut followed by the metallic scrape of a bar being drawn across the entrance from the outside. Every head turned toward the source of the sound, water still dripping from their chins as they realized their situation had fundamentally changed.

They were no longer guests being shown hospitality. They were prisoners, secured in a chamber deep within an impregnable fortress, completely at the mercy of captors whose intentions remained utterly mysterious.

The next few hours passed in tense silence and men sat with their backs against the carved stone walls, weapons within easy reach.

Finally, the sound of the massive bar being drawn back

sent every hand to sword hilts, though Scipio's sharp gesture kept weapons sheathed as the great doors swung open once again. What happened next was so unexpected that several soldiers wondered if exhaustion and stress had finally caused their minds to snap.

A line of elegant women entered the chamber, their flowing garments dyed in brilliant colours and worked with intricate patterns. Gold and silver ornaments adorned their necks and arms, whilst their hair was dressed in elaborate styles that required considerable time and skill to achieve.

Each woman carried rolls of woven cloth that they spread across the stone floor with practiced efficiency, creating a series of dining areas arranged around the chamber's perimeter. The textiles were works of art in themselves, geometric patterns in rich blues and deep reds, animal motifs rendered with startling realism, and abstract designs that seemed to move and flow like living things.

The soldiers watched this domestic activity with growing bewilderment, their military training providing no guidance for how to respond to such unexpected hospitality. They remained motionless as the women completed their work and filed out of the chamber with the same quiet dignity that had marked their entrance.

'What in Jupiter's name,' someone began, but Scipio's raised hand cut off the question before it could be completed.

'Stay alert,' the veteran commander warned quietly. 'This could be some sort of ritual preparation. Don't let your guard down just because they're treating us like honoured guests.'

Before anyone could respond, the doors opened again to admit another procession that challenged their perception even further. More women entered, but these carried baskets overflowing with fruits whose colours and shapes defied easy identification. Alongside the exotic produce came platters of cooked meat that filled the chamber with aromas rich enough to make empty stomachs growl with desperate hunger.

The food was arranged carefully on the spread cloths as a hopeful murmur rippled through the Roman ranks. Men who had shared their last scraps of hardtack that morning now stared at enough provisions to feed them for days, but none moved toward the tempting display.

'Hold position,' Scipio commanded, noting how several younger soldiers were beginning to shift restlessly toward the food. 'Nobody moves until we understand what's happening here.'

The women completed their arrangements and departed as silently as they had arrived, leaving the Romans alone with the most elaborate meal any of them had seen since departing Alexandria. The fruits gleamed like jewels in the torchlight, whilst the aroma of perfectly seasoned meat made concentration increasingly difficult for men who had been surviving on field rations and whatever game they could hunt.

As the great doors began to close once more, a single figure entered the chamber before they clanged shut behind him. This was clearly not one of the warriors who had led them through the ruins, nor was it another servant attending to their needs, his skin was pale, and he wore what was undoubtedly a toga, though made from the same fabric that had adorned the women.

The figure limped badly, relying heavily on a walking stick carved from some dark wood and polished to a mirror finish. One arm hung useless at his side, whilst a livid red scar ran from his left eyebrow to his jaw.

The chamber fell into absolute silence as the man

walked slowly forward towards them before stopping and looking around.

'Well,' he said in fluent Latin, a hint of amusement creeping into his tone as he studied the Romans' obvious confusion, 'what are you waiting for? Let's eat.'

The effect of the stranger's words was immediate and transformative as military discipline, already strained by exhaustion and uncertainty, finally gave way to the basic human need for sustenance and the Romans fell upon the feast with desperate hunger. Men who had been fighting for their lives just a few hours earlier, now gorged themselves on provisions that would have graced an emperor's table.

'Easy, lads,' Scipio warned as he watched younger soldiers stuffing themselves with obvious desperation. 'You'll make yourselves sick eating too fast. Take smaller bites, and let your bodies adjust.'

But the advice was largely ignored as the men grabbed the opportunity to fill their empty bellies. Some managed to maintain a measure of restraint, but others ate until they could barely move.

As the initial feeding frenzy subsided, the more experienced soldiers began applying their experience and wounds that had been ignored during the desperate flight through the valley were finally examined and treated with whatever medical supplies remained in their packs.

Decimus and Sica moved through the chamber providing assistance where they could, their varied campaign experience making them invaluable for treating injuries that ranged from infected cuts to the more urgent needs of open wounds. They worked with materials salvaged from their equipment, strips of cloth torn from spare tunics, fresh water used to clean wounds, and the contents of personal medical kits that had somehow survived the journey through desert and jungle.

'Hold still,' Sica murmured as he cleaned the nasty gash on Marcus's forearm where the crocodile's claw had found a gap in his armour. 'This needs proper attention, or it'll fester in this climate.'

An hour or so later, the women returned, moving through the chamber with the same quiet efficiency they had shown earlier. They collected empty platters and baskets whilst leaving behind piles of blankets, and as the chamber filled with the quiet sounds of men settling down for rest, Seneca joined the expedition's senior leadership around their mysterious host.

The man had positioned himself against one of the carved walls where the torchlight revealed the full extent of his injuries. The scar that marked his face was only the most obvious sign of trauma, though his useless arm showed evidence of multiple breaks that had healed badly, and his damaged leg hardly bore his weight.

'My name is Corvus,' he said as the Romans settled into a rough circle around him. 'Once a serving Optio of the Twenty-First Rapax.

The formal military introduction carried weight that went beyond mere identification. Here was proof that their expedition had succeeded in its primary objective, they had found a survivor of the missing legion, someone who could provide answers to the questions that had driven them over a thousand miles of hostile territory.

'Optio Corvus,' Scipio acknowledged with the respect due to a fellow soldier. 'What happened to your legion? How did you come to be here?'

'We came for the same reasons you did, I suppose,' began Corvus, 'following rumours of gold, lost cities, or whatever glory the empire thought we might find in these gods-forsaken lands. We had three hundred men when we left Alexandria, maybe two hundred when we reached the waterfall after crossing the desert.' His good hand moved unconsciously to his scarred face as he continued. 'The descent was treacherous, and we lost men to falls and accidents, but the real horror began when we reached the valley floor. We thought we were prepared for hostile natives, but what we encountered...' He shook his head slowly. 'No amount of training prepares you for enemies who fight like demons and show no fear of Roman steel.'

'The cannibals,' said Flavus grimly, remembering the bone pile they had discovered.

'Cannibals, yes,' replied Corvus, 'but not the crude primitives you might expect. They struck our column with coordinated attacks, using the terrain and their knowledge of local conditions to devastating effect.' He paused, gathering himself for the most difficult part of his account. 'I was wounded early in the fighting, my arm shattered by a war club, my leg nearly severed by an obsidian blade. When our formation broke and men scattered into the forest, they left me behind, but I managed to crawl into dense undergrowth where the natives couldn't find me.'

His eyes took on the distant look of someone reliving traumatic memories.

'From my hiding place, I watched them systematically hunt down the survivors. Those they captured alive were brought back to their main camp and...' He swallowed hard before continuing. 'They didn't kill them quickly. They kept them alive while they worked on them, one limb at a time.

Cauterizing wounds with burning brands to prevent death from blood loss.'

The Romans listened in horrified silence as Corvus described atrocities that challenged even their experience of frontier warfare.

'Some of those men lived for days, watching their own body parts being consumed by their captors. The sounds they made... the screams... those are sounds no man should ever have to hear.'

'How did you escape?' asked Seneca.

'After three days of watching my comrades being butchered and eaten, I couldn't take any more. I crawled away from my hiding place and headed toward these ruins, thinking I'd rather die than wait for them to find me.'

'But you made it here.'

'Barely. I passed out from blood loss and exhaustion and when I woke up, I was in this very chamber being tended by healers who had somehow found me and brought me to safety.'

Flavus leaned forward with obvious interest.

'These people who rescued you? Are they the same ones who saved us today?'

'The very same. Along with one other survivor they had also found and brought here.' Corvus's expression grew more complex. 'He was here only few weeks but then stole a necklace and fled the city under cover of darkness. That's why they have locked you in, they don't trust you.' He looked around with sudden understanding. 'I suppose the very fact that you are here means that he actually made it back?'

'He did,' said Scipio. 'Well, most of the way.'

'But why the conflict?' asked Seneca, his tactical mind seeking to understand the strategic situation they had stumbled into. 'What drives these cannibals to attack a city this well-defended?'

Corvus shifted painfully, adjusting his position against the stone wall before responding.

'The natives are called the Makatani,' he replied, 'and don't actually live in the valley. They come from the jungle regions above the caldera, following seasonal migration patterns that have brought them into conflict with Panthera's people for generations. They covet these ruins, not just for their defensive value, but because they believe conquering them will grant them the power of the ancestors who built them.'

He gestured toward the carved walls around them with his good arm.

'Panthera's ancestors built this city when the world was young, or so the stories go. His people are the last remnants of that ancient civilization, but they're dying out. Each generation produces fewer children, each year sees more of the old knowledge lost. The Makatani know this, they can sense weakness the way predators scent wounded prey.'

'How long before they're overrun?' asked Scipio.

'Soon, perhaps within a generation, but not yet. Panthera still commands enough warriors and trained beasts to hold them at bay, especially when they're foolish enough to attack in the open as they did today.' Corvus's scarred face showed something approaching admiration. 'You saw what those cats can do in coordinated assault. The Makatani fear them more than they fear Roman steel.'

Marcus leaned forward, his curiosity piqued by the cultural implications.

'These cannibals,' he said, 'I have heard of such practises but thought eating human flesh drove men mad.'

'They do not just exist on human meat only,' said

Corvus. 'But they do believe that eating a warrior's flesh transfers his strength and courage to the consumer. They probably devoured my comrades because they recognized them as formidable opponents worthy of such honour.'

The explanation sent chills through the listening Romans, who understood that their own fighting prowess had likely marked them for similar treatment if they had fallen during the day's battle.

'What about the gold?' asked Scipio. 'The rumours that brought you here in the first place, vast treasures hidden in an ancient African city?'

Corvus looked genuinely confused, his brow furrowing as he processed the question.

'Gold? What gold? I've been here for... gods, it must be three years now, and I've seen no evidence of any significant treasure. Perhaps there was wealth here once, in the distant past, but if so, it's long gone.'

Scipio's face darkened with suspicion and growing anger.

'You're lying,' he said flatly. 'We've all seen the serving women who brought the food. They wear necklaces and bracelets that would be worth a fortune in any Roman market.'

Corvus dismissed the observation with a wave of his good hand.

'Trinkets,' he said simply. 'Personal ornaments passed down through families, small pieces that reflect their artistic heritage rather than vast wealth. Nothing approaching the sort of treasure that would justify mounting an expedition of this scale.'

'They may be small pieces,' said Scipio, 'but those weren't trinkets, they were evidence of far more significant resources.'

'Perhaps your eyes saw what your hopes wanted them to see,' replied Corvus, his own voice cooling as he recognized the accusation implicit in Scipio's words. 'I've lived among these people for years. If there were vast hoards of gold hidden somewhere in this complex, don't you think I would know?'

The tension in the chamber grew palpable as Scipio and Corvus stared at each other across the flickering torchlight.

'You expect me to believe,' said Scipio slowly, 'that we've travelled across half of Africa, lost hundreds of good men, and risked everything on an expedition based on lies and legends?'

'I expect you to believe the evidence of three years' observation over the fantasies that drove you to undertake this journey,' replied Corvus with equal coldness.

The bad mood that settled over the group was almost tangible, poisoning the atmosphere of their temporary sanctuary with the bitter taste of disappointed greed and challenged authority. Seneca intervened before the confrontation could escalate further.

'What happens now?' he asked, directing the question to Corvus whilst deliberately shifting attention away from the inflammatory topic of treasure. 'What can we expect from our hosts?'

Corvus seemed grateful for the change of subject, his tension easing slightly as he addressed more practical concerns.

'You'll remain here for a few days while Panthera decides what to do with you,' he said simply. 'He's not cruel, but he's also not naive about the dangers of allowing armed Romans to move freely through his domain.

'Panthera?' said Flavus. 'I thought the city was called Panthera.'

'It is,' Corvus confirmed. 'But the leader of these people,

the man you saw commanding those great cats today, he also bears that name. Whether he was named for the city, or the city was named for him, I've never been able to determine. But they are connected in ways that go deeper than you or I will ever understand. I suspect that you'll continue to be fed, your wounds treated and given time to recover from your ordeal.'

'And then?'

'Then Panthera will make his decision about whether you represent a threat to his people's survival or a potential asset in their struggle against the Makatani. Depending on what he concludes...' Corvus shrugged with his good shoulder. 'You might find yourselves free to leave or joining your predecessors in ways you'd prefer not to contemplate.'

The words hung in the torchlit air like smoke from a funeral pyre, carrying implications that none of the Romans wanted to examine too closely. Their rescue from certain death had come with a price that had yet to be determined, and their survival now depended on the judgment of a man who commanded panthers and ruled over the remnants of a civilization older than Rome itself.

Chapter Twenty-Six

The City

Several days passed in the secured chamber with agonizing slowness. At first, the Romans had been grateful for the respite, soft blankets instead of rocky ground, unlimited fresh water instead of carefully rationed sips, and food that actually tasted of something other than leather and mould. The daily arrival of servants bearing platters of exotic fruits and perfectly prepared meat had seemed like luxury beyond their wildest dreams after months of brutal survival, but as the days stretched on, gratitude gave way to restlessness, and restlessness to barely contained frustration. These were soldiers, men of action who had endured impossible hardships to reach this hidden valley, and being confined like valuable prisoners, no matter how comfortable their accommodation, grated against every instinct they possessed.

'How much longer?' Falco muttered on the eighth day, pacing the chamber's perimeter for what must have been the hundredth time. 'I feel like a prize bull being fattened for sacrifice.'

'At least prize bulls get to see sunlight before they're slaughtered,' replied Marcus grimly, noting how the eternal torchlight was beginning to affect everyone's mood. 'We don't even know if it's day or night out there.'

Scipio maintained his professional composure, but even his weathered patience was beginning to show strain. He had spent the previous evening checking and rechecking their meagre equipment, anticipating the moment they may have to fight for their lives.

'Eight days,' he said quietly to Seneca during one of

203

their whispered conferences. 'Long enough to decide whether we're guests, prisoners, or something else entirely. Whatever they're planning, it should happen soon.'

As if summoned by his words, the familiar sound of the great bar being drawn back echoed through the chamber and the Romans immediately formed up in their customary positions, not quite military formation, but ready to respond to whatever new development their captivity might bring.

Corvus entered with his characteristic limping gait, his scarred face showing an expression that mixed relief with nervous anticipation. Behind him came two of Panthera's warriors, their presence adding formal weight to what was clearly an official summons.

'Legatus Flavus, Prefect Scipio, Tribune Seneca,' he announced. 'Panthera will see you now.'

The three senior officers exchanged glances. Whatever judgment their mysterious host had reached about their fate, they would learn it within the hour.

'The rest of you remain here,' Scipio ordered his men. 'Maintain discipline and be ready for anything.'

The journey through the ruins proved to be a revelation that challenged every assumption they had formed about their hosts during their confinement. Instead of the primitive accommodations they might have expected, the complex revealed itself to be a functioning city whose inhabitants had adapted ancient architecture to meet modern needs with remarkable ingenuity.

Side chambers that had once served ceremonial or storage functions now housed families whose lives seemed to follow simple domestic routines. Children's voices echoed from hidden courtyards, whilst the sounds of normal daily activities providing a backdrop that spoke of a community rather than a fortress under siege.

'How many people live here?' Seneca asked Corvus as they passed another intersection where corridors led deeper into the cliff face.

'Perhaps three hundred souls,' the Optio replied. 'Enough to maintain their traditions and defend their territory, but not enough to expand beyond what the valley can support.'

Doorways led onto high balconies that jutted from the cliff face like stone gardens suspended in space. These elevated platforms had been transformed into carefully cultivated growing areas where exotic plants flourished in the abundant light and moisture and the Romans caught glimpses of vegetables and fruits whose species they couldn't identify, all thriving in soil that must have been carried up from the valley floor basket by basket over generations.

'Ingenious,' Flavus observed. 'They've created an entire agricultural system in the sky.'

Water was everywhere, not just the ceremonial fountains they had encountered in their chamber, but practical systems that captured and distributed the moisture that seeped continuously through the ancient stonework. Channels carved directly into the rock carried fresh springs to every level of the complex, whilst carefully positioned vessels collected condensation and rainwater for storage during drier periods.

The deeper they travelled into the cliff face, the more obvious it became that they were approaching something significant. The shaped stones gave way to natural rock formations that had been enhanced rather than completely altered, suggesting they were entering chambers that predated even the ancient construction that surrounded them.

Finally, their guides led them through an archway

205

carved from living stone into a chamber that defied every expectation they had formed about their destination. Natural light flooded the space from carefully carved openings in the rock above, creating shafts of golden illumination that centred on a single focal point with mathematical precision.

At the heart of the chamber, bathed in the light from above, sat a throne carved directly from the bedrock itself, and seated upon it was the magnificent chieftain they had witnessed commanding the great cats during their rescue.

Up close, his presence was even more overwhelming, a man whose physical power was matched by an aura of absolute confidence that marked natural leaders.

At his feet, sprawled his two black panthers, their yellow eyes tracking every movement the Romans made, whilst their bodies remained relaxed but ready to explode into lethal action at the slightest signal from their master.

But it was the assembled court that truly drove home the magnitude of the moment. Around the chamber's perimeter stood two dozen warriors, each dressed in ceremonial finery. Gold ornaments caught and reflected the natural light, whilst elaborate headdresses created silhouettes that seemed to belong to gods rather than mortal men.

Each warrior held a leopard on a chain, the great cats displaying the same trained docility as the panthers and the sight was both beautiful and terrifying, a display of power that used living weapons as casual decoration.

The entire arrangement had been carefully designed to inspire awe, and it succeeded completely. The Romans found themselves in the presence of authority that predated their civilization by millennia, surrounded by evidence of power that operated according to rules they barely understood.

Chapter Twenty-Seven

The Throne Room

The throne chamber fell into absolute silence as the three Roman officers were escorted forward by their guards. Panthera remained motionless upon his carved throne, his magnificent presence dominating the space with an authority that required no words or gestures. The great cats at his feet tracked every movement with predatory interest, their yellow eyes reflecting the golden light that streamed through the carefully positioned openings above.

But it was what lay directly before the throne that drew every Roman eye and held their attention with magnetic force. A chest, ornately carved from some dark wood and bound with bands of pure gold, sat open to display contents that would have ransomed an emperor. Gold bracelets and necklaces from a dozen different nations spilled over the container's edges like water frozen in motion, whilst precious stones the size of dove eggs caught the light and threw it back in brilliant fragments of emerald, sapphire, and ruby.

Necklaces of intricate workmanship lay draped across the treasure's surface, their links so fine they seemed crafted by gods rather than mortal hands and rings set with stones that had no names in Roman gemmology glittered amongst chains of silver so pure it seemed to glow with inner light.

The display was clearly deliberate, positioned to catch maximum light whilst remaining within easy reach of the man who commanded this hidden realm. It was wealth beyond calculation, a demonstration of resources that made everyone present stare in amazement.

'Sweet Jupiter,' said Scipio, his voice barely audible.

Beside them, Corvus shifted uncomfortably on his damaged leg.

'I have never seen this before,' he said quietly to Flavus. 'This must be the treasure you spoke of.'

All four men waited patiently, their gaze flicking between Panthera and the chest.

He's waiting for you to speak,' the Optio said eventually, 'Panthera understands Latin perfectly, but he considers it beneath his dignity to use foreign languages in his own hall. You speak and I'll translate his responses back to you.'

Flavus stepped forward and nodded his respect to the chieftain.

'Great Panthera,' he began, his voice carrying clearly through the vast chamber, 'we are grateful for your hospitality and the lives of our men that you preserved from certain death. We come as representatives of Rome, seeking information about the fate of our lost comrades.'

Panthera listened without visible reaction, his magnificent features showing neither interest nor displeasure. Finally he responded, his voice surprisingly soft for a man who wielded so much power.

'He asks why you have come so far from your own lands to seek men who are already dead,' Corvus interpreted, his tone carefully neutral.

'We needed confirmation,' Flavus replied. 'Roman leaders requires proof of death before soldiers can be declared lost. The testimony of a single survivor, no matter how credible, cannot satisfy the demands of military procedure.'

The translation process continued with the same formal precision, each exchange requiring careful conversion between two languages that had developed in complete isolation from each other. But as the conversation progressed, Panthera's attention began to focus on Scipio with growing intensity. The camp prefect had been unable to tear his gaze away from the open treasure chest since entering the chamber. Finally, Panthera spoke again, his words carrying a note of amusement that required no translation.

'He says,' Corvus began, his voice showing reluctance to relay the observation, 'that one among you seeks more than simple confirmation of his comrades' fate. He says this one covets the river stones his people use for adornment, and that such hunger makes men dangerous.'

Scipio's head snapped up as he realised he was being observed and discussed. His scarred face flushed with something between embarrassment and anger.

'River stones?' he repeated. 'We both know they are not merely river stones, that's more wealth than most Roman governors see in a lifetime of service.'

Corvus looked shocked at the bluntness, but Panthera's reaction was merely to smile, an expression that somehow made his magnificent presence even more intimidating.

Scipio continued, his manner growing more aggressive as he warmed to his theme.

'We have travelled thousands of miles across hostile territory to reach this place' he said, 'and are representatives of the greatest empire the world has ever known. We have lost many men yet killed many of his enemies who threaten his people's very survival, and common courtesy, if not gratitude, suggests that such service merits substantial reward rather than dismissive comments about river stones.'

Scipio's words seemed to take longer to absorb but when he finished, Panthera's response was delivered with the sort of calm finality that brooked no argument.

'He says,' Corvus reported, his voice carrying obvious reluctance, 'that you have already received your reward. You received your lives when his warriors saved you from the Makatani. No debt exists between his people and yours, and no payment is required for services that were never requested. He says you will be allowed to regain your strength from your ordeal, and then you will leave his territory by the same route you entered. This audience is concluded.'

Flavus opened his mouth to deliver the sort of diplomatic response that might preserve their dignity, but Scipio's voice cut across his words with the sharp authority of someone making a command decision.

'Wait,' the camp prefect said, his tone causing Panthera to regard him with renewed interest. 'I have a proposition that might benefit both our peoples.'

Corvus looked alarmed at this development, and he looked between Scipio and Flavus, trying to indicate they were treading a dangerous path. But when Panthera spoke again, his tone carried curiosity rather than anger, though his magnificent presence seemed to grow more imposing as he leaned forward on his ancient throne.

'He asks what you could possibly offer that would interest the ruler of this realm,' Corvus interpreted.

Scipio's mind worked furiously.

'The men who attacked us today,' he said, his voice growing stronger as he developed his argument. 'They'll return in greater numbers, better organized, more determined to capture this city. Your people saved our lives, but we could repay that debt by eliminating the threat permanently. Tell him that Roman military doctrine excels at exactly this sort of problem. We don't just defeat enemies, we destroy them so completely that they can never threaten civilised peoples again.'

Panthera listened with obvious attention, his yellow eyes never leaving Scipio's face as he considered the proposition. When he finally responded, his words were directed to one of his senior warriors rather than to the Romans themselves.

The conversation that followed was conducted entirely in their musical language, but the passion and urgency of the exchange made its importance clear even to those who couldn't understand the words. Finally, Panthera turned his attention back to the Romans to respond.

'He asks,' Corvus translated, 'what reward you would expect for undertaking such a task.'

Scipio's gaze flicked toward the open treasure chest with obvious hunger before returning to meet Panthera's steady stare.

'Gold,' he said simply. 'Enough to compensate my men for the additional risks we would be undertaking on your behalf.'

The response seemed to amuse their host, whose sarcastic laugh conveyed more than mere scepticism. Finally. He spoke again, his stare never leaving Scipio.

'He says,' Corvus reported, 'that the Makatani have a great war chief who coordinates their attacks from a stronghold deep in the swamplands. His position is well defended and has never been successfully assaulted by Panthera's warriors. If you bring him the chief's head as proof of death, this chest and all it contains is yours, along with safe passage out of here.'

The terms hung in the chamber's golden air like incense from a temple altar. Flavus and Seneca exchanged glances that communicated their shared understanding of what was being proposed.

'Scipio,' Flavus began, his voice carrying the authority of overall command, 'this requires considerable discussion

211

amongst ourselves before...'

'We agree,' Scipio interrupted, his words cutting through the Legatus's diplomatic caution like a blade through silk. 'We accept your terms, great Panthera. One chief's head for that chest of Gold. So it will be.'

Flavus stared at the camp prefect with obvious horror as the reality of the situation sunk in, but before anyone could voice their objections or attempt to modify the agreement, Panthera rose from his throne and gestured toward the entrance. The audience was over, the bargain had been struck, and as guards moved to escort them back to their chamber, Flavus and Seneca understood that Scipio had just committed them to a course of action that would test their skills, their courage, and quite possibly their lives in the swamplands where an unreachable war chief waited with hundreds of cannibalistic followers.

Chapter Twenty-Eight

The Chamber

Back in the chamber, the great doors slammed shut behind them with the finality of a tomb being sealed, the metallic scrape of the massive bar sliding into place echoing like a death knell. For several moments, the Romans stood in stunned silence, the magnitude of what had just transpired settling over them like a shroud. The young Legatus's face was flushed with anger and frustration, his carefully maintained composure finally cracking under the pressure of command decisions he felt powerless to influence.

'*You madman!*' he hissed, wheeling on Scipio with fury that had been building throughout their return journey. 'You've just committed us to a suicide mission without consultation, without consideration of tactical realities, without any thought beyond your own greed! The target is an unreachable war chief, in an unknown position, deep in swamplands where they have every advantage and we have none, against enemies who eat the bodies of defeated opponents!'

Scipio remained unmoved by the tirade, unimpressed by the anger of a much younger and inexperienced man.

'We came here for a reason, Legatus,' he said quietly, emphasising the rank with just enough edge to suggest the position did not impress him. 'Not just to confirm the death of a missing legion, but to investigate reports of vast wealth hidden in the African interior.' He gestured toward the chamber around them. 'Look at what we've found. A city that makes Roman engineering look primitive, people who command trained predators as casually as we command horses, and

213

wealth that potentially exceeds anything in the imperial treasury. This isn't just another barbarian settlement to be pacified and forgotten, it is one to be examined, dominated and if necessary, absorbed into Rome's dominions.'

Seneca stepped forward, his own anger barely contained despite his usual diplomatic restraint.

'And how exactly do you propose we survive long enough to report these discoveries to anyone?' he demanded. 'You've committed us to assault an unknown position defended by warriors who've been fighting in this terrain since childhood!' They've already defeated us once, let alone what they did to the Rapax.'

'I've committed us to a mission that offers the possibility of substantial reward rather than slinking home empty-handed with tales of failure,' replied Scipio coldly. 'Consider the strategic implications, not just the immediate tactical challenges.'

He began pacing the chamber with the restless energy of someone developing arguments under pressure, his weathered hands gesturing to emphasise his points.

'If we return to Claudius with confirmation of this place's existence, along with samples of the wealth to be gained here, we could return with a proper expeditionary force. A fully trained legion, more perhaps, better prepared for the terrain and conditions, and equipped to not just occupy this city but establish permanent Roman presence throughout the region.'

His eyes took on a covetous gleam, imagining advancement and glory beyond his previous dreams.

'This could be another province, Flavus. Egypt was nothing but desert and primitive mud farmers before Roman administration transformed it into the Empire's granary. What we've found here could become something similar, a source of wealth and strategic position that would secure the southern frontiers for generations. All we need to do is gather proof and report back to Claudius.'

Flavus shook his head with obvious disgust.

'Assuming any of us survive to deliver such reports,' he replied bitterly. 'Which seems increasingly unlikely given the insane commitment you've made on our behalf. No, I will not order these men to undertake a mission that amounts to nothing more than suicide for the sake of your personal enrichment. We'll find another way to negotiate our departure.'

The conversation was interrupted by Corvus, who had been listening to the exchange with growing unease.

'I'm afraid it's too late for that, Legatus,' he said quietly. 'The agreement has been made in Panthera's presence before witnesses. He will expect it to be honoured.'

'And if we refuse?' asked Flavus.

Corvus smiled, but the expression held no warmth or reassurance.

'Look around,' he said simply, gesturing toward the chamber that had become their world for the past eight days. 'This door is locked from the outside. The walls are solid granite, carved from living rock. It would take weeks to break through even if you had proper tools, which you don't.'

He moved to the water basin, running his fingers along the carefully carved channel that supplied their needs.

'All they have to do is block this water supply and wait. No food, no water, no possibility of escape. You'd last perhaps five days before dehydration drove you to accept whatever terms they chose to offer. And even if you agreed to honour the bargain but then attempted to renege once you were outside,' he continued, anticipating their next line of thought, 'you'd never escape the valley alive. They know every path, every hiding place, every source of water. The city is surrounded by the Makatani, the crater is surrounded by dangerous territory, and they have allies among peoples you've never heard of.'

The implications of his words settled over the Romans like poison spreading through their bloodstream. They had walked into a trap whose walls were carved from stone older than their civilisation, and whose bars were forged from their own desperation.

'Panthera is not cruel,' continued Corvus, 'but he is absolutely practical. He gave you an opportunity to serve his interests whilst potentially benefiting your own. If you're unwilling to accept that opportunity...' He shrugged expressively, the gesture encompassing all the unpleasant alternatives that awaited them.

The chamber fell into brooding silence as each man contemplated the magnitude of their situation. Somewhere in that hostile landscape, their survival would be decided by factors beyond any Roman military doctrine, in terrain they'd never seen, against enemies whose tactics adapted to conditions no legion had ever encountered.

Hours passed in uncomfortable contemplation before most of the men settled into their sleeping arrangements, but rest proved elusive for those burdened with command and as the chamber filled with the quiet sounds of sleeping men, Scipio rose from his own blankets and approached the corner where Flavus sat with his back against the ancient stone wall.

The young legatus stared at him coldly, still angry at his earlier insubordination.

'Legatus,' said Scipio, quietly, 'I accept that my earlier actions were hasty, but there is a way in which we can make this work.'

'I don't see how,' said Flavus, 'but continue.'

'The answer is right before us,' said Scipio, 'All we have to do is use the Occultum.'

'The Occultum?' said Flavus. 'I have heard rumours of such men but how can they help us all the way out here.'

'Oh they are not far away,' said Scipio, staring across the room to where Seneca and his men were resting. 'In fact, I know there are six of them right here in this very room and I think it is about time we saw exactly what they are made of.'

Chapter Twenty-Nine

The Chamber

Halfway through the night, Flavus called Seneca to the far wall to join him and Scipio, their voices kept to whispers that wouldn't disturb the exhausted soldiers who had finally found sleep amongst their borrowed blankets.

'Seneca,' said Flavus, 'I'll bet straight to the point. Scipio has a proposal that could sort out this whole sorry mess. I have been informed that you and your men have certain skills that you can bring to bear to provide the service that Panthera has requested. To be clear, I am talking about the head of the Makatani chieftain.'

Seneca glanced across at Scipio, obviously the source of the reveal before looking back to Flavus. It was pointless trying to deny the reality.

'We have been known to do similar things,' he said, 'but this is unlike anything we have tried before. How do you suppose we get in there?'

'Scipio has a plan,' said Flavus. 'Scipio, myself and our remaining men, will leave here and advance to the edge of the swamplands to establish a defensive position where the Makatani can't help but notice our presence. Once there, we make as much noise as possible to draw their attention and when they respond, we engage them fully while you and your men skirt around the edge of the swamp and find their camp.'

'A diversion?' said Seneca.

'Exactly.'

Seneca stared at the two men.

'Six men against potentially hundreds of enemies, deep in hostile territory with no support or extraction possible if things go wrong. The numbers aren't exactly encouraging.'

'Perhaps not,' said Flavus, 'but a conventional assault is not possible. We've seen what happened to the Twenty-First so a direct advance into their chosen terrain is suicide. But I am led to believe this so-called Occultum has operated behind enemy lines before.'

'This isn't Germania or Britannia,' said Seneca. 'This is different terrain, different enemies, different stakes entirely.'

'The stakes are what they are,' said Scipio. 'If we do nothing, everyone dies anyway. At least this way, we're taking action rather than waiting for circumstances to decide our fate.'

Despite his obvious scepticism about the plan's chances of success, Seneca found himself considering possibilities that conventional wisdom suggested were impossible. The reality was inescapable, conventional assault was suicide, retreat was blocked, and inaction meant slow death through starvation or eventual discovery. But they had faces similar odds before and had come out the other side intact.

'I need to discuss this with my men before I make any decision,' he said finally.

'Of course,' said Flavus. 'But the longer we wait, the less likely we are to succeed.'

Seneca rose from his position and looked across the room to his comrades.

'Give me time with my men,' he said quietly. 'Then you'll have an answer.'

As Flavus and Scipio settled back into contemplative silence, Seneca joined his men on the far side of the chamber.'

'Well?' asked Falco as Seneca sat down amongst them, 'your face says you have news, and that is seldom good.'

'Scipio has a plan,' said Seneca without preamble, his

voice kept low enough to avoid carrying to the other men 'He wants to use the main force as a diversion while we infiltrate the Makatani camp and eliminate their leadership.'

The Occultum looked between themselves. Although there was little detail. In principle it was exactly the sort of surgical operation they had perfected through years of desperate circumstances.

'It's insane,' said Marcus eventually. 'But it's also probably our only chance of completing this mission and getting home alive.'

'The terrain will be the challenge,' said Sica. 'Swampland, hostile wildlife, and enemies who know every path and hiding place. We'll be operating blind in conditions designed to kill outsiders.'

'But that's exactly why they won't expect it,' Falco added. 'Maybe unconventional thinking is what this situation requires.'

'Which is why we need more information before making any decisions,' agreed Seneca. 'I'll talk to Corvus. If we're going to attempt this, we need to understand exactly what we're walking into.'

Seneca found Corvus sitting alone near the chamber's water basin, the scarred Optio staring into the clear liquid.

'Corvus,' he said, sitting beside him, 'I need you to tell me about the Makatani. Everything you know about their numbers, their capabilities, their methods of warfare.'

Corvus adjusted his position against the stone wall, and looked up to the ceiling as he retrieved the information about the people who had almost ended his life.

'They're usually seasonal raiders,' he began quietly. 'They don't live in the valley permanently but migrate here during the dry months when hunting becomes difficult in their traditional territories. But this season has been different. Instead of the usual raiding parties that strike and withdraw, they've established a permanent camp in the heart of the swamplands. Something has changed in their leadership or their circumstances that's made them more aggressive than previous years.'

'How many warriors are we talking about?'

'Difficult to say with certainty,' replied Corvus. 'Raiding parties have ranged from twenty to fifty men, but those are just the ones who venture close enough to the ruins to be counted. Their main camp probably holds more than a hundred fighters, possibly more if they've been reinforced by allies from other tribes.'

'What about their defences? Palisades, earthworks, anything that would complicate a direct assault?'

'Few artificial defences,' Corvus admitted. 'But they don't need them. Their main camp is located at the heart of the swamplands, in a place Panthera's people believe is protected by malevolent spirits.'

'Meaning?'

'Meaning that warriors who venture too deep into those waters don't return. The few who have been recovered were found days later, their bodies bearing signs of death that couldn't be explained by conventional weapons or known predators.'

'How would we identify their leader?' asked Seneca.

'His face,' replied Corvus immediately. 'The war chief is marked with complete facial tattoos, serpent patterns that cover everything from forehead to jaw.

'Serpent patterns?'

'Scales, rendered with such precision that his face

appears to be covered with snakeskin. It's a mark of rank that's earned through combat and confirmed through ritual scarification that few men survive.'

'What about the camp itself? Layout, approaches, anything that might help a small unit get close without detection?'

Corvus considered the question carefully.

'Apparently it's built on a series of interconnected islands, with the main settlement on the largest. Wooden walkways connect the different areas, but they're designed to be destroyed quickly if the camp is threatened.'

Seneca absorbed this information while working through tactical possibilities that might enable a small unit to penetrate such defences. The picture Corvus painted was challenging but not impossible, assuming they could reach the camp undetected and identify their target accurately.

'One more question,' he said quietly. 'If someone were to eliminate the war chief, what would happen to his followers?'

'Chaos,' replied Corvus without hesitation. 'The Makatani follow strength, not political structures. Remove their leader, and they'd probably fragment into smaller groups fighting each other for succession. At a minimum, it would break up their current unity.'

The conversation continued for another hour, before Seneca finally returned to his men. The whispered briefing that followed painted a clear picture of what they would face if they agreed to attempt Scipio's plan.

'Perhaps a hundred men or more in a position, protected by terrain that's killed everyone who's tried to assault it conventionally,' he summarized quietly. 'One primary target, identifiable by facial tattoos, surrounded by personal guards in a camp designed for quick defence.'

'Sounds familiar,' Sica observed with characteristic pragmatism. 'Different environment, but the same basic challenge. Get close, identify the target, eliminate him cleanly, and extract before organized response becomes possible.'

'The terrain is what makes this different,' Marcus pointed out. 'We'll be operating at a severe disadvantage from the moment we enter their territory.'

'But with stakes that make the risk worthwhile,' Seneca added. 'If we succeed, we complete our mission and potentially save everyone's life. If we fail, we die attempting something rather than waiting for death to claim us through inaction.'

The final vote was unanimous, and when they had reached consensus, Seneca rose and walked back toward where Scipio and Flavus waited with obvious tension.

'We'll do it,' said Seneca without preamble. 'But the tactical details are ours to determine. We'll need a guide who knows safe routes through the terrain, and we'll need precise timing to coordinate with your diversion.'

'What do you need from us?' asked Flavus.

'Exactly what you proposed initially,' said Seneca. 'Draw them out and give us some time where the camp is lightly defended. We'll do the rest.'

'Timing?'

'We'll depart at dusk tomorrow, allowing us to reach our laying-up position during the night. Your diversion should begin at dawn the following morning, giving us time to approach the camp while they are distracted.'

'And after?'

'Once we are in place, we'll wait until they return to camp. As soon as we can, we'll infiltrate under the cover of darkness and carry out the mission.'

'What about getting back?'

'Leave that up to us. We need to stay flexible and react to whatever the circumstances throw at us. If we succeed, the enemy should be too disorganized to mount effective pursuit. If we fail...' He left the sentence unfinished, but the implications were clear enough. Failure would leave the expedition exactly where it had started, except with six fewer men.

The eastern sky was beginning to show the first pale hints of dawn when they finally agreed the last of the details. Within the next few days, the Occultum would test their skills against the strangest foe they had ever faced, but this time, failure would doom not just themselves but every Roman who had followed them into this hidden realm.

Chapter Thirty

The City

The following day, the Occultum isolated themselves in the far corner of their chamber, their equipment spread across blankets in careful arrangements of importance. Seneca sat cross-legged before his opened sarcina, every item receiving scrutiny that would determine its value against the weight it would add to an already impossible mission. The standard legionary pack that had served him well through conventional campaigns now seemed grotesquely overloaded for what lay ahead.

'We'll take just one sarcina,' he said eventually, 'with equipment for two days only. Once we are at our insertion point we'll ditch it and from that moment forward, we carry only weapons and water.'

'Standard evasion tactics for withdrawal?' asked Marcus, though the question was largely rhetorical. They had used the same methods for escaping hostile territory since their first mission together.

'Standard tactics,' Seneca confirmed. 'If we accomplish the mission, we move fast and quiet back toward the ruins. If everything has gone to plan, Scipio should be there with his men to cover our withdrawal. Once there, well, we'll see if Panthera is as good as his word but if we don't succeed…' He left the sentence unfinished, but the implication was clear enough. Failure would likely eliminate the need for any evasion tactics whatsoever.

The plan they had developed was deliberately simple, almost to the point of being crude by the standards of Roman military doctrine. But experience had taught them that complex plans rarely survived contact with reality, especially when operating in terrain they had never seen against enemies whose capabilities remained largely unknown.

'We get close,' he continued, 'we identify the target, we eliminate him as quickly and quietly as possible. Everything else is contingency that we'll deal with as it develops. Any questions?'

There were none. Each member of the Occultum understood exactly what they were undertaking and why conventional forces couldn't attempt it. Six men could accomplish what a hundred could not, assuming they possessed the skills, the courage, and the luck necessary to survive whatever awaited them in the swamplands.

As dusk approached and the ancient city settled into its evening routines, the familiar sound of the bar being drawn back echoed through their chamber. The massive doors swung open to reveal Corvus, accompanied by a man dressed differently from Panthera's people.

'This is Kesi,' Corvus announced, introducing their escort with obvious respect. 'He knows every safe path through the terrain you'll need to traverse, every source of fresh water, every location where predators gather to hunt. He's ready when you are.'

The guide nodded acknowledgment but said nothing, his attention focused on assessing the six men who would depend on his knowledge for their survival.

Seneca rose and shouldered his reduced pack, the lightened load feeling strange after months of carrying standard military equipment.

'In that case,' said Seneca, 'let's go.'

As they filed toward the chamber entrance, Falco

paused to glance back at the soldiers they were leaving behind. Every eye in the chamber was fixed on the departing elite unit. Some faces showed confusion at being excluded from whatever operation was planned, others displayed obvious concern for comrades heading into unknown dangers.

But every face showed respect. Whatever they were planning to undertake in the hostile darkness beyond the valley walls, they would do so with the accumulated expertise of campaigns fought across the known world.

The Occultum was on the move, but as they followed their silent guide through passages that led toward the world beyond the ancient walls, each member of the unit understood that they were walking toward their greatest challenge yet.

Chapter Thirty-One

The City

The massive entrance doors stood open like the mouth of some primordial beast, their ancient timbers creating a gateway between the civilised world of Panthera's city and the hostile wilderness that stretched beyond.

Kesi waited for them in the gathering darkness, his slight figure almost invisible against the weathered stone until movement revealed his presence.

Corvus limped forward to join them on the threshold.

'Kesi will take you to a position near the swamp's western edge,' he explained quietly. 'It's a route the Makatani seldom use, but it offers a good approach to their main camp without being seen.'

'How long to get there?' asked Seneca.

Corvus translated the question and Kesi's response was brief but seemed to encompass more information than the simple words might suggest.

'You will be there by dawn, if conditions remain favourable,' Corvus interpreted. 'Longer if you encounter patrols or predators that require detours.'

'And what about him?'

'He knows paths that will bring him back to the city. You won't need to worry about him once he's completed his task.'

As the last traces of daylight faded from the sky above the crater's rim, Kesi gestured toward the entrance with quiet authority. The time for departure had arrived, carrying them from the safety of ancient stones into a world where human presence was neither welcomed nor tolerated.

The descent proved much easier than their first experience with the steps and their guide moved with fluid efficiency, his knowledge of every stone and handhold making navigation possible even without the benefit of torchlight that might betray their presence to watching enemies.

'Stay close,' Seneca whispered to his men as they began following Kesi down the shadowed stairway. 'Single file, maintain contact with the man ahead of you.'

The transition from worked stone to natural rock formations was gradual but unmistakable, and what had begun as formal staircases soon gave way to rougher paths. The city's influence was fading, replaced by the sort of raw wilderness that had existed here since the world's creation.

'Smell that?' Marcus whispered as they paused on a narrow ledge to assess the route ahead.

The air stank of stagnant water and abundant vegetation, the rich organic odours that marked wetland environments where life flourished in forms unknown to Mediterranean climates. But underneath those natural perfumes lurked something else, the sort of organic decay that suggested death in quantities that went beyond normal ecological processes.

'The swamp,' Seneca confirmed grimly. 'We're getting close.'

Their guide froze in position ahead of them, his body language suggesting the need for absolute silence and stillness. For long moments, the Occultum remained motionless whilst Kesi listened to sounds that their untrained ears couldn't detect or interpret.

Finally, he resumed movement with careful steps, and the Occultum followed with equal caution, trusting his knowledge whilst remaining alert for threats that might appear without warning until finally, the rocky floor gave way to softer earth that showed the first signs of moisture from the wetlands ahead. Trees pressed closer to their route, their canopy blocking out most of the starlight whilst creating shadows that could conceal any number of dangers.

Kesi began moving with a different rhythm now, advancing in short stages that ended with him dropping flat against the ground whilst his ears strained to detect sounds that might indicate hostile presence. Each pause lasted several minutes, during which the Romans maintained absolute stillness whilst their guide assessed conditions that could mean the difference between safe passage and violent discovery.

The pace was maddeningly slow, but it was appropriate for their circumstances. Speed would be useless if it led them into ambushes or compromised their mission before it could begin. It was far better to arrive at their destination hours late than to be discovered during approach and alert the entire enemy camp to their presence.

In the distance, barely visible through the intervening vegetation, a faint glow began to appear on the underside of low-hanging clouds. The light was too steady to be natural, and too localised to be anything other than the reflection of numerous fires burning in close proximity to each other.

'There,' Decimus whispered, pointing toward the distant illumination. 'That's got to be their main camp.'

Kesi had noticed their attention to the distant glow and nodded confirmation before resuming his careful advance through terrain that grew progressively more treacherous with each step. The ground beneath their feet was becoming softer, whilst the air grew thick with moisture.

Another hour passed in careful navigation through increasingly difficult conditions. Trees gave way to scattered vegetation that offered less concealment, whilst solid ground became a memory, and they found themselves moving through terrain where each step might sink them deep into mud or standing water.

The guide's expertise became even more crucial as they entered this marginal environment where the boundary between land and water had been erased by centuries of seasonal flooding. He seemed to know instinctively which surfaces would support their weight and which would trap them in quicksand or bog, leading them along routes that might have been invisible to anyone lacking his accumulated knowledge.

Finally, after what felt like an eternity of careful progress through increasingly hostile terrain, Kesi stopped and gestured for them to gather around his position. The Occultum formed a tight circle, each man close enough to hear whispered instructions whilst maintaining the sort of vigilance that had kept them alive through countless dangerous missions.

Their guide pointed directly ahead, his gesture encompassing a vista that had been hidden by the undergrowth until this moment. Before them stretched an expanse of still water that reflected the stars like a dark mirror, its surface broken only by occasional ripples that suggested movement in the depths below.

The swamp proper lay before them, a world of standing water and hidden dangers that had protected the Makatani camp for generations. Somewhere beyond that deceptively peaceful surface, the war chief slept in confidence knowing that his camp had never been successfully challenged by outside forces.

Kesi raised his hands to mime the action of drawing a

bow and sending an arrow toward the distant firelight, then held up all ten fingers to indicate distance.

Talorcan immediately grasped the implications, his experience with both archery and difficult terrain allowing him to calculate the practical realities.

'The distance of ten arrows,' he said. 'Perhaps two thousand paces through swampland.'

The guide seemed to understand that his message had been received and interpreted correctly and without further ceremony, turned away to begin retracing his steps through the treacherous terrain they had just traversed. Within minutes, he had vanished into the darkness, leaving the Occultum alone at the edge of a hostile environment that stretched between them and their ultimate objective.

'Form a perimeter,' Seneca ordered quietly. 'All-round defence, and maintain contact with the men on either side of you. We wait here until dawn.'

The Occultum deployed into their familiar patterns, each man taking position according to skills that had been refined through years of working together while somewhere back in the city, Scipio was preparing his own force for the diversionary assault that would draw enemy attention away from the Occultum's infiltration route.

The timing had to be perfect. Too early, and the deception would be discovered before they could exploit it; too late, and they would miss their opportunity to penetrate the enemy stronghold while defences were reduced.

But for now, they could only wait and watch, six men alone in hostile territory, preparing to attempt what conventional forces could never accomplish.

Chapter Thirty-Two

The Valley

Dawn came slowly, with golden light creeping over the crater's rim to illuminate a landscape that seemed caught between paradise and hell, and in the ruins at the base of Panthera's ancient city, the surviving legionaries prepared for battle.

Scipio moved through the ranks, checking equipment and adjusting formations while behind him, Flavus conducted his own inspection.

'Double file,' Scipio said quietly as the hundred survivors formed up in the shadow of ancient stones. 'Standard marching order and don't worry about maintaining silence. We're not trying to hide our presence today.'

The column that emerged from the ruins bore little resemblance to the motley collection of volunteers and criminals who had departed Alexandria months earlier. Hard experience and necessity had now forged these men into something approaching the legendary efficiency of regular legionaries.

They retraced their route through the valley with deliberate visibility, making no attempt at concealment whilst following paths that would take them back to the edge of the swamplands where their previous ordeal had begun almost two weeks earlier. The morning air carried sounds of their passage, the rhythmic tramp of hobnailed caligae on packed earth, the clink of equipment adjusted during movement, the sort of noise that announced Roman presence to anyone within miles of their position.

'Good,' Scipio observed with satisfaction as birds

exploded from cover ahead of their advance. 'Let every creature in this valley know we're coming. The more attention we draw, the better the chances Seneca and his men will succeed.'

They quickly reached the ground that overlooked the wetlands where crocodiles lurked, and poison darts had taken their toll and the swamp stretched before them like a cracked brown mirror, its deceptively peaceful surface concealing depths that had swallowed Roman soldiers without trace.

'Deploy into line abreast,' Scipio ordered as they reached their final position. 'Three ranks deep, maintain proper intervals. This is where we make our stand.'

The transformation from marching column to battle formation was executed with impressive efficiency. The men spread across the available frontage in perfect alignment, their shields locked edge to edge whilst gladii remained sheathed but ready for immediate use. It was Roman military doctrine at its most fundamental, disciplined soldiers in proper formation, presenting an unmistakable challenge to any enemy who chose to accept it.

Scipio took his position in the centre of the front rank, his scarred features scanning the swamplands ahead whilst his mind calculated distances and timing that would determine the success of their deception. Somewhere in those wetlands, the Occultum was beginning their own approach to the enemy stronghold, depending on this diversion to draw away the warriors who might otherwise detect their infiltration.

'Share the water,' he commanded, noting how the morning heat was already beginning to take its toll on men wearing armour under the African sun. 'Drink your fill now, because it may be hours before you get another chance.'

Water skins passed from hand to hand, each man taking what he needed whilst ensuring his comrades received their share.

'Listen to me,' Scipio called as the preparations neared completion. 'You know why we're here. You know what's expected of us. The men who went into those swamps last night are depending on us to draw enemy attention away from their mission. You've earned your rations through blood and suffering that would have broken lesser men but now it's time to step up. Last time, they caught us unprepared after an exhausting march. This time it is different. We may be few, but if you follow my orders without compromise, most of us will make it back to the city. Now, let's show these barbarian cannibals what Roman steel can accomplish when wielded by soldiers who refuse to surrender!'

The response was immediate and overwhelming. A hundred voices raised in the battle cry that had echoed across three continents, the sound rolling across the valley like thunder.

'Ready?' Scipio shouted, 'on my mark... *begin!*'

The sound that erupted from the Roman formation sent flocks of birds soaring into the sky as hundred gladii struck a hundred shield bosses simultaneously. The metallic percussion carried across the swamplands like their own version of the jungle drums that had tormented their nights, but this was Roman thunder rather than primitive beating.

For half an hour, the demonstration continued, the formation remaining perfectly aligned whilst their weapons created a wall of sound that announced Roman presence to every creature within miles. Sweat poured from faces already reddened by exertion and heat, but discipline held firm whilst the message was driven home with relentless efficiency.

Eventually, Scipio saw what he had been waiting for, movement in the depths of the swampland, dark shapes that emerged slowly from concealment. The enemy was taking the bait, drawn by the noise generated by Roman confidence rather than fear.

'Stop!' commanded Scipio, his voice cutting through the rhythmic thunder.

The sudden silence was almost shocking after the prolonged cacophony and a hundred men stood motionless in perfect formation whilst the echoes of their demonstration faded across the wetlands.

'Get ready, lads,' Scipio called into the sudden stillness, his tone carrying grim satisfaction at the success of their deception. 'They'll be here before you can say Jupiter's hairy arse!'

The shadows in the swampland were resolving into recognisable shapes now, warriors paddling their war canoes through their natural element. The Makatani were coming, just as the plan required and somewhere in the wetlands behind them, the Occultum would be waiting to start their own infiltration.

The diversion was working exactly as intended, though whether either group would survive to appreciate their tactical success remained to be determined.

Chapter Thirty-Three

The Swamp

The swamp erupted into motion as if some primordial god had stirred the depths with a massive spear. What had appeared moments before as empty wetland now teemed with dark figures like demons materializing from the depths of hell itself. Water cascaded from their painted bodies as they jumped from the canoes and waded toward the solid ground where Roman steel waited in disciplined ranks.

'Archers forward!' Scipio commanded, his voice cutting through the growing din of enemy war cries. 'Take them while they're exposed!'

The surviving bowmen stepped through gaps in the shield wall, their numbers pitifully reduced by the casualties sustained during months of brutal campaigning. Perhaps two dozen men remained from what had once been a full century of specialist troops, each carrying just a few arrows each.

They drew and loosed nonetheless, their arrows arcing across the intervening distance to strike targets who couldn't take cover whilst struggling through waist-deep water.

The missiles found their marks with satisfying accuracy. Warriors stumbled and fell beneath the surface with screams that were quickly muffled by the brown water, whilst others pressed forward despite wounds that would have felled lesser men. But for every man who dropped, three more seemed to take his place, emerging from hiding spots that had been invisible until movement revealed their presence.

'Ten arrows each,' the senior archer reported grimly as his men continued their methodical work. 'After that, we're down to gladii like everyone else.'

The reality was brutal but unavoidable. Even perfect accuracy wouldn't eliminate enough enemies to meaningfully reduce the odds facing the Roman formation. The archers could slow the enemy advance and eliminate selected targets, but they couldn't win the battle through missile fire alone.

'Make every arrow count,' replied Scipio coldly. 'Every man you kill is one less to face our gladii.'

The remaining arrows were loosed into the oncoming hoard and when the final shaft was expended, the archers melted back through the formation to take their positions in the rear ranks, their short bows replaced by gladii that would serve them well enough in close combat.

The Makatani continued emerging from the swamplands in numbers that exceeded every previous estimate of their strength. Hundreds of warriors gained the solid ground and spread out across the available frontage, their weapons ranging from fire-hardened spears to captured Roman equipment.

But instead of launching an immediate assault, they paused to wait for reinforcements who continued arriving from hidden positions throughout the wetlands. The delay was both tactically sound and psychologically devastating for the waiting Romans.

'Sweet Jupiter,' someone muttered from the ranks behind Scipio. 'There must be five hundred of them.'

'More like six,' another voice corrected grimly. 'And they're still coming.'

The Makatani formation continued growing and a chant began to rise from their ranks, starting as a low murmur that gradually built into a rhythmic chorus of voices that seemed to make the very air vibrate with primitive power.

This was something primal, the sort of sound that

connected these warriors to ancestors who had fought with stone weapons when Rome was still a collection of mud huts beside the Tiber. The chanting built and built until individual voices were lost in a wall of sound and fearless determination.

Individual warriors broke from the chanting to roar war cries that defied description, sounds that seemed to come from the throats of wild beasts rather than human beings. The challenges were delivered with faces painted in patterns that created the illusion of serpent scales, ritual scarification that transformed them into something beyond ordinary mortality.

The psychological impact was immediate and devastating, and several younger Romans shifted nervously in their ranks, their faces pale beneath bronze helmets. These weren't civilised opponents who fought according to recognisable rules, but something that seemed to have emerged from nightmares about humanity's savage past.

'Steady the line!' Scipio barked, noting how the formation was beginning to waver as men absorbed the full magnitude of what they faced. 'Eyes front! Trust your training!'

But even veteran soldiers were struggling to maintain composure when confronted with enemies who outnumbered them at least ten to one, and expected to die in battle but welcomed the prospect. The Roman formation held, but barely, discipline maintained through willpower rather than confidence.

Scipio stepped forward to address his men.

'Listen to me!' he roared, his tone cutting through the fear and uncertainty. 'Each one of you is worth ten of them! We have the training, the weapons, and the discipline that built an empire!' He gestured toward the enemy formation with obvious contempt, his movements designed to project confidence rather than reveal the concern that gnawed at his professional

assessment of their tactical situation. 'We are Romans! Our predecessors fought greater numbers than this with fewer advantages, yet they came through. Remember your training, trust your comrades, and we will endure.'

The words were familiar, drawn from the repertoire of speeches that had rallied legions facing impossible odds throughout Roman military history. But familiarity didn't diminish their power when delivered by a commander whose own courage was beyond question.

'Let the first wave come,' Scipio continued, his voice growing stronger as he relayed the tactical plan that would preserve as many lives as possible. 'We will repel them as Roman steel has always repelled barbarian fury. But when they break away, and they will break away, we withdraw in good order.' He pointed toward the distant ruins behind them where Panthera's warriors waited to support their retreat. 'Each group retreats twenty paces while the others provide cover. We repeat this manoeuvre over and over again, covering each other as we return to safety. No man breaks formation, no man runs. If any of you abandons his comrades, I swear I will kill you myself before the enemy gets the chance.'

The threat carried weight because every man knew Scipio would carry it out without hesitation. But more important than fear of punishment was the plan itself, which offered hope of survival rather than glorious but futile last stands.

'Stick to the plan and most of us will see this through,' he concluded. 'Now face your front. *Here they come!*'

The Makatani charge erupted with shocking violence as hundreds of warriors surged forward across the open ground that separated the two forces. Their war cries reached a crescendo that seemed to shake the earth itself, whilst weapons flashed in the morning sunlight as they closed the distance with terrifying speed.

The moment of truth had arrived. Roman discipline would be tested against primitive fury in circumstances that would determine whether any of them lived to see another sunset. But behind the advancing tide of enemies, the swamplands stretched toward horizons where the Occultum pursued their own desperate mission, depending on this diversion to keep enemy attention focused away from their infiltration route.

The false battle was about to become terrifyingly real.

Chapter Thirty-Four

The Swamp

On the far side of the swamp, dawn had brought the Occultum to the launch point. The pre-dawn darkness had been spent in methodical final checks, each man ensuring that weapons were secure, water carefully rationed, and equipment reduced to the absolute minimum necessary for survival in hostile terrain.

The sarcina now lay abandoned, hidden beneath thick undergrowth where it could be recovered during withdrawal if circumstances permitted. Each man carried only the personal weapons they had become comfortable with over years of campaigning, some dried meat, and a single water skin each.

They positioned themselves at the water's edge, each man finding cover amongst the tangled vegetation that lined the swamp's margin, their positions offering good observation of the route ahead whilst providing protection from detection by enemies who might still be in the area.

The morning air carried sounds from across the valley with crystalline clarity, the metallic thunder of gladii striking shield bosses echoing across the wetlands like their own version of the primitive drums that had tormented their nights.

'There it is,' said Talorcan quietly. 'A hundred men making enough noise to wake the dead. It should get the Makatani's attention well enough.'

The demonstration continued for what felt like hours, each crash of metal on metal carrying across the water like a challenge that no warrior culture could ignore indefinitely, but when the distant thunder stopped, the sudden cessation was more ominous than the noise itself, suggesting that contact had been made, and violence was about to erupt with all the fury that desperation could inspire.

Seneca looked along the line of his companions, seeing his own thoughts reflected in faces marked by years of dangerous living. Once again, they were being asked to accomplish what conventional forces couldn't attempt, to penetrate enemy strongholds that had never been successfully assaulted, to eliminate targets whose death might break the resistance of an entire people.

'Are we ready for this?' he asked.

The responses came without hesitation.

'Ready.'

'Always ready.'

'Let's finish this.'

The chanting reached its peak and transformed into the distinctive roar of hundreds of men charging into battle. The Makatani assault had begun.

Chapter Thirty-Five

The Swamp

The water embraced them, closing around their legs as if reluctant to release anything that entered its domain. Seneca felt the bottom give way beneath his feet with each step, soft sediment and rotting vegetation creating treacherous footing that could trap an unwary man or twist an ankle with devastating consequences.

The Occultum moved in single file through the brown mirror of the swamp, each man maintaining a calculated distance from the soldier ahead whilst their eyes constantly scanned for threats that could emerge from any direction. The water rose and fell with the hidden contours of the bottom, sometimes reaching their knees, other times climbing to their waists as they navigated depressions that had been carved by centuries of seasonal flooding.

In the distance, carried on the still air like the voices of distant gods, came the sounds of battle erupting across the valley. The clash of weapons against shields, the screams of wounded men, and the noise of Romans selling their lives as dearly as possible against overwhelming odds.

'They're buying us time with their blood,' Marcus whispered, his voice barely audible above the gentle lapping of water against their legs. 'We'd better make it count.'

The swamp seemed to swallow sound with hungry efficiency, their movements creating barely perceptible ripples that spread outward before vanishing into the organic maze that surrounded them. Ancient trees rose from the water like the pillars of some primordial temple, their trunks disappearing into a canopy so thick that precious little sunlight penetrated to the surface below.

Hanging moss draped from every branch in grey curtains that stirred without any detectable breeze, creating the illusion of movement where none should exist, and the air itself felt heavy with moisture.

They had been moving for perhaps twenty minutes when Seneca raised his hand, the silent signal for absolute stillness. The rest of the Occultum froze instantly, six men becoming as motionless as the dead trees around them whilst their eyes tracked something that had caught Seneca's attention.

The creature that emerged from a tangle of submerged roots was smaller than the monsters they had encountered in the main river, but still easily large enough to take down any man who wasn't paying attention. The crocodile moved with unhurried an apex predator in its own territory, its prehistoric eyes scanning the water for disturbances that might indicate prey.

For long moments, predator and soldiers regarded each other across ten paces of brown water, neither moving whilst both assessed the threat the other represented. The reptile's brain, unchanged since the world's creation, processed the strange vertical shapes as potential food whilst calculating the energy required to attack against the likelihood of success.

Finally, the crocodile submerged and disappeared into the murky depths, leaving only ripples to mark its passage.

'Keep going, said Seneca quietly as they resumed their careful advance. 'They're not looking for trouble if we don't give them reason to hunt us.'

The water level rose steadily as they pressed deeper into the swamp's heart, forcing them to advance with increasingly careful steps whilst the bottom beneath their feet became a treacherous maze of fallen logs, tangled roots, and soft patches that could swallow a man if he stepped wrongly.

Strange fish moved through the murky water around their legs, some no larger than a man's thumb whilst others approached the size of small dogs. Most seemed more curious than aggressive, but their alien appearances served as constant reminders that this was an environment governed by rules no Roman had ever learned.

One of the larger specimens approached Marcus with obvious interest before being discouraged by a gentle movement of his gladius beneath the surface. The fish departed without apparent alarm, but its boldness suggested these waters contained predators that had never learned to fear human presence.

The canopy above their heads teemed with life whilst birds with plumage of impossible brilliance flashed between the trees like living jewels. But it was the spiders that drew the most nervous attention from the advancing Romans. Creatures the size of a man's hand suspended themselves over the water on webs that gleamed like silk in the filtered light, their bodies poised to drop onto anything that passed beneath their hunting grounds.

'Don't touch the webs,' Talorcan warned quietly as they navigated between particularly dense clusters of the gleaming snares. 'Some of those beauties are large enough to consider us prey rather than threat.'

The smell of the swamp was overwhelming, not the clean scent of flowing water they were accustomed to, but the rich organic perfume of an environment where everything that died remained to nourish what came after. Rotting vegetation mixed with the earthier odours of mud and stagnant pools, whilst underneath it all lurked something else, a smell from things better left undisturbed.

Their progress slowed as the water deepened, and the bottom became increasingly treacherous. What had begun as difficult walking transformed into something approaching swimming as they encountered pools where the bottom disappeared.

'How much further?' Falco asked during one of their brief pauses.

Seneca studied the route ahead, noting how the canopy seemed to thin slightly in the distance.

'Not far now,' he replied, 'we're approaching some sort of clearing.'

The chorus of frogs that had provided constant background noise since entering the swamp began to take on a different quality as they advanced, individual calls becoming distinguishable from the general din. Some were deep enough to vibrate through the water itself, whilst others created piercing notes that seemed designed to penetrate human consciousness with almost physical force.

The cacophony was simultaneously beautiful and maddening, a symphony of sound that spoke of life flourishing in conditions that would kill most creatures within hours. But underneath the natural music lurked something else, the occasional splash or movement that suggested larger predators moving through their territory with patient hunger.

A snake passed within arm's reach of Sica's position, its body easily as thick as a man's leg whilst its length disappeared into the murky water without revealing its full extent. The serpent showed no interest in the Romans, but its casual proximity served as another reminder that they were visitors in a realm where no human belonged.

The battle raging in the distance began to take on a different character as they penetrated deeper into the swamp's embrace.

'Scipio's conducting his retreat,' Marcus observed, noting how the sounds of combat seemed to be moving steadily away from their position. 'Drawing them back toward the ruins just as planned.'

The smell of rot grew stronger as they advanced, no longer the healthy decomposition of natural cycles but something more ominous, the sort of organic decay that suggested death in quantities that went beyond normal ecological processes. Mixed with the sweetness of rotting vegetation came hints of something else, the unmistakable odour of human habitation in close proximity.

'We're getting close,' Seneca whispered quietly.

The water began to shallow again as they approached what appeared to be rising ground ahead, the muddy bottom giving way to something more solid. Finally, after more than four hours of punishing progress through some of the most hostile terrain any of them had ever encountered, Seneca raised his hand and pointed toward a low island that rose from the swamp like the back of some sleeping monster.

The patch of solid ground was perhaps fifty paces long and half as wide, its surface covered with vegetation, offering concealment from observation whilst providing a position where they could rest and assess their situation before the final approach to their target.

Without words, the Occultum began the final effort required to drag themselves from the brown water onto the blessed relief of dry land. Each man emerged from the swamp like some primordial creature crawling from the depths of creation, their bodies streaming with organic matter.

They collapsed onto the muddy earth with grateful silence, their minds processing the magnitude of what they had just accomplished. They knew they were close but for now, they could only rest and gather strength for whatever trials awaited them in the hours ahead. The real test was yet to come.

Across the swamp, the clash of steel against bone echoed across the wetlands as Scipio's gladius punched through flesh to silence another Makatani warrior. Around him, the Roman formation maintained its deadly precision despite being outnumbered by odds that would have broken lesser troops.

'*Second rank, advance!*' he commanded, his scarred voice cutting through the din of combat. 'First rank, fall back twenty paces!'

The front rank disengaged from their enemies, their shields locked in defensive positions whilst gladii discouraged pursuit through short, vicious thrusts that opened throats and severed arteries.

Behind them, fresh soldiers stepped forward to take their place, their weapons already bloodied from the sustained engagement that had been raging for hours. The rotation allowed exhausted men to recover whilst maintaining constant pressure on enemies who had never faced such disciplined opposition.

Flavus watched from his position in the centre of the formation. Despite his youth and inexperience, he could appreciate the masterful way Scipio was managing their resources, using superior training and discipline to hold back forces that should have overwhelmed them through sheer numbers.

The Makatani fought with fearless determination that

bordered on religious frenzy, throwing themselves against the Roman shields with complete disregard for personal survival. Their war cries echoed across the valley as painted warriors wielded captured gladii alongside primitive clubs, their serpent-faced leaders driving them forward with examples of courage that defied rational understanding.

But now, instead of the piecemeal attacks they had been conducting, hundreds of warriors surged forward simultaneously, their combined weight testing the formation's ability to absorb such concentrated pressure.

The impact sent shock waves through the ranks as Romans found themselves fighting multiple opponents whilst trying to maintain the spacing and coordination that had kept them alive so far.

'Hold the line!' Scipio roared, his blade carving through a warrior's neck.

But even as he spoke, the tactical situation was deteriorating with terrifying speed. The Makatani weren't just pressing their frontal assault, dark figures emerged from the swamplands on both sides of the formation, warriors who had used the engagement to mask their own movement into positions where they could strike the Romans from unexpected directions. The disciplined retreat that had been working so effectively suddenly became a death trap as enemies appeared where none should exist.

'Enemy left!' someone screamed as Makatani warriors erupted from concealment to strike the formation's exposed flank. 'They're everywhere!'

The left flank buckled under the assault as men who had been maintaining perfect discipline, suddenly found themselves surrounded.

'Defend the flanks!' Scipio roared, trying to adapt their

formation to meet threats from multiple directions. *'Form testudo!'*

But the manoeuvre required time and space they no longer possessed and the Makatani warriors pressed their advantage with savage efficiency, sensing weakness in enemies who had suddenly lost the initiative.

'Close in!' bellowed Scipio, but the damage was spreading like poison through the ranks and one of the younger soldiers turned to flee back towards the city.

'Hold your positions,' roared Scipio, as the young man was swamped by three warriors, *'no one runs,'* but panic was more contagious than plague when men were already stretched beyond their limits and another soldier broke the line, running away from the battle as fast as he could... Then another.. and another!

'Nooo!' Scipio's voice carried desperation rather than authority as he watched his carefully managed withdrawal transform into something far more dangerous. He needed a rallying point, but there were no standards or eagles here, and the formation that had held against impossible odds disintegrated in moments, discipline evaporating like morning mist before the desert sun. What had been an orderly tactical withdrawal now became a rout as soldiers abandoned their positions to seek individual survival through flight rather than collective strength.

Scipio's reaction was immediate and brutal. His gladius took the nearest fleeing soldier between the shoulder blades, punching through mail rings to emerge from the man's chest in a fountain of blood and the body dropped to the muddy ground as the camp prefect sought his next target.

'Cowards!' he roared, his scarred face twisted with fury as he struck down another deserter. *'I'll kill every man who abandons*

his post!'

But even his legendary ferocity couldn't stem the tide of collapse that was consuming his command. Men who had survived impossible hardships together were now trampling each other in their desperation to escape enemies who sensed victory and pressed their advantage with savage enthusiasm.

The Makatani war cries reached a crescendo as painted warriors surged forward to exploit the Roman collapse as what had been a disciplined formation holding them at bay became a collection of individuals fleeing in whatever direction offered the best chance of survival.

Scipio found himself surrounded by enemies whilst his own men fled past him without offering assistance. His gladius continued its deadly work, opening throats and piercing hearts with automatic precision, but he was one man against dozens of opponents who showed no fear of Roman steel.

A war club connected with his helmet, sending him staggering whilst stars exploded across his vision. Another blow struck his shoulder, numbing his sword arm whilst blood ran down his face from a scalp wound that painted his world red.

For a moment that stretched like eternity, the veteran commander wavered between duty and survival, his professional instincts warring with the animal need to preserve his own life. Around him, the last vestiges of Roman order were disappearing into the distance as his soldiers chose flight over formation until finally, with a curse that would have impressed any veteran… *he turned and ran!*

Chapter Thirty-Six

The Swamp

After regaining their breath and allowing their bodies to recover from the brutal ordeal of the swamp crossing, Seneca gestured for his men to form up for the final stage of their approach. They slipped back into the brown water with reluctant acceptance, but this time their senses sharpened by proximity to their objective.

The character of the swamp began to change as they pressed deeper into territory that showed signs of regular human habitation. The water remained treacherous, but pathways had been cleared through the worst tangles of vegetation, whilst broken branches and disturbed mud spoke of frequent passage by people who knew how to navigate this hostile environment.

They advanced with painful slowness, testing each step before committing their weight whilst their eyes constantly scanned for threats that could emerge from any direction. The canopy above their heads got thinner and eventually, the faint but unmistakable scent of burning wood drifted through the humid atmosphere, mixing with the earthier odours they had been breathing for hours.

'Smoke,' announced Seneca quietly, 'we're getting close.'

The smell grew stronger as they continued their cautious advance, and through a gap in the vegetation ahead, he caught sight of something that made him signal immediately for absolute stillness. All the Occultum stared forward and what they saw exceeded their most optimistic expectations whilst simultaneously confirming their worst fears about the magnitude of their undertaking. The Makatani settlement sprawled across a substantial island that rose from the swamp, its elevated position providing natural defence against the floods that regularly swept through the wetlands.

Several dugout canoes lay drawn up against the muddy shoreline, and beyond the beached vessels, they saw semi-permanent structures that had been integrated into the living landscape with remarkable ingenuity.

The huts were formed from the branches of massive trees that had been carefully bent and woven into frameworks that supported walls of woven reeds and palm fronds. The integration was so complete that from any distance greater than a few hundred paces, the settlement would be virtually invisible to observers who didn't know exactly where to look. Only the smoke rising from carefully concealed cook fires and the occasional glimpse of the dugout canoes betrayed the presence of human habitation.

But what drew their immediate attention was what they didn't see... people. The settlement appeared completely deserted, its pathways empty and its structures showing no signs of current occupation.

'They're all gone,' said Falco quietly. 'They must have responded to Scipio's demonstration just as we hoped.'

'Or it's a trap,' Sica added pragmatically, refusing to accept that anything could be as simple as it appeared.

Seneca studied the settlement through narrowed eyes. The absence of visible defenders was encouraging, but it could just as easily indicate a more sophisticated trap than anything they had anticipated.

'We need to get closer,' he decided finally, 'and find concealment where we can observe their return and identify our targets before we commit.'

The search for a suitable observation post proved more challenging than they had anticipated, but finally, after nearly an hour of careful scouting, Talorcan spotted what they needed. A substantial mat of floating vegetation had broken away from some distant shore to drift against a fallen tree perhaps fifty paces from the settlement's edge.

The natural raft was large enough to conceal their entire unit whilst thick enough to support their weight, creating a perfect hide that would appear to be nothing more than one of the countless pieces of organic debris that drifted through the swamp's waters. More importantly, it offered clear observation of the settlement whilst remaining far enough away to avoid detection by returning warriors.

'That's it,' Seneca confirmed, and finally, after what felt like hours of careful progress, they reached the floating island and hauled themselves onto its deceptively solid surface.

They arranged themselves in a rough circle with each man facing outward to provide all-round observation. Water skins were passed around, and the last of dried meat consumed without conversation as the afternoon heat pressed down on them like a physical weight.

When darkness fell and the warriors returned from their engagement with Scipio's forces, the six men would attempt to eliminate a chief whose death might break the power of an entire people.

Chapter Thirty-Seven

Near The city

The collapse had come with shocking suddenness, terror spreading through the Roman ranks like wildfire through dry grass. What had been disciplined soldiers conducting a tactical withdrawal transformed in moments into a mob of desperate men fleeing for their lives without regard for comrades or consequences.

Arrows whistled through the air with deadly accuracy as Makatani archers targeted the fleeing Romans and men stumbled and fell with screams that were quickly cut short by obsidian points punching through mail rings to find vital organs.

The poison darts that had tormented them during their first encounter with the swamp proved even more deadly during the rout as warriors emerged from concealment to send their whispered death at close range, leaving victims helpless before pursuing enemies.

'Retreat!' Flavus screamed, his young voice cracking with panic as he abandoned all pretence of military bearing. *'Everyone run!'*

But the command was unnecessary. Every surviving Roman was already fleeing with the desperate speed that only absolute terror could inspire, their heavy equipment abandoned as they sought whatever speed their legs could provide.

Behind them, the Makatani pursued like predators who had scented blood and knew their prey was broken. War cries echoed across the valley as painted warriors closed the distance with terrifying speed, their intimate knowledge of the terrain allowing them to overtake Romans who stumbled over unfamiliar ground.

The killing was methodical and horrifying. Warriors caught fleeing soldiers from behind, war clubs rising and falling with lethal efficiency as they struck down enemies who could no longer defend themselves. But instead of delivering killing blows, many of the attacks were calculated to disable rather than destroy, stunning impacts that dropped men unconscious but left them breathing.

'They're taking prisoners!' someone screamed in horrified realisation. 'Sweet Jupiter, they're taking prisoners!'

The knowledge of what awaited captured Romans added fresh urgency to their flight, with memories of the bone pile they had discovered driving them to find reserves of speed they didn't know they possessed.

Scipio found himself running alongside men he had commanded with absolute authority just minutes before, his scarred face showing the same naked terror that marked every other survivor. His gladius remained in his hand through instinct rather than intention, the weapon forgotten in the animal desperation to reach safety before pursuing death could claim him.

The ancient stairway that had brought them down from Panthera's city now represented their only hope of survival, but the distance that separated them from its base seemed to stretch like an eternity of exposure to enemies who moved faster and knew the ground better.

The sounds of combat gave way to something far worse, the screams of soldiers who had been overwhelmed, their cries of torment echoing across the valley with soul-destroying clarity, as many begged for mercy that would never come. Some called out names of comrades still fleeing, others simply screamed wordlessly as pain beyond description was inflicted by

257

enemies who viewed their suffering as entertainment rather than cruelty.

'*Don't listen!*' Flavus called to the surviving runners, though his own voice showed how the sounds affected him. '*Don't look back! Just run!*'

The base of the cliff face drew closer with agonizing slowness, each step requiring maximum effort whilst pursuit grew ever nearer. Arrows continued to fall amongst the fleeing soldiers, claiming victims who had almost reached safety before toppling forward onto stone that had been carved by hands that predated Rome by millennia.

Finally, gasping and sobbing with exhaustion and terror, the survivors reached the ancient steps and began their desperate ascent toward whatever sanctuary Panthera's city might provide. The narrow path that had seemed treacherous during their descent now offered blessed protection from the arrows that clattered harmlessly against stone walls.

But the climb was brutal for men already exhausted by combat and flight, their legs trembling with fatigue whilst their lungs burned from the effort of sustained , desperate running.

Step by step they climbed, each man driven by the knowledge that stopping meant certain death. Behind them, the sounds of systematic slaughter continued as the Makatani finished their work amongst the fallen, their victory cries echoing off the cliff face as painted warriors celebrated the destruction of enemies who had dared to challenge them in their own territory.

Scipio hauled himself up the steps, his command destroyed, and his professional reputation shattered beyond repair.

Flavus climbed beside him with similar desperation, the young Legatus's carefully maintained composure completely evaporated in the face of catastrophe that exceeded his worst nightmares. The tactical withdrawal that should have preserved his men's lives had become a rout that had consumed them all.

Above them, the massive doors of Panthera's city stood open like the mouth of salvation itself, ancient timber promising safety from the nightmare that had consumed their carefully planned operation. They could see Panthera himself standing in the gateway, his magnificent presence flanked by warriors who held their great cats on golden chains.

'The cats,' someone gasped hopefully. 'Panthera's cats can stop them!'

But even as they spoke, it became apparent that the tactical situation was beyond salvation by any intervention the city's defenders could provide. The Makatani were ascending the cliff face in numbers that would overwhelm even the trained predators, whilst their victory had transformed them into a frenzied mob that would accept any losses necessary to complete their triumph.

Panthera seemed to reach the same conclusion. The panthers and leopards at his warriors' sides were magnificent killers, but they were not numerous enough to stop hundreds of enraged enemies climbing an open slope.

The first Romans reached the gateway and Scipio stumbled through the entrance with his breath coming in ragged gasps, whilst Flavus collapsed against the ancient stones with complete exhaustion.

More survivors staggered through the doors in ones and twos, each arrival marking another man who had somehow outrun death across the valley floor and up the treacherous cliff face. But their numbers were devastatingly reduced and where over a hundred men had begun the morning's engagement, just over a dozen remained to seek sanctuary behind Panthera's

259

walls.

'Close the doors!' one managed to gasp as the last stragglers reached safety. 'They're right behind us!'

Panthera's warriors threw their strength against the ancient wood and the massive timber barriers began to swing shut with the groaning protest of bronze hinges that had supported their weight for millennia. Some of the surviving Romans added what little effort they could muster to help seal the entrance before pursuit could prevent it.

The doors slammed shut with thunderous finality just as the first Makatani warriors reached the gateway, pounding their weapons against the doors in frustrated rage at being denied their complete victory.

Only fourteen men remained alive. Fourteen survivors from an expedition that had numbered in the hundreds when it departed Alexandria, reduced now to this handful of broken soldiers who had witnessed the destruction of everything they had worked to build.

They stood in the torchlit passage like the walking dead, their minds overwhelmed by experiences beyond their capacity to process. Some still clutched weapons they would never need again, whilst others had lost even the most basic equipment during their desperate flight.

The walk back through the ancient corridors felt like a funeral march, and though each step carried them further from the catastrophe that had consumed their comrades, they offered no comfort for the magnitude of their failure. The city's inhabitants watched their passage with frustration, each fully aware that that yesterday's allies had become tomorrow's burden.

When they finally reached their familiar chamber, the sight of food and water waiting for them seemed like a mockery rather than hospitality and men who had fought and run and climbed beyond all reasonable endurance simply collapsed against the carved walls, too exhausted even to care about sustenance that would restore their physical strength.

They sat in stunned silence, unable to comprehend the magnitude of their disaster, whilst somewhere in the hostile swamp beyond the valley walls, six of their comrades continued a mission that might be their only remaining hope of salvaging anything from the wreckage of their overwhelming disaster.

The Occultum were on their own now, as they had always been when the impossible needed to be accomplished, but their survival and that of every man in the chamber now depended entirely on the outcome of their mission.

Chapter Thirty-Eight

The Swamp

Dusk settled over the swamplands as the Occultum maintained their vigilant positions on the floating vegetation mat.

The first sounds reached them whilst the western sky still held some light, but these weren't the subdued murmurs of defeated warriors returning to lick their wounds, they were the triumphant calls of victorious hunters celebrating a successful expedition. The chanting grew louder as the first dugout canoes appeared through the gathering darkness, their hulls low in the water with burning torches flickering at the prows of the vessels.

Within minutes of landing, the warriors began re-feeding the smouldering fires, with pre-dried wood, sending sheets of flame soaring into the gathering darkness. More men joined them over the next hour, their wild celebrations sending them into a religious frenzy, building into patterns that seemed to make the very air vibrate with primitive power.

Dancing began around blazing fires, their flames leaping toward the canopy whilst casting wild shadows that transformed painted warriors into creatures from nightmares. But it was the figure who emerged from the largest dwelling that drew every eye and confirmed their worst fears about the magnitude of their undertaking. The man was enormous, not just tall but massively built. His entire body was a canvas of tattooed serpents, that covered him from forehead to feet in patterns of such intricate complexity that they seemed to form a living skin of reptilian imagery.

'That's him,' said Falco quietly, his voice carrying absolute certainty despite the distance and flickering light.

'That's our target.'

The war chief's presence dominated the celebration, his warriors making way for his passage.

'He's huge,' Marcus observed grimly. 'Getting close enough to take him down is going to be considerably more difficult than we anticipated.'

The Occultum withdrew into the centre of the vegetation where they could talk a little more freely without fear of being seen, forming a tight circle whilst the sounds of primitive celebration echoed across the dark water.

'We can't go in yet,' said Seneca quietly. 'We'd be dead before we reached the first hut. When the celebration ends, when the warriors are exhausted and drunk on whatever they use to fuel these rituals, then we move. Not before.'

The men nodded their agreement. Patience and stealth were their greatest assets and only by using both would they have the slightest chance of successfully carrying out their mission.

Around them, the swamp continued its ancient rhythms, whilst the sounds of tribal celebration grew more intense with each passing hour. But it was when the screaming began that the Occultum's discipline was tested beyond all reasonable limits.

The first cry cut through the night air, a Roman voice suffering agony beyond description.

'*They've got prisoners,*' gasped Marcus.

More screams followed, individual voices joining in a chorus of agony that defied rational understanding as the prisoners were subjected to some sort of cruelty yet unseen to the Occultum's eyes.

Seneca felt his men's discipline wavering as the torture

263

continued, saw hands moving toward weapons whilst bodies tensed for some sort of rescue assault that would accomplish nothing except adding their own deaths to the night's toll. His own instincts screamed for immediate action, every fibre of his being demanding that he lead his men forward to die fighting rather than listen to comrades being systematically destroyed. But he knew the only chance any of the prisoners had of getting out of alive was if he and his men could get in there unseen.

'Hold position,' he said quietly. 'Nobody moves. That's an order.'

'Seneca...' began Marcus, but Seneca cut him short.

'I said hold!' he hissed. 'Do you think I want to listen to this? You think any of us wants to sit here whilst they work on our people? But charging in there accomplishes nothing except getting us all killed!'

The distant screaming continued, individual voices fading only to be replaced by others as the Makatani worked through their captured prizes with methodical efficiency. Some cries spoke of physical torture, whilst others carried the sort of psychological terror that broke minds before bodies gave way.

Falco buried his face in his hands, his massive frame shaking with the effort of not racing to their aid. Around him, his companions struggled with similar internal battles, each man fighting the basic human instinct to act even when action was futile.

'This is what they did to the Twenty-First,' said Decimus quietly. 'This is how two hundred experienced legionaries lost their lives in this stinking swamp.'

The knowledge didn't make the sounds easier to bear, but it provided context that helped explain why conventional military approaches had failed so completely in this environment. The Makatani weren't just enemies to be defeated, they were predators who had refined cruelty into an art form that served both practical and spiritual purposes.

The celebration continued through the deepest hours of the night, but gradually, even the most frenzied celebration began to show signs of exhaustion. The dancing became less coordinated, the chanting more sporadic, whilst the crowds around the central fire began to thin as warriors sought rest or simply collapsed where they stood.

The screaming had stopped some time earlier, leaving only the crackling of flames and the distant chorus of night creatures to fill the oppressive silence. Whether the cessation meant death or unconsciousness for their captured comrades remained unclear, but the absence of sound was almost worse than the agony that had preceded it.

'Now?' Marcus asked quietly as they watched the settlement settle into inactivity.

'Soon,' replied Seneca, his eyes tracking the movement of sentries who patrolled the camp's perimeter. 'Let them get completely settled. We need them asleep, not just tired.'

Another hour passed in agonizing patience whilst the Occultum waited and the fires burned lower, creating pools of shadow that could conceal approaching enemies.

'It's time,' Seneca announced finally. 'We'll get in and out as quickly as we can. But whatever happens, that chieftain dies tonight. Agreed?'

The men nodded their agreement. It was the least they could do in retribution for the horrors the Makatani had inflicted on their fellow Romans.

The Occultum slipped back into the brown water, their eyes constantly scanning for threats that could emerge from any direction. The water that had tormented them during daylight now provided concealment from observation, its dark surface hiding their progress from anyone who might glance out from the camp.

They moved in single file towards the camp. Fallen logs provided cover whilst patches of vegetation broke up their human outlines.

The final approach required infinite patience as they tested each step for stability whilst ensuring their emergence from the water produced no sounds that might alert nearby enemies and one by one, they hauled themselves onto the muddy shore where the Makatani's dugout canoes lay drawn up like sleeping beasts.

From this close, the settlement's sophistication became even more apparent. The structures weren't crude shelters thrown together from available materials, but carefully designed dwellings that had been integrated into the living landscape with remarkable skill. Pathways had been cleared and maintained, while drainage systems channelled excess water and human waste away from the living areas.

They crawled forward slowly, each movement calculated to minimize noise. The mud beneath their bellies was warm and organic, teeming with life forms that viewed human intrusion as either threat or opportunity, until finally, after what felt like hours of careful progress, they reached the settlement's edge and paused to assess what awaited them in the dying firelight ahead.

What they saw would haunt them for whatever remained of their lives.

Chapter Thirty-Nine

The City

The chamber that had once offered sanctuary now felt like a tomb as the fourteen survivors of the morning's catastrophe sat in stunned silence against the ancient stone walls. The torches that provided their only illumination flickered with dying flames, casting dancing shadows that seemed to mock their presence with reminders of how far they had fallen from the confident force that had departed Alexandria months earlier.

Scipio sat apart from the others, his gladius still stained with blood from the desperate fighting that had consumed his command.

Over four hundred legionaries had followed him and Flavus from Syene, trusting their leadership to see them through whatever challenges awaited in the hostile territories beyond Roman authority. Now, including him and Flavus, just fourteen remained, their presence in this chamber serving as testament to the complete failure of everything they had worked to accomplish.

The reality of their situation was unavoidable. They had suffered a catastrophic defeat and although there was another mission being carried out by the Occultum deep in the heart of the swamp, it was too late. If a hundred legionaries conducting a simple diversionary defence had been destroyed so completely by an army of primitives, what chance could six men possibly have against the same opponents in their own stronghold?

'They're dead,' he said quietly, his voice carrying across the chamber with the finality of a funeral pronouncement. 'All of them. The Occultum, Seneca, every man who went on that insane mission.'

Several of the surviving soldiers looked up from their own contemplation of disaster.

'You don't know that,' one of them said weakly. 'They're good soldiers. Better than good. Maybe they found a way…'

'To do what?' Scipio interrupted, his tone cutting through the false optimism with surgical precision. 'To accomplish what a full century could not? To defeat an entire settlement with six men when we couldn't hold our ground with over ten times their numbers?'

The silence that followed his words was profound and terrible, each man forced to confront the reality that their situation had moved beyond merely desperate into realms of impossibility that offered no hope of conventional salvation.

'So what happens now?' asked one of the men, his young voice showing the strain of the defeat. 'Do we wait here for Panthera to decide our fate? Beg for his mercy and hope he's willing to escort us back to the frontier?'

Flavus's sudden laugh from across the chamber held no humour, only the bitter recognition of the realities that would determine their future.

'Look around you,' he said, gesturing toward the chamber that had become their prison. 'Scipio promised to eliminate his enemies and solve his tactical problems. Instead, we've demonstrated that Roman soldiers can be defeated by painted savages, and that our vaunted military superiority means nothing in terrain where our enemies hold every advantage. Panthera expected results that would justify his trust in us. What he got instead was proof that Romans are as vulnerable as anyone else when they're stupid enough to fight on terms dictated by their enemies.'

'So he'll want us gone,' said one of the men, following the logic to its inevitable conclusion.

'He'll want us dead,' Flavus corrected flatly. 'Better that we simply disappear into the wilderness, leaving behind just bones and legends about the fate that awaits those who challenge his authority, than take word of his existence back to Rome.'

The brutal assessment sent uncomfortable stirrings through the listening soldiers, each man understanding that their survival now depended on factors beyond their control or influence. They had become liabilities rather than assets, burdens that their host would be better off eliminating than preserving.

After a few minutes, Scipio got to his feet and looked around the chamber.

'There is another way,' he announced suddenly, the simple statement sending a flickering of hope into the hearts of every man present. 'We take our fates back into our own hands.'

'And how do we do that?' sneered Flavus from the far wall. 'It's your stupidity that got us into this situation in the first place, Scipio, so spit it out. Tell us of this new masterplan that can be accomplished with just fourteen men.'

Scipio studied the young legatus with calculating eyes, his mind working through possibilities that had been developing since the magnitude of their disaster became clear. When he spoke again, his words carried the weight of command decisions that couldn't be reversed once implemented.

'We do what we should have done the first day we got here,' he said simply. 'We take the gold that justified this entire expedition in the first place, the treasure that will make our survival worthwhile to Rome.'

'What gold?' Flavus replied with obvious frustration. 'That small chest in the audience chamber? Even if we can get to it, and then escape and manage to make our way back to Rome, which is extremely unlikely, how will that justify the deaths of so many men to Claudius?

'Because we were sent here originally on the evidence of a single necklace,' said Scipio. 'So if we can prove there is more, we will be welcomed back as heroes not failures. Besides, I don't believe for a single moment that we saw Panthera's entire wealth in that chamber, this city is too big and was certainly once hugely powerful which means there has to be more.'

'Corvus has told us there isn't any significant treasure here. Yes, we've seen some ornaments, some decorative pieces, but nothing approaching the wealth that would justify mounting a full invasion.'

'Corvus has been here for three years,' Scipio observed, his tone growing more confident as he developed his argument. 'Three years during which he's become dependent on Panthera's hospitality for his very survival. Do you really think he'd tell us about wealth that might tempt us to actions that could endanger his comfortable arrangements?'

The logic was persuasive, offering hope to men who had been contemplating only their own mortality only minutes earlier. Several began nodding agreement, their faces showing the beginnings of desperate hope.

'Even if there is treasure,' Flavus continued, 'how exactly do you propose we acquire it? We're outnumbered by hundreds, locked in a chamber deep within their stronghold, with hardly any weapons and no support?'

Scipio moved slowly to the centre of the chamber.

'Legatus,' he said slowly, 'could you approach, I need to speak with you quietly.'

Flavus looked around the chamber with obvious uncertainty, noting how the surviving soldiers were watching the exchange with growing interest. Something in Scipio's tone suggested this wasn't merely another tactical discussion, but a conversation that would determine the future of their entire group.

'Here?' he asked, gesturing around the room.

'Here,' Scipio confirmed with finality.

The young legatus rose from his position against the wall and walked across the chamber to stand before his camp prefect, his bearing some remnants of the dignity of command.

'What is it, Scipio?' he asked quietly. 'What couldn't wait for a more appropriate moment?'

The answer came without warning or hesitation as Scipio's pugio suddenly punched upward between Flavus's ribs.

The young Legatus's eyes widened in shock and disbelief as steel found his heart, his mouth opening in a gasp that emerged as blood rather than words. His hands moved toward the wound with automatic reflex, but his strength was already fading as his life's blood fountained from the precisely placed cut.

The surviving soldiers scrambled to their feet with obvious alarm, their hands moving toward weapons whilst their minds struggled to process what they had just witnessed. But before any of them could react effectively, Flavus collapsed to the stone floor in a spreading pool of crimson, his young life ended by the man he had trusted absolutely.

Scipio spun around to face his men with the bloody pugio still in his hand, his scarred features showing no emotion.

'*From now on, I command this unit,*' he hissed, 'and anyone who has problems with that arrangement can join our former legatus on the floor.'

The chamber fell into horrified silence as the twelve exhausted soldiers contemplated the corpse of their commanding officer and the man who had just murdered him without apparent provocation or regret. Each understood that their situation had just transformed from merely desperate into something far more dangerous.

'Scipio…' began one, his voice carrying obvious shock at what he had witnessed.

'Centurio Scipio,' the older man corrected sharply, his arm lifting to point his pugio at the man who had spoken. 'And consider carefully what you have to say next lest it costs you your life. We're getting out of this death trap, and we're taking enough wealth with us to justify our survival to anyone who might question our methods.'

'You've just murdered a Roman officer,' another soldier said, his young voice cracking with the magnitude of what they had witnessed. 'That's treason, mutiny, a capital crime that…'

'That will be irrelevant if we're all dead,' Scipio shouted. 'And we *will* all be dead unless we take action that goes beyond conventional military thinking.'

He gestured toward the chamber around them.

'Look around you. We're prisoners in everything but name, completely at the mercy of these people. We have no value to Panthera anymore and it is only a matter of time before he does what those natives out there could not. Kill us all.'

He bent over to clean his pugio on Flavus's toga before returning it to its sheath, the casual nature of the action emphasising his complete lack of regret about what he had just done.

'We owe Panthera nothing,' he continued, his tone growing more confident as he developed his justification. 'But we owe ourselves everything. Survival, wealth, and whatever future we can carve out of this disaster with action rather than talk.'

'What are you suggesting?' asked one of the men.

'I'm saying, we don't wait for them to come to kill us, we take the initiative and take the fight to them.'

'Just us?' asked another, looking around the survivors.

'Just us,' said Scipio, 'and the element of surprise.'

The room fell into contemplative silence as each man processed the magnitude of what their new commander was proposing, but as they looked around the chamber that had become their prison, and contemplated the alternatives, the choice began to seem less impossible than inevitable. Conventional thinking had brought them to this situation, perhaps unconventional thinking was required to escape it.

Chapter Forty

The Makatani Camp

The scene that greeted the Occultum in the dying firelight challenged every assumption about the boundaries of human cruelty. What hung from the thick branch wasn't recognisable as having once been a Roman soldier, it was the systematically prepared remains of something that had been transformed from man into meat through methods that defied civilised understanding.

The body dangled head-down from vine ropes, naked flesh blackened and blistered where flames had done their methodical work. What remained of the arms hung toward the smouldering coals like charred sticks, whilst exposed ribs gleamed white where meat had been carefully carved away for whatever feast had followed the torture. The face was gone entirely, burned away to reveal the skull beneath whilst empty sockets stared blindly at the mud below.

Around the central fire lay further evidence of the macabre feast, bones picked clean, and the remains of charred flesh scattered on the floor. But as the full horror of the scene settled over them, a heart wrenching sound cut through the night air, a low, keening cry of human suffering beyond endurance. The voice was weak but unmistakably alive, coming from somewhere deeper in the settlement where shadows concealed whatever horrors were still unfolding.

'*Sweet Jupiter,*' gasped Marcus, his voice carrying desperate hope mixed with terrible understanding. 'Someone's still alive.'

The knowledge transformed their tactical situation completely. This was no longer just a mission to eliminate an enemy leaders it was now a rescue operation where Roman soldiers were suffering unimaginable torment.

Seneca felt the weight of command settle on his shoulders like a lead cloak. The mission that had brought them across half of Africa demanded they eliminate the war chief whose death might break Makatani power permanently, but the cries echoing through the darkness spoke of men who would die in agony if immediate action wasn't taken.

'We can't save them all,' he said quietly, 'but we can try to save some whilst still completing our mission.'

He studied the settlement through narrowed eyes, noting how the structures were distributed across the elevated ground whilst trying to identify where prisoners might be held and where their primary target would be sleeping.

'The big chief will probably be in the largest dwelling,' he continued, his tactical mind working through approaches, 'we'll look for him there.'

Another cry echoed from the darkness, weaker than before but carrying the unmistakable accent of a Roman soldier pushed beyond all reasonable limits of endurance.

'Time's running out,' said Marcus. 'We need to move… *now!*'

'We split up,' Seneca decided finally. 'Sica and Talorcan, the chief is your responsibility. Use whatever methods necessary, but make sure he dies tonight.'

The two men nodded acknowledgment.

'The rest of us will locate and extract whatever prisoners we can,' continued Seneca. 'We'll rendezvous at the boats as soon as we can but no later than first light, regardless of mission status.'

'And if we're compromised?' asked Decimus.

'Then we sell our lives dearly,' replied Seneca. 'Make it

cost them everything we can before they bring us down, but whatever happens, nobody gets taken alive. I won't have any of us ending up like these poor bastards.'

Another scream echoed through the settlement interrupting the briefing.

'Enough talking,' said Seneca, unsheathing his blade, 'let's move.'

Chapter Forty-One

The Chamber

The transformation in the chamber was remarkable. Where moments before there had been a group of broken soldiers contemplating their own mortality, there now stood a unit of determined men. Scipio's brutal demonstration of leadership had shocked them from despair into action.

'Remember,' said Scipio quietly as his men gathered around him, 'we move fast, we move silent, and we kill anyone who gets in our way. No prisoners, no mercy, no hesitation.'

The remaining soldiers nodded their understanding, their minds processing the magnitude of what they were about to attempt. They were planning to steal from their hosts, murder anyone who discovered them, and escape into hostile territory with wealth that belonged to people who had only recently saved their lives.

'The route is simple,' Scipio continued. 'We head straight to the audience chamber where that treasure chest sits waiting. We take it and anything else of value we can carry, then find our way out of this death trap.'

'And if we're discovered?' asked one of the men.

'Then we fight our way out,' replied Scipio flatly. 'Those people defeated us in the swamp because they knew the terrain and we were operating according to conventional military doctrine. In here, on solid ground with steel in our hands, we're still Romans.'

The logic was brutal but compelling. They had been broken in the wetlands by enemies who held every tactical advantage, but within the confines of Panthera's city, their superior weapons and training might prove decisive against opponents who wouldn't be expecting sudden violence.

Scipio moved to the great doors and pressed his ear against the ancient timber, listening for sounds that might indicate guards or other activity beyond their chamber.

'Ready?' he asked, looking back at his men who had formed up behind him with weapons drawn.

When they nodded confirmation, he took a deep breath and began hammering on the doors with the hilt of his gladius, his voice raised in apparent desperation.

'*Help!*' he called, his words echoing through the corridors beyond. 'We need help! Someone's dying in here!'

The sound reverberated through the ancient stonework, but no immediate response came from beyond the chamber. Scipio waited several moments before repeating his performance, this time with even greater urgency.

'*Help!*' he shouted again, adding a note of panic to his voice. 'The legatus is wounded! He needs immediate attention!'

Still nothing. The silence stretched uncomfortably whilst Scipio's men waited with weapons ready, until finally, the sound came they had been waiting for, footsteps approaching through the corridors beyond. Within moments, he metallic scrape of the great bar being drawn back echoed through their chamber and they looked amongst each other, knowing that there was no turning back.

The doors swung open to reveal two warriors, their eyes focused on the apparent emergency.

Scipio pointed toward Flavus's corpse with apparent distress, his performance convincing enough to draw both men several steps into the chamber.

'He collapsed,' said Scipio urgently. 'Started convulsing, then just fell. He's not breathing properly.'

The warriors approached the body with obvious

concern, their attention focused entirely on the apparent medical crisis rather than the Romans who were positioning themselves for coordinated action. When they knelt beside Flavus to assess his condition, they exposed themselves completely to the trap that had been prepared and two of Scipio's men drove their pugios into the warriors' backs simultaneously.

Both men collapsed beside Flavus's corpse, their blood mingling with that of the young legatus in spreading pools that stained the ancient stones.

'Finish them,' Scipio commanded, his gladius already in his hand as he approached the wounded warriors.

The executions were swift and brutal. Steel found throats and hearts and within moments, their corpses joined Flavus on chamber floor.

'Follow me,' Scipio ordered, moving quickly toward the open doorway. 'Stay close, stay quiet, and kill anything that moves.'

They left their chamber, moving through corridors that had seemed merely ancient during their previous passage but now felt actively hostile. The torches that provided illumination cast dancing shadows that could conceal threats, whilst the maze of passages offered countless opportunities for ambush or discovery.

But their route was direct and their purpose clear. Scipio remembered his previous journey and led them through the winding corridors, his memory sharpened by desperation, following the path that would take them back to the audience chamber where wealth beyond calculation waited on casual display.

Within moments they encountered one of Panthera's guards coming from a side corridor and Scipio cut him down within seconds, the body crashing to the floor before he could raise the alarm.

'*Drag him aside,*' hissed Scipio, 'get him out of the main passage.'

Once the body had been hidden, they continued deeper into the complex, their confidence growing with each corridor they navigated without detection. The city seemed to sleep around them, its inhabitants unaware that death stalked their sacred halls bearing Roman steel.

Another man emerged from what appeared to be sleeping quarters wearing only a loincloth, his weapons nowhere in sight as he tried to determine what had awakened him, but one of the legionaries killed him with a thrust to the heart that dropped him instantly. The execution was silent and professional, adding another victim to their trail of systematic murder.

'How much further?' someone whispered as they paused at another intersection.

'Not far,' replied Scipio, 'The audience chamber is just ahead.'

The final approach proved easier than they had dared hope. The massive space where they had first encountered Panthera lay empty and unguarded, its carved walls rising into shadows whilst the throne waited in solitary splendour at the chamber's heart.

But it was what stood before the throne that drew every eye, the ornate chest Scipio had observed during their audience, still positioned in casual display of wealth that exceeded anything they had imagined possible. Gold and precious stones gleamed in the torchlight, a king's ransom left apparently unguarded in the confidence that no one would dare steal from Panthera's personal collection.

'There it is,' said Scipio. 'Everything we need to buy our way back into imperial favour.' He nodded to two men who made their way over and closed the lid before picking it up with obvious effort. The weight was substantial but manageable, a fortune that could transform their circumstances completely.

'Time to go,' said Scipio, turning back toward the entrance. 'We've got what we came for.'

As they began their withdrawal from the chamber, each man understood that they had just committed a heinous act. They had murdered their hosts, stolen sacred treasure, and violated every principle of military honour that had been drilled into them since recruitment. But they were alive, they were armed, and they were carrying wealth that might enable them to disappear into whatever future they could create beyond the reach of imperial justice. It wasn't honourable, but it offered possibilities that staying to face Panthera's judgment would never provide.

Chapter Forty-Two

The Makatani Camp

The approach to the largest dwelling tested every skill Sica and Talorcan had developed through years of operating behind enemy lines. The structure dominated the settlement's central area, its elevated position providing natural observation whilst its size spoke of the importance of whoever slept within its woven walls.

They moved with painful slowness across the muddy ground, sometimes crouching behind scattered equipment, other times crawling on their bellies whilst the dying fires cast unpredictable shadows that could either conceal or betray their presence. Each step was calculated to avoid the debris that littered the area, including weapons carelessly dropped by warriors too intoxicated to maintain proper discipline.

The settlement showed limited signs of life despite the early hour, but it was sluggish movement from people struggling with the aftereffects of whatever substances had fuelled their celebration. Warriors stirred occasionally beside dying fires, whilst others emerged from dwellings to relieve themselves before returning to their rest. But their movements were slow and unfocused, suggesting they remained under the influence of drink or drugs that had sustained their ritual frenzy.

The final approach to their target required crossing twenty paces of open ground where discovery would mean immediate death. But the dying fires provided pools of shadow between areas of illumination. Dropping to the ground, both men crawled inch by painful inch across the ground, made muddy be so many dancing feet in the night. It was excruciatingly slow, but eventually they reached the structure's base without detection, pressing themselves against woven walls that had been designed more for comfort than defence, and through gaps in the latticework, they could observe the interior where oil lamps provided dim illumination that revealed their objective in all his tattooed magnificence.

The war chief lay sprawled across a sleeping mat, his massive bulk rising and falling with the deep breathing of someone lost in drugged slumber.

'*Alone,*' whispered Sica, noting the absence of guards or companions who might complicate their approach. '*They're confident the camp is secure.*'

The entrance to the dwelling was a simple flap of treated hide that could be lifted without sound, and they slipped inside like shadows, their movements so careful that even a light sleeper would have struggled to detect their presence.

The war chief continued his deep slumber, unaware that death had entered his sanctuary. His weapons lay within easy reach beside the sleeping mat, but unconsciousness rendered them useless whilst his killers positioned themselves for coordinated action.

Talorcan drew his hunting knife with infinite care, the steel emerging from its scabbard without the slightest whisper of metal against leather. His movements were automatic, based on countless similar operations where surprise had been everything, and discovery meant failure. But as he prepared to deliver the killing stroke, Sica's hand closed over his wrist with gentle but insistent pressure.

'*Wait,*' the Syrian whispered coldly, his voice barely audible whilst his eyes remained fixed on the sleeping chieftain's face. '*I want him awake for this.*'

Talorcan hesitated for a moment, recognising

something in his comrade's tone that was personal rather than tactical, but he also wanted the chief to experience more than just death, he wanted him to suffer. With a nod, he adjusted position, his hands moving to where they could silence any cries that might alert the settlement.

Once done, Sica moved his arm across the war chief's throat whilst lowering his weight onto the massive torso. The war chief's eyes opened with alarm but as he tried to cry out, Talorcan's iron grip closed over his mouth whilst Sica's forearm pressed against his windpipe.

'I want you to know exactly what's happening,' hissed Sica coldly. *'This is the price you pay for all the blood on your hands.'*

The curved dagger appeared in his free hand with a fluid grace, its blade catching the lamplight whilst the war chief's eyes widened with growing terror. The weapon moved with deliberate slowness, its point finding the soft flesh beneath the ribs whilst Sica's face remained inches from his victim's painted features.

'This is for our comrades,' he continued, his voice never rising above a whisper whilst steel began its methodical work. *'And for all the others you butchered like animals.'*

The blade pushed forward with agonising slowness, parting flesh and muscle whilst carefully avoiding vital organs that would end the torment too quickly. The war chief's body convulsed with pain, his muffled cries absorbed by Talorcan's grip.

'Feel it?' Sica whispered, his face so close to his victim's that they shared the same breath.

The torture continued with methodical precision, steel working deeper whilst avoiding anything that would cause immediate death. The war chief's struggles grew weaker as pain overwhelmed his nervous system, but consciousness was maintained through careful application of techniques that Sica had learned over many years as an assassin.

Finally, when the victim's eyes showed the glazed acceptance of someone who had abandoned hope of survival, Sica's voice carried a different quality.

'This is for the man on the fire,' he said with absolute finality, and taking a deep breath, eased his blade directly but slowly into the war chief's heart.

The massive body convulsed once more before settling into the stillness that marked the transition from life to death and the painted eyes that had witnessed countless atrocities stared sightlessly at the dwelling's woven ceiling, whilst blood pooled beneath his corpse in spreading darkness.

For long moments, both men stared at their handiwork, the weight of personal vengeance settling over them with complex emotions. This hadn't been the clean, professional killing that marked most of their operations, it had been something darker, more personal, driven by images of what their comrades had endured.

'Take his head,' said Sica finally, 'let's get out of here.'

Chapter Forty-Three

The Makatani Camp

On the other side of the camp, the sounds of suffering men had drawn the rest of the Occultum through the settlement like a malevolent beacon, leading them between the dwellings toward whatever horrors had generated the cries that echoed through the night. Seneca led his reduced team with weapons ready, expecting to encounter guards protecting valuable prisoners, but what they found defied every tactical assumption they had formed.

The holding area lay completely undefended, a simple clearing where their captured comrades lay untethered in the filth. No sentries patrolled the perimeter, and no guards stood anywhere near. But the reason soon became apparent and as Seneca and his men drew closer, they could see each man's legs had been systematically destroyed with methodical precision, their kneecaps shattered by club blows.

The brutality was overwhelming. Eight men lay scattered across the muddy ground, each one semi-conscious and painfully aware of their circumstances despite injuries that had transformed them from soldiers into helpless victims. Their faces showed the sort of pain that went beyond physical trauma into realms where hope itself became a burden too heavy to bear.

One of them looked up as the Occultum approached, his eyes focusing with obvious difficulty on figures that might represent salvation or merely additional torment. When recognition dawned, his cracked lips curved into the sort of ironic smile that marked men who had moved beyond despair into darker territories.

'You're too late,' he whispered, his voice barely audible despite the silence that surrounded them. The words carried neither accusation nor surprise, just the flat acceptance of someone who had witnessed systematic destruction of everything he had once believed about human nature.

'We'll do something,' replied Seneca quietly, his voice carrying desperate conviction despite the evidence of his own eyes. 'We'll find a way to get you out of here.'

But even as he spoke, his tactical mind was processing the impossibility of what he was suggesting. Eight men with destroyed legs, each requiring carriers to move even short distances, whilst pursuit by hundreds of enemies became inevitable the moment their presence was discovered.

The other prisoners began stirring as the voices penetrated their pain-induced stupor, heads turning with obvious agony toward figures that represented the first hope they had experienced since capture.

'There's nothing you can do,' hissed the man, stating the obvious with devastating clarity. 'We can't walk, you can't carry us, and those animals will be awake soon enough. But there is something you can do. End our suffering. Give us clean deaths instead of what they have planned. We've seen what they do to their prisoners, and we don't want to go that way.'

'No,' said Seneca immediately. 'We don't abandon comrades. We'll find another way.'

'What other way?' snapped the man. 'Look at us. Really look. We're finished, but you can save us from ending up like the poor bastards hanging over their fires.'

Decimus moved closer to Seneca, his pragmatism cutting through any emotional response to focus on tactical necessities that couldn't be ignored indefinitely.

'He's right,' he said quietly. 'We can't save them, but we

can give them honourable deaths.'

The silence that followed was profound and terrible, broken only by the quiet breathing of men whose pain had moved beyond vocal expression. Each member of the Occultum understood what was being asked of them, and each struggled with the moral implications of killing their own comrades in the name of mercy.

'I won't order it,' said Seneca finally, 'I can't.'

'You don't have to,' replied Falco, stepping forward, 'I'll do it. Quick, clean and with honour, the way we used to do it in the arenas.'

The first prisoner nodded with genuine gratitude, his features showing relief rather than fear at the prospect of ending his torment through Roman steel rather than primitive cruelty.

'Thank you,' he whispered, his words carrying the weight of absolute sincerity. 'That is how soldiers should die.'

What followed tested every principle the Occultum had developed about the obligations of military brotherhood. Each prisoner was approached individually, the situation explained with gentle honesty whilst they were given the opportunity to make whatever peace their circumstances allowed.

Some wept quietly as they contemplated endings that had come sooner than expected, whilst others maintained a stoic dignity despite facing inevitable death. But all of them showed understanding of why this mercy was necessary, and a gratitude that it would be delivered by comrades rather than enemies.

Decimus and Marcus positioned the first man with careful gentleness, supporting his weight whilst avoiding pressure on injuries that sent waves of agony through his destroyed legs. He winced with obvious pain but maintained consciousness through sheer determination.

Seneca knelt before him, taking the man's hands in his own whilst speaking quietly about family, honour, and whatever afterlife awaited soldiers who had served Rome faithfully. His words carried the sort of formal dignity that marked funeral orations, transforming execution into a ceremony that preserved human dignity even in circumstances that challenged every assumption about civilised behaviour.

'Are you ready?' asked Falco gently, his massive frame positioned behind the victim whilst the point of his gladius rested lightly between the man's shoulder blades.

The man nodded once, his eyes closing whilst his lips moved in silent prayers to whatever gods might be listening.

Falco took a deep breath and a few heartbeats later, thrust the blade downward with professional precision, the point finding the gap between vertebrae quickly and cleanly. The gladius plunged downward through the flesh and Cartlidge, severing the spinal cord, to bring immediate unconsciousness followed by almost an instant death.

The process was repeated with methodical efficiency, each prisoner receiving the same careful attention whilst their comrades ensured that death came as mercy rather than punishment. Some spoke final words about families they would never see again, whilst others simply nodded acknowledgment that their time had come.

But it was the youngest prisoner who tested their resolve most severely. Barely old enough to grow a proper beard, he had been recruited from some provincial town where military service represented adventure rather than the brutal realities they had all discovered in the African wilderness.

'*Please,*' he whispered, his voice breaking with fear as he watched his comrades receive their merciful deaths. '*Don't kill* me. I'll get better, I'll be able to walk again. I have a family back in Rome that needs me.'*

Seneca felt his own resolve wavering as he looked into eyes that still held hope despite everything they had witnessed. This wasn't a veteran who understood the cruel necessities that governed their situation, this was a boy whose mind refused to accept the finality of his circumstances.

'It's going to be all right,' said Seneca gently, moving close. 'We're not going to leave you behind. We'll find a way to get you out of here.'

The young soldier's face brightened with desperate relief, his arms reaching out to embrace the commander who had just promised salvation from the nightmare that had consumed his world. But as he pressed against Seneca's chest with grateful tears, the older man's eyes met Falco's with the sort of communication that required no words.

Seconds later, the gladius found its mark with the same professional precision that had ended the other prisoners' suffering, bringing merciful unconsciousness to someone whose youth had made acceptance impossible. The boy died believing he had been saved rather than executed, his final moments unmarked by the terror that would have made his death infinitely more cruel.

When the grisly work was completed, eight Roman soldiers lay still and peaceful in the mud of a hostile settlement, their suffering ended by comrades who had respected them enough to provide honourable deaths rather than abandoning them to systematic torture.

The Occultum stood in silence for long moments, each man processing the magnitude of what they had just accomplished whilst struggling with emotions that had no names in military vocabulary. They had committed what any Roman judgement would consider murder, but they had also provided mercy that circumstances had made necessary.

'Time to go,' said Seneca finally, and they moved toward the boats that represented their only hope of escape from the hostile settlement. The night was far from over, and dawn approached with the inexorable certainty of judgment itself.

Chapter Forty-Four

The Swamp

The dugout canoe moved through the dark water with a steady rhythm, six paddles cutting the surface in silence whilst the Occultum fled from the scene of their merciful butchery.

Seneca stared ahead toward their destination, his paddle working automatically whilst his mind replayed images of young faces accepting death as preferable to whatever torment awaited them in Makatani hands. The actions had been unavoidable, but that fact provided little comfort when measured against the weight of Roman blood on their hands. The irony was devastating, they had succeeded in their rescue mission, but not before killing everyone they had tried to save.

The sound reached them when they were perhaps halfway across the treacherous waters, a rhythmic pounding that carried across the swamp with unmistakable urgency. Drums, beaten in patterns of coordination rather than celebration, echoing from the settlement they had just left with their struggling consciences and the head of the murdered chieftain.

'They've found the bodies,' said Seneca, his voice breaking the oppressive silence. 'Increase the speed.'

The canoe surged forward under their desperate efforts, brown water streaming from the paddles as behind them, the sounds of alarm continued building and torches appeared in the distance like angry fireflies seeking their trail.

When they finally reached solid ground, the evidence of the previous day's catastrophe lay scattered before them in devastating clarity. Roman bodies dotted the landscape, their equipment scattered across ground that had been churned into bloody mud by the systematic slaughter that had followed Scipio's rout.

'Mother of gods,' gasped Decimus, studying the carnage that stretched between their position and the distant ruins. 'They butchered everyone.'

They moved through the devastation with grim efficiency, their boots splashing through mud that had been mixed with Roman blood whilst their eyes scanned constantly for threats that might emerge from the scattered debris. Each body they passed had been someone they knew, men who had shared their rations and fought beside them through impossible hardships during the long journey that had brought them all to this hostile valley.

The trail of destruction continued all the way to the base of the ancient stairway, where the final stand had apparently taken place amongst stones that had witnessed countless previous tragedies. Here the bodies lay thickest, evidence of Romans who had turned to fight rather than continue running when pursuit had finally overtaken them.

But it was the sight that greeted them at the top of the stairs that transformed concern into something approaching terror. The massive doors of Panthera's city stood wide open, revealing the entrance like the mouth of some mythical monster, their ancient timber revealing the darkness beyond whilst no guards were visible at their posts.

More bodies lay scattered across the stepped approach, not Roman corpses but the painted warriors of Panthera's people. The evidence of desperate fighting was everywhere, blood staining ancient stones whilst weapons lay abandoned where they had fallen from dying hands.

Sica stared at the carnage around them, realising the head of the chieftain was probably now surplus to requirements, and as he threw it to one side to roll back down the ancient steps behind him, his comrades drew their weapons.

Behind them, the drums from across the swamp continued their urgent rhythm, growing louder as pursuit was organised amongst enemies who had discovered the full magnitude of the death filled night. But ahead, the city that should have offered sanctuary, might now prove even more dangerous than the enemies pursuing them, as the massive doors beckoned like an invitation to hell itself, promising answers to questions they weren't certain they wanted answered.

'Whatever's in there,' said Decimus staring through the doors, 'it's not going to be pleasant.'

'No,' Seneca agreed, moving toward the open entrance with his weapon ready. 'But we need to know what happened to our people. And we need to find out if there's another way out of this death trap.'

Chapter Forty-Five

The City

The corridors that had once echoed with the dignified footsteps of an ancient civilisation now reeked of blood and betrayal. Bodies lay scattered throughout the passages like leaves after a storm, their positions telling a story of systematic slaughter that had caught the inhabitants completely unprepared for violence within their own sanctuary.

Sica knelt beside one of the fallen warriors, studying wounds that painted a disturbing picture of the night's events. The man's throat had been opened with surgical precision, whilst his ornate weapons remained undisturbed in their sheaths, evidence of someone killed by trusted allies rather than enemies in open combat.

'Roman blade work,' he announced grimly. 'These people were murdered by someone they had no reason to fear.'

'But not all of them,' said Decimus, pointing toward evidence of different weapon types scattered throughout the carnage. 'Look at these, club wounds, arrow strikes, spears.

The trail of destruction led them deeper into the complex, each corridor revealing fresh horrors that challenged their understanding of what had occurred during the hours they had spent in the hostile swamplands. The methodical nature of some killings contrasted sharply with the frenzied violence that marked others, suggesting multiple phases of slaughter conducted by different groups with different objectives.

When they finally reached the chamber where they had spent so much time, Marcus immediately walked over to Flavus's corpse, kneeling down to examine the cause of death. The wound that had killed him was unmistakably Roman, a pugio thrust delivered with professional precision between the ribs to find the heart with surgical accuracy.

'Sweet Jupiter,' he said. 'One of our own men must have murdered him in cold blood.'

The implications were staggering. Roman soldiers turning on their officers was a complete breakdown of every principle that had sustained Roman military organisation through centuries of conquest and expansion.

'Leave him,' said Seneca eventually, 'we need to keep going.'

They continued into the complex, and the further they went, the more obvious it became that a catastrophe of huge proportions had occurred. Women and children lay amongst the fallen warriors, their bodies showing a vast array of brutal injuries carried out in a frenzied attack.

'This doesn't make sense,' said Marcus, studying a family group that had been killed whilst apparently trying to flee toward the city's interior. 'Even if Scipio and his men went rogue, a few Romans couldn't have done all this.'

The discovery that proved his assessment came when they rounded a corner to find the corpse of one of Panthera's magnificent panthers, the great cat's jet-black hide bristling with arrows. The animal's claws were extended and bloody, evidence that it had died fighting whilst defending its home against invaders.

'Makatani arrows,' said Decimus, recognising the distinctive shafts. 'This wasn't just Roman treachery, it looks like they got inside somehow.'

The whisper that froze them in their tracks came from somewhere above their heads, a human voice raised in desperate communication that suggested some survivors might still exist. Each member of the Occultum immediately adopted defensive positions whilst their eyes scanned the shadows for threats that might accompany whoever was trying to contact them.

'Up here,' the voice called again, and they spotted a figure moving carefully along a high ledge that overlooked their position. 'I'm coming down.'

Corvus descended with obvious difficulty, his damaged leg making the climb treacherous. When he reached ground level, his condition was revealed to be even worse than their initial impression, with fresh wounds marking his arms and torso, whilst his clothing was stained with blood that might or might not be his own.

'*Seneca,*' he gasped, 'thank the gods you made it back alive.'

'What happened here?' Seneca demanded immediately, 'where is everyone?'

Corvus struggled to organise his thoughts whilst his eyes constantly darted toward the shadows as if expecting enemies to emerge at any moment. When he spoke, his words tumbled over each other with the frantic urgency.

'It was Scipio,' he began, his voice cracking with strain. 'After you left for the swamp, he and his men carried out the diversion, but they were overrun by the Makatani. Only a few of his men survived to make it back but when they arrived, Scipio killed Flavus in front of all his men, then announced they were taking the treasure chest and leaving. They murdered the guards, stole the chest, and fought their way past anyone who tried to stop them. But that wasn't the worst of it.' Corvus paused, gathering strength for the most damaging part of his account. 'When they left, they sabotaged the doors, destroying the mechanisms that would have allowed them to be closed quickly. We were completely exposed, defenceless against whatever might come from outside.'

'The Makatani,' said Falco with dawning understanding. 'They must have had scouts watching the city, waiting for exactly such an opportunity.'

'A war party was already moving through the valley when Scipio's treachery gave them their opening,' Corvus confirmed. 'Before we could organise a proper defence, they were inside the walls, killing everyone they could reach. The leopards were released to stop them, but there were too many and not enough time.'

The tactical picture was devastatingly clear. Scipio's betrayal had created the vulnerability that the Makatani had exploited with devastating efficiency, transforming the ancient sanctuary into a slaughterhouse where civilised people had been butchered by primitive enemies.

'Is anyone still alive?' asked Seneca.

'Yes,' replied Corvus. 'Many managed to escape by other tunnels but Panthera and perhaps fifty of his people are trapped in the audience chamber, surrounded by Makatani warriors.'

Seneca considered the situation carefully. The implications were clear enough. The enemy forces that had exploited Scipio's treachery were now in complete control of the city, holding a few dozen survivors for whatever systematic torture they considered appropriate for such a significant victory. He looked around at his men, seeing his own thoughts reflected in faces marked by months of impossible hardships. They had completed their mission by eliminating the war chief whose death might have broken Makatani power, but Scipio's betrayal had negated any tactical advantage their success might have provided. Now they faced a choice that would define them for whatever remained of their lives. Abandon the survivors to whatever fate awaited them and attempt their own escape through hostile territory, or risk everything in a final attempt to rescue people who had shown them hospitality despite every reason for suspicion.

'Lead the way, Corvus,' he said finally. 'Our work here is not over.'

Chapter Forty-Six

The Audience Chamber

Seneca led his men quickly through the corridors with weapons drawn, their movements silent despite the knowledge that stealth would soon become irrelevant to their survival.

They reached the door into the audience chamber and his men took cover in the shadows while Seneca peered through the gap. Inside, Panthera sat upon his carved throne, his magnificent presence undimmed despite the impossible circumstances that had reduced his ancient realm to this final tableau.

Around him, arranged like a human shield, stood the remnants of his people, women whose elegant robes were torn and bloodstained, children whose faces showed the blank terror of innocents confronting adult violence, and elderly men whose dignity remained intact despite the systematic destruction of everything they had worked to preserve. Perhaps fifty souls in total, all that remained in a city that had endured for millennia.

The floor of the chamber was littered with corpses that told the story of desperate resistance overcome by overwhelming numbers. Panthera's warriors lay where they had fallen, their ornate weapons soaked in blood pooled on ancient stones that had never witnessed such systematic slaughter.

Around them, the remaining Makatani forces numbered at least forty warriors, their weapons held with casual confidence, spears and clubs that had proven their effectiveness against more civilized opponents.

Seneca studied the situation. They were just six men against forty enemies in a confined space where their opponents held every advantage, whilst innocent civilians would probably suffer regardless of the engagement's outcome.

The calculation was brutal, but it was also irrelevant. Some situations became matters of honour that demanded action regardless of the likely consequences. He withdrew from the doorway and gathered the Occultum around him in a side corridor. Each man present understood that whatever they decided now, would determine not just their own fates but those of everyone trapped in the chamber ahead.

'There's not much we can do,' said Seneca quietly. 'We're heavily outnumbered and any assault we attempt will likely get us all killed without saving anyone.'

'And if we do nothing?' Falco asked.

'Then good people will die whilst we hide in shadows like cowards,' interjected Marcus flatly. 'Same result for them, but we get to live with the knowledge that we abandoned the innocents when they needed us most.'

The silence that followed was profound. They had spent years conducting impossible missions, and killing countless enemies, but this situation challenged even their accumulated experience with desperate circumstances.

It was Falco who finally voiced what they were all thinking, his directness cutting through tactical complexity to reach the essential truth about their situation.

'I've had enough of hiding and plotting,' he said. 'We came here as soldiers, we've fought as soldiers, and if we're going to die, we should die as soldiers. Not skulking in corridors whilst innocent people suffer.'

'Agreed,' said Sica immediately. 'Better to die fighting than live with dishonour.'

Marcus nodded his confirmation, his veteran's experience telling him that some battles had to be fought regardless of their tactical merit. Around him, the other members of the Occultum showed similar resolution.

'In that case,' said Seneca finally. 'We end this now, one way or another.'

Decision made, they formed up in the corridor outside the door to the audience chamber, each man checking his weapons whilst processing the tactical realities that would govern the next few minutes of their lives. The chamber ahead contained innocents whose survival depended on six Romans accomplishing what conventional wisdom suggested was impossible.

'No more subterfuge,' said Seneca, 'We move fast and inflict overwhelming violence on anyone who stands before us.'

It wasn't much of a plan, but it was all they had. Six against forty in circumstances that would test every skill they had developed through campaigns across three continents. But they were the Occultum. The impossible was what they did, even when success required miracles rather than mere professional competence.

'Right' said Seneca, taking a deep breath, 'let's do this,' and without any more hesitation, pushed the door open wide to charge into the chamber.

Chapter Forty-Seven

The Audience Chamber

The Occultum burst in like a maelstrom of fury and death, their blades scything through those unfortunate enough to be close to the door. For precious seconds, painted warriors froze in shock at the sight of armed Romans materializing from shadows where no enemies should exist, and as some reached reflexively for weapons, others simply stared in disbelief at the intruders who should not be there.

The Occultum exploited those critical heartbeats with ruthless efficiency, their blades opening bellies and severing arteries whilst some of the Makatani still struggled to process the impossibility of their situation.

For perhaps five heartbeats, the element of surprise transformed the Occultum into an unstoppable force of destruction, working their way through opponents who couldn't coordinate any serious resistance to threats they hadn't anticipated. But shock could only last so long against experienced warriors, and the Makatani were nothing if not adaptable predators.

A serpent-faced war leader's roar shattered the paralysis, and his scattered warriors began responding, their individual panic transforming into coordinated fury as tribal discipline reasserted itself over primitive terror.

What followed was battle in its purest form, no formations, no tactics, just the elemental savagery of predators and prey locked in mortal combat where only the strongest and most ruthless would survive. The Makatani warriors threw themselves forward with the desperate fury of cornered beasts, their primitive weapons seeking Roman flesh with single-minded determination. War clubs whistled through the air with bone-crushing force, whilst obsidian-tipped spears thrust and slashed with the sort of primal violence that had sustained these people through millennia of tribal warfare.

Marcus found himself pressed back against ancient stones as three warriors attacked simultaneously. His gladius worked with desperate efficiency, opening a throat here, severing a wrist there, but for every enemy who fell, another seemed to take his place from the seething mass of painted flesh that filled the chamber.

Sica moved through the chaos like death incarnate, his Syrian agility allowing him to flow between spear thrusts whilst his curved dagger found the gaps between ribs with surgical precision. But even his legendary skills were being pushed beyond reasonable limits as the sheer weight of numbers began telling against superior Roman training.

The air grew thick with the metallic scent of spilled blood and the acrid smoke of torches knocked askew during the melee. Ancient stones that had witnessed countless ceremonies now ran red with gore whilst the dying screams of men echoed off walls that had never been designed to contain such primitive violence.

Falco's roar rose above the din as a war club connected with his shoulder, the impact sending jolts of pain through his massive frame whilst his gladius continued its grizzly work of ending men's lives. His eyes took on the glazed intensity that marked berserkers entering a combat trance, whilst his massive frame advanced through enemy ranks with the inexorable momentum of an avalanche.

A weapon appeared in each of his hands, his gladius in the right, a captured war club in the left, and he began cutting through Makatani warriors with the sort of methodical brutality that had once entertained crowds in the Circus Maximus.

'Come on, you painted bastards!' he bellowed, 'come and die on Roman steel! I'll feed your serpent gods with your own blood!'

Warriors threw themselves at him with desperate courage, but courage without skill was insufficient against a man who had survived hundreds of arena contests through superior technique and absolutely ruthless application of violence.

Bur the element of surprise that had carried the Occultum's initial assault quickly faded as the enemy numbers started to tell, and Marcus staggered as a spear point found the gap between his shield and shoulder armour, the blade drawing blood whilst sending jolts of pain through his sword arm. Beside him, Decimus grunted with effort as multiple enemies pressed their attack simultaneously, and they knew that despite their ferocious attack, there could only ever be one outcome.

'We can't hold them much longer!' shouted Seneca, withdrawing his knife from the face of a fallen warrior. 'Fall back to the corner, we'll make a stand there.'

The Occultum responded, working their way backwards in a solid line, but as they retreated, something happened that changed the whole situation as one of the Makatani turned away from the melee and drew his bow to send an arrow straight toward Panthera. The ruler's reflexes proved equal to the threat but as he twisted aside, the arrow sped past to strike down something infinitely more precious, and a child crumpled without a sound, the arrow protruding from his chest.

Panthera's response was immediate and terrible. The roar that erupted from his throat seemed to come from the depths of hell itself, a cry of parental rage elevated to divine fury. His magnificent frame bent to retrieve a fallen axe, and he plunged into the battle with devastating efficiency, splitting skulls and severing limbs in a storm of pent-up rage.

The sight of their leader joining the combat stirred something primal in Panthera's surviving people. These weren't warriors trained for battle, but they were human beings pushed beyond all reasonable limits by the systematic destruction of everything they held sacred, and the chamber erupted into complete chaos as the battle transformed from organized combat into something far more primitive, a struggle for survival where every person fought with whatever weapons they could find and whatever strength remained in bodies pushed beyond all reasonable limits.

It was slaughter on both sides. The Makatani warriors were experienced fighters with weapons designed for killing, but they were unprepared for the sort of desperate resistance that came from people who had lost everything except the will to make their deaths cost their enemies dearly.

The serpent-faced leader tried to retreat, but Falco's reflexes proved faster, and his blade took the man's head in a single stroke that sent the tattooed skull bouncing across bloodstained stones.

With their leader dead and their numerical advantage eroded by Roman steel, the surviving Makatani began to break as individual warriors sought escape rather than glory, but the chamber's confines offered no retreat.

The final slaughter was brief but comprehensive. Every invader who had violated the ancient sanctuary paid for that transgression with his life, their painted corpses joining those of the defenders who had died protecting what they loved most, but when silence finally settled over the blood-soaked chamber, the cost of victory became apparent. Bodies lay scattered across stones that had been transformed from ceremonial space into charnel house, whilst the survivors stood amongst the carnage with the blank expressions of people who had witnessed the destruction of their world.

The Occultum had survived the impossible battle, though not without cost. Marcus favoured his wounded shoulder whilst Decimus tested a leg that had taken a spear thrust during the melee's final phase. But they were alive, they were armed, and they had accomplished what conventional wisdom suggested was impossible.

A gathering crowd in one corner of the chamber drew Seneca's attention and he pushed through the small group with growing dread, knowing instinctively that whatever lay at their center would transform this moment of military triumph into something far more complex.

At the heart of the crowd, a woman knelt in spreading crimson whilst cradling a small form against her chest. The boy who had taken the arrow meant for his father lay still and pale in her arms, his young life seemingly cut short by something he had never done anything to deserve.

Panthera stood beside them like a statue carved from grief itself, his magnificent presence diminished by loss that went beyond anything tactical victory could compensate. The ruler whose authority had commanded great cats and controlled ancient wealth was reduced to something far more basic, a father confronting the imminent death of his only son in circumstances where all his power meant nothing.

The chamber fell into absolute silence as everyone present absorbed the magnitude of what had been lost. They had won the battle, but at a cost that made victory feel like just another form of defeat.

Chapter Forty-Eight

The Audience Chamber

The boy lay still as death in his mother's arms, the arrow protruding from his small chest. Blood seeped around the shaft with each shallow breath as Sica pushed through the gathered crowd.

'Give him to me,' he said firmly. 'I can help.'

The woman looked across towards Panthera, with eyes that showed desperate hope mixed with maternal protectiveness, her arms tightening around her son.

Panthera nodded once and the mother slowly released her son with obvious reluctance, her hands trembling as she placed the most precious thing in her world into the care of violent strangers.

Sica lifted the child with infinite care, his movements designed to avoid jarring the arrow that had found its mark with devastating precision. The Syrian's face showed none of the emotion that marked everyone else in the chamber, only the cold professionalism that had sustained him through years of violence and survival across the empire. With the child safe in his arms, he turned away, carrying his small burden toward the corridors that led back to their original detention chamber while behind him, the Occultum and the boy's mother followed in anxious silence.

The chamber where they had spent so many days awaiting their fate now served a different purpose entirely. Several sarcinae remained scattered around the walls, their contents varied depending on who had survived the long trek from Syene.

'Search everything,' Sica ordered as he carefully placed the boy on one of the woven mats. 'Medical kit, personal supplies, anything that might be useful.'

The Occultum scattered through the chamber, their hands rifling through equipment and a few moments later, Marcus emerged from his search carrying an assortment of items that represented their best hope for preserving young life. A proper Roman medical kit containing bronze instruments designed for battlefield surgery, needles and thread for closing wounds, and leather strips that could serve as tourniquets.

But the centrepiece of their makeshift surgical arsenal was a collection of herbs and powders that Sica himself had brought on their journey, Syrian remedies learned from desert nomads, Egyptian preparations acquired in Alexandria's markets, and precious substances that had cost him a large amount of silver over many years of campaigning.

'Hold him steady,' Sica commanded as he prepared to remove the arrow. 'This is going to be brutal, but the shaft has to come out.'

Talorcan positioned himself to secure the child's torso whilst Decimus held his legs, their combined strength ensuring that involuntary movements wouldn't drive the arrow deeper during the extraction process. Around them, some of Panthera's people watched in horrified fascination as foreign soldiers prepared to conduct surgery that would determine their prince's survival.

The removal was every bit as brutal as Sica had predicted. The arrow had lodged between ribs in a position that required careful manipulation to avoid damaging vital organs, whilst the barbed flint point had to be worked free without tearing additional tissue during its withdrawal. Had it been an adult, they would have driven it straight through but with a child, the trauma would have been just too brutal.

The boy's small body convulsed with agony despite his unconscious state, blood flowing more freely as the foreign object was extracted from the flesh that had closed around it, but Sica's hands remained steady throughout the procedure, his years of battlefield experience allowing him to work with clinical precision despite the emotional weight of operating on a child.

When the arrow finally came free, the Syrian immediately began the more delicate work of cleaning and dressing the wound. Clean water flowed liberally over the injury, washing away debris whilst Sica's potions provided antiseptic protection against the infections that killed more soldiers than enemy weapons.

Marcus appeared with additional supplies as the surgery continued, clean cloth torn from spare tunics, bronze implements that had been heated in the flames of oil lamps to sterilise them, and precious medicines that represented their best hope for preventing the fever that claimed most patients who survived initial trauma.

The process took over an hour of slow, meticulous work, life-or-death surgery performed under impossible conditions. Sica's hands worked with steady efficiency whilst sweat poured from his face, the strain of concentration combining with emotional pressure to test his reserves of strength and skill.

Finally, the wound was cleaned, treated, and bandaged with materials that provided protection whilst allowing the injury to drain properly. The boy's breathing had stabilised during the procedure, his colour improving slightly as his young body began responding to professional medical attention.

'Now we wait,' Sica announced quietly, settling beside his patient. 'The next few days will determine whether he lives or dies.'

The Occultum arranged their sleeping arrangements around the surgical area, creating a protective circle, providing security against any further threats that might emerge during the boy's recovery. Blankets were distributed and guard schedules established, transforming the chamber into a makeshift hospital where Roman discipline served military as well as medical purposes.

The vigil that followed tested even Sica's extraordinary endurance beyond all reasonable limits. For three days and nights, the boy burned with fever as he struggled against infection and trauma, his small frame wracked by delirium that kept him crying out for parents who watched helplessly from the chamber's edges.

Throughout it all, Sica stayed his patient's side, checking the wound's condition with obsessive frequency whilst administering medicines according to strict schedules that he maintained despite his own exhaustion. The Syrian's face grew gaunt with fatigue as Panthera's people brought their own remedies to help with the rest of the wounded and got rid of the dead bodies throughout the city.

The fever broke on the fourth morning with shocking suddenness. One moment the child was burning with unnatural heat whilst muttering words that made no sense, the next his eyes opened for the first time since his injury.

'Water,' he whispered, his voice barely audible.

The mood in the chamber transformed instantly. Where there had been quiet desperation and vigil-like atmosphere, suddenly there was a celebration of victory snatched from the jaws of defeat.

A messenger was immediately dispatched to inform Panthera that his son had awakened, and the ruler's response was immediate, his magnificent presence appearing in the chamber doorway within minutes.

'Where is the man who saved my son?' he asked, speaking in Latin for the first time.

But Sica was nowhere to be seen. The Syrian had simply vanished, leaving behind only the evidence of his medical competence.

A search of the chamber revealed nothing until Falco's booming laughter echoed off the ancient stones.

'The lazy bastard,' he declared with obvious affection, pointing toward a shadowed corner where Sica lay curled among discarded blankets. 'Look at him. Saves a prince's life and then falls asleep in the corner, snoring like a dog that's too tired to find a proper bed.'

Sica lay in exhausted slumber, his reserves depleted beyond all reasonable limits. But even unconscious, his hand remained positioned where he could reach his medical supplies instantly if emergency treatment became necessary.

The sight of their comrade sleeping like the dead after days of tireless service brought gentle smiles to faces that had witnessed too much violence and death during their time in this hidden realm.

As they watched, Panthera approached quietly. The ruler who commanded great cats and controlled ancient wealth beyond measure now stood in humble silence beside a sleeping soldier whose skilled hands had preserved what emperors' treasures could never purchase, the life of a beloved child in a world where death came too easily to the innocent.

Chapter Forty-Nine

The Plains

The sun was a pale disc in the morning haze when Scipio led the column away from the jagged rim. Behind them, the caldera brooded in silence, its secrets buried once more, save for the hoard strapped in bundles across the backs of the surviving legionaries. Every step took them further from the place that had almost claimed their lives, yet the relief was tempered by uncertainty.

The route out had been far from the waterfall and the land beyond was unlike anything Scipio recognised. The ridges rolled in strange, sweeping arcs, dotted with clusters of dark, wind-stunted trees.

'We head north,' said Scipio, squinting up to the sun. 'And if the gods are kind, we'll eventually reach the Mare Nostrum.'

They marched in silence for hours, every man wrapped in his own thoughts. The treasure they carried was both a blessing and a curse, wealth beyond measure, but a burden that slowed them down.

The day grew hotter, the ground underfoot baked and brittle and more than once they found themselves circling a dry riverbed, its cracked floor littered with the bones of animals that had not made it to water. They rationed their own supply carefully, each man sipping only when his tongue began to stick to his teeth.

By mid-afternoon, the landscape began to rise again, forcing them into a narrow defile between walls of red stone. The air was close, the sun's heat trapped until it shimmered and somewhere far above, a hawk wheeled lazily, its shadow flickering over them like a silent omen.

'Keep moving,' said Scipio, his voice carrying no hint of doubt, though his mind was a constant tally of risks and when at last the defile widened, they found themselves looking out over a vast plain where the wind combed the grass in silver waves. It was beautiful, but it was also vast, exposed, and unwelcoming.

They halted only long enough to take their bearings as Scipio scanned the sky again, noting the position of the sun as it dipped slightly westward.

'North,' he said again, pointing into the distance, and this time there was steel in his voice. 'We keep moving and if we survive, the Mediterranean will be waiting for us, even if it takes weeks.'

The men fell into motion once more, their shadows stretching long before them as the land swallowed them whole.

The first sign of the river was the change in the air. Scipio smelled it before he heard it, cooler, fresher, with a faint tang that suggested animal life. The brittle grass underfoot gave way to greener blades, and insects buzzed in sudden abundance. Then came the murmur, low at first, swelling to a steady rush as they topped a gentle rise and saw it glinting below.

The men halted as one, staring in disbelief. A ribbon of water, wide enough for two triremes to pass side by side, sliding northwards through a bed of pale sand and stone. Sunlight flashed off ripples where the current curled around bends, and stands of willow and acacia leaned over the banks, their roots drinking greedily.

'By all the gods,' breathed one of the men. 'We're saved.'

Scipio allowed himself a smile.

'Not yet,' he said, 'but it does head north and could be our road to the sea.'

The change in mood was instant. They laughed as they knelt to drink, sluicing away the grime and salt of the march and for the first time since leaving the caldera, the weight of the treasure felt less like a curse and more like a promise.

They followed the river's meandering course, and each day the world seemed kinder. Fish leapt in the shallows, birds flitted from tree to tree, and the air grew softer, the nights cooler. Scipio even caught himself thinking:

'We're going to make it.'

By the fifth day, confidence had settled into the column like a welcome guest. Men talked more, shoulders loosened, and the pace grew brisk. They moved as soldiers again, not fugitives clinging to the edge of survival.

As they continued on their journey, one of the men stopped, his gaze fixed on a low ridge to their right.

'Centurio,' he said, 'look.'

Scipio followed his eyes and felt the small hairs rise on the back of his neck.

Up on the ridge stood no more than a dozen figures, tall men standing in a tight line against the sky. Warriors, by their stance and their weapons: long spears, round hide shields, and bodies daubed with ochre and white. The wind stirred the feathers in their hair, but otherwise they did not move. They simply watched.

The river's murmur seemed suddenly loud in the stillness.

'Do we keep moving?' asked one of the men quietly.

Scipio didn't answer at once. His gaze stayed locked on

the ridge as the warriors began to descend, slow and deliberate, their eyes never leaving the Romans.

The column bunched up behind him, men shifting uneasily, hands finding the grips of shields and hilts of swords. The laughter of the past days was gone, replaced by a taut silence.

No one spoke as the gap closed. They just stood waiting on the riverbank, hearts pounding, as the strangers came steadily closer, the outcome of the meeting as yet unwritten.

Chapter Fifty

The City

The weeks that followed their desperate battle had transformed the ancient city from a place of death into something approaching normalcy, though the scars of violence remained etched into stones that had witnessed too much suffering. The Occultum and many of Panthera's people had mainly recovered from their injuries whilst those who had fled the violence began to return.

But beneath the surface calm lay currents of change and as the Occultum sat around a platter of fruit, talking quietly amongst themselves, Corvus limped through their quarters with news that would reshape everything.

'They're leaving,' he announced without preamble. 'Panthera and his people. The city is no longer safe, not after what happened. Too many know about it now, and too many enemies have seen its weaknesses.'

Seneca looked up.

'Where will they go?'

'Far to the south, hundreds of miles into territory where no outsider has ever ventured. They have other settlements, other strongholds that remain secret from the world.' Corvus paused, gathering himself for the more important part of his message. 'But first, Panthera wants to see Sica... *alone.*'

The Syrian looked up from his own tasks with obvious wariness. In his experience, private audiences with powerful men rarely ended well. He looked across to Seneca, receiving a nod of permission in reply.

'Lead the way,' said Sica with a sigh, rising to his feet.

They departed through corridors that had become

familiar during their extended residence, passing chambers where the evidence of recent violence was being systematically erased, but the route Corvus selected soon led away from the main passages, instead following smaller tunnels that none of the Occultum had used previously.

'He wants to thank you properly,' Corvus explained as they navigated increasingly narrow passages. 'What you did for his son... it goes beyond military alliance or political cooperation. It was personal, and he responds to such things in personal ways.'

The tunnels grew smaller and more obviously ancient as they penetrated deeper into the cliff face, their walls showing primitive tool marks from eras when bronze was precious and iron unknown. Oil lamps provided minimal illumination creating just enough illumination to light their way.

Finally, they emerged into a chamber that had clearly been hollowed from solid stone by hands that possessed infinite patience but limited tools.

At the cave's heart stood what appeared to be a statue, a crude representation of a panther, carved from weathered stone, but barely recognisable as the magnificent predator it was supposed to represent.

Panthera himself stood beside the ancient sculpture, and when he saw Sica enter the chamber, he nodded once to the four men by his side.

The men strained against the statue with a coordinated effort and despite its size, it slid to one side revealing a small entrance, leading into darkness that swallowed the feeble light from their oil lamps. Panthera gestured for Sica to follow, then squeezed through the opening.

Sica followed, intrigued by what may lay ahead, and within a few moments, they entered another cavern that stole his breath and challenged his sanity with a single devastating revelation. Before him was the hidden truth that had cost the lives of hundreds of Roman soldiers who had been convinced by promises of wealth beyond their wildest dreams and lost their lives as a consequence.

All around him, gold gleamed from every surface in quantities that made the tribute of conquered provinces seem like copper coins scattered by beggars. Statues carved from precious metals stood in neat rows whilst gemstones the size of birds' eggs caught the torchlight and threw it back in brilliant fragments of every colour imaginable.

Necklaces that would have ransomed emperors hung from wooden frames like common rope, whilst rings set with exquisite jewels lay scattered in casual piles so vast that individual pieces had lost all meaning. Coffers overflowed with coins from civilisations that predated Rome by millennia, their gold content undimmed by the centuries that had accumulated above this hidden sanctuary.

'Sweet merciful Jupiter,' Sica breathed, his voice barely audible, 'this is... this is *impossible.*'

But the evidence of his eyes couldn't be denied. Here was the treasure that had drawn expeditions across continents and inspired legends that survived in whispered tales told around tavern fires. Here was wealth that could purchase entire provinces, arm a hundred legions, or transform any man who possessed it into the equal of gods themselves.

Panthera spoke for the first time since entering the chamber.

'Take all what you want,' he said simply, his Latin heavily accented but perfectly clear. 'It is yours to do with as you wish.'

The offer hit Sica like a physical blow, his mind

319

struggling to process the magnitude of what was being placed at his disposal. A lifetime of discipline warred with human avarice whilst his eyes tracked over wealth that represented more purchasing power than entire kingdoms could muster.

His first instinct was refusal, the automatic response of someone who had been trained to accept only what he had earned through service rather than what had been offered through generosity. But he knew that rejection of such a gift would insult Panthera and he had to make a decision.

He moved through the chamber like a man walking in a dream, his hands trailing over treasures that would have inspired wars if their existence became known to the outside world. Everywhere he looked, new wonders revealed themselves from civilisations that spanned millennia, with precious metals worked into forms that challenged every assumption about primitive capabilities.

Finally, his attention was drawn to one of the many chests that lined the chamber's walls. The container itself was a work of art, carved from some dark wood and bound with gold fittings, but on top of the chest, displayed with casual elegance amongst all the other treasures, lay a pendant that seemed to call to him with almost magnetic attraction. A golden panther wrought with such artistic precision that it seemed ready to spring from its chain, its form encrusted with precious stones that created patterns of light and shadow across its surface.

The craftsmanship was extraordinary, not the crude work that marked most barbarian attempts at metalworking, but something that would have graced an emperor's personal collection. The panther's eyes were emeralds that seemed to hold inner fire, whilst its spotted coat was rendered in tiny gems that created texture approaching that of living fur.

Sica lifted the pendant with reverent care, feeling its

substantial weight whilst studying details that revealed new marvels with each moment of examination. This wasn't just jewellery but art that connected whoever wore it to the power and majesty of the great cats that had once roamed these territories in numbers beyond counting.

Panthera nodded approval as the Syrian made his selection, his yellow eyes showing satisfaction that the gift had been chosen with appreciation for its artistic rather than merely monetary value. The pendant represented wealth that could purchase estates, but more importantly it embodied the spirit of a people whose connection to their environment went beyond mere survival.

Once done, they departed the treasure chamber in silence, the ancient statue once again sealing the entrance and resuming its role as guardian of secrets that could reshape the known world. But Sica carried with him proof that such wealth existed, tangible evidence of mysteries that lay hidden in the depths of Africa.

When they returned to the chamber where his comrades waited, Sica concealed the pendant beneath his military cloak, the weight of the golden panther pressed against his chest like a secret that challenged every principle he had developed about the proper relationship between soldiers and wealth.

'Where have you been?' Falco asked immediately, noting something different about his comrade's manner.

'Nowhere important,' Sica replied carefully. 'He just wanted to express his gratitude for services rendered.'

'That's all?'

'There's nothing to tell,' said Sica. 'At least not yet.'

'I bet he gave you a woman,' said Falco, 'that pretty one

who brings the fruit.'

Sica sighed and shook his head. Apart from fighting, women and wine were always just a moment's thought away for the giant gladiator.

'No Falco,' he said, 'no woman. 'But even if there was, you would be the last person I would tell.'

The following dawn brought their departure from the ancient city that had witnessed so much violence and sacrifice as the guides that Panthera had promised waited at the base of the great stairway.

The Occultum gathered their equipment and made their way to the entrance. They were leaving as different men than they had arrived, marked by choices that would define them for whatever remained of their lives and as they reached the valley floor, Falco turned to look up at the city one last time.

'Look,' he said quietly, pointing toward the highest terrace. 'He's watching us leave.'

Up above, Panthera stood silhouetted against the morning sky like a statue commemorating the end of an age, his magnificent presence undimmed despite everything he had lost during their time in his realm. But it was what he carried in his arms that transformed the moment from a simple farewell.

A small black panther cub rested against his chest, its fur so dark it seemed to absorb light rather than reflect it. The young predator's yellow eyes tracked their movement with curiosity whilst its tiny form promised to grow into the same deadly magnificence that had once protected this ancient sanctuary.

The symbolism was unmistakable, life continuing despite loss, and power adapting rather than surrendering, the eternal cycle that had sustained this hidden civilization through millennia of challenges. In the cub's fierce gaze lay the promise that Panthera's legacy would survive whatever trials awaited in the unknown territories where his people would build their new home.

'A new beginning,' said Marcus quietly, understanding that they were witnessing something far more significant than mere departure.

'For all of us,' said Seneca. 'Now, let's go home.'

Chapter Fifty-One

The Valley

The route chosen by their guides bore no resemblance to the path they had taken into the hidden valley weeks earlier. Gone were the treacherous swamps and the precipitous waterfall that had tested every measure of their strength and spirit. Instead, they now travelled along a hidden artery carved from the very bones of the earth, tunnels shaped by unknown hands that had chiselled their legacy into the living rock with a skill refined over generations.

Smooth-walled corridors, some large enough to accommodate pack animals in pairs, wound through chambers where fresh air circulated in whispering currents and vertical shafts, cunningly bored through layers of stone, reached to the world above drawing air down into the depths below.

'Incredible,' murmured Marcus, his voice echoing softly against the stone. He ran his hand along the wall as they passed. 'This must have taken decades.'

The others made no reply, the awe too great, the silence too sacred to break but when at last they emerged onto the open plain, the sudden flood of light struck them like a hammer. The heavens above stretched open, vast, and merciless in their clarity and after the intimacy of the tunnels, the sky felt overwhelming, beautiful and alien.

Yet the land before them was unfamiliar. This was not the landscape they had crossed on their approach to Panthera's domain. Here, the terrain was gentler and low stone cairns, weathered by centuries, marked the path ahead. Occasionally, carved symbols and small stone totems, barely perceptible to the untrained eye, revealed an ancient trail, worn by the feet of countless generations.

Their guides continued at a measured pace, unhurried yet unwavering, following the contours of the land with instinctive precision. The ground rose and dipped in slow undulations, guiding them steadily toward the sound of running water. The murmur began as a whisper, but with every passing mile it grew stronger, until by late afternoon it became unmistakable, the voice of another river.

When they reached its banks, the water revealed itself in full. It was a substantial river, wide and flowing with quiet strength, heading northward. Waiting at the shore were two dugout canoes, long, sleek vessels hewn from massive trunks, and hollowed by fire and labour. Though simple in design, they were capable of carrying heavy loads and navigating the shallows where larger boats would falter.

Seneca, gestured toward the river and asked a question in halting fragments of their shared vocabulary.

The elder of their guides responded with a stream of melodic syllables. Though the precise meaning eluded them, the message was clear. The river would take them away from this hidden place, down to the great waterway that carved its path through the heart of Africa. It would carry them, eventually, toward the known world, to where Roman influence began again.

There was something like hope in the air and for the first time in what felt like years rather than months, as the men of the Occultum sensed the pull of home. The mystery of their journey might never fully leave them, but the way ahead at least seemed open.

They loaded their gear into the canoes, checked the balance, and pushed off, the current embracing them like an old friend, its steady flow easing the labour of paddling.

Silence settled over them all, a peaceful hush not born of fear, but of relief but as they rounded a bend, the world changed.

'What's that?' asked Falco, withdrawing his paddle into the canoe and staring towards the riverbank.

The figure hung between two trees, suspended by thick rope tied at the wrists and ankles, limbs stretched wide and twisted unnaturally. It swayed slightly in the breeze, like some obscene parody of a scarecrow, not designed to frighten crows, but men, and there was no doubt about the message, it was just too familiar.

Flesh blackened by the fire below clung to bone and skin peeled back in long ribbons, exposing the muscle and sinew beneath. The torture had been applied with precision, not rage, every mark deliberate, every wound an act of communication. This was not the product of vengeance alone, this was vengeance.

As they drifted closer, the horror took on a terrible familiarity as Falco's voice cracked.

'Sweet merciful Jupiter.,' he gasped, *'that's Scipio.'*

The camp prefect's identity was unmistakable despite the damage. His silhouette, the remnants of his uniform, the particular angle of his jaw, these details remained. But it was the object protruding from his mouth that drew their full attention and hammered the meaning home.

A golden chain, glinting in the sunlight, its bejewelled links shimmering like a serpent's tongue. The gems had been polished and sparkled with cruel mockery, reflecting the light like the eyes of a predator. This was no mere execution. It was an announcement.

Scattered at the base of the grisly monument were the remains of the rest of his men. Their weapons lay broken beside them, shields cracked and discarded, corpses sprawled in final gestures of agony. Vultures had already found them and the stench of rot curled through the air.

No words were spoken as the canoes drifted past. The river did not pause and neither did their guides, but eventually, Falco found his voice.

'The Makatani must be around here somewhere,' he said, staring up the nearby hills. 'They must have caught Scipio before he could get away.'

Seneca did not answer at once. His eyes had not left the two guides. He studied them carefully, measured every blink, every twitch of expression. There was no surprise in their faces, no shock, not even disdain. Their eyes remained fixed on the river ahead, their hands never faltering in their rhythmic paddling. *They had known.*

'I don't think it was the Makatani,' said Seneca at last. 'I think it was Panthera's men.'

The Occultum absorbed the reality of the situation. Scipio's betrayal had not merely been punished by Panthera, it had been turned into a warning, one that would echo in the hearts of all who might one day mistake courtesy for weakness.

The river continued its steady course, and as the grim spectacle faded behind them, the Occultum sat in heavy silence, the air thick with unspoken truths.

The current bore them northward, toward the vast Nile that would eventually carry them home. But behind them, suspended in the trees, Scipio's contorted form remained, forever screaming, and forever a reminder that not all justice wore the robe of a magistrate, and not all debts were settled in coin.

Chapter Fifty-Two

Rome

The familiar clamour of Rome's harbour came as a shock to the Occultum, an overwhelming collision of noise, smell, and motion after so many months immersed in silence, hardship, and survival. The Tiber, the ancient lifeblood of the city, shimmered in the sunlight as it bore the perfume of civilisation: the scent of warm bread wafting from bakeries that never closed, the tang of fermenting wine from amphorae stacked in neat rows along the quayside, and the more pungent, human aroma of a city where half a million souls lived, fought, bargained, and dreamed within stone's throw of one another.

The six members of the Occultum stood motionless upon the sun-warmed timbers of the quay, absorbing it all. They had returned to a world unchanged, yet no longer familiar. Around them, dockhands bellowed to one another over crates of grain and olive oil, merchants haggled, and slaves toiled as the machinery of empire ground on, indifferent to the return of men presumed dead.

None of the onlookers paid them any heed. To the bustling port, they were just another handful of legionaries returned from service, certainly not the last survivors of an expedition that had vanished into the African interior.

Marcus watched the ordinary chaos unfolding around him, his gaze distant.

'Feels strange,' he murmured. 'As if we're visitors now, like this isn't our city anymore.'

He was right, of course. They had changed, not merely in appearance, though their hardened expressions, sun-worn tunics, and subtle wounds bore testament to what they'd endured, but in spirit. They had crossed thresholds no Roman map acknowledged, glimpsed civilisations long thought mythical, and borne witness to truths the empire was neither ready for nor deserving of.

'Report to the Palatine within the hour,' barked a harbour official, not even glancing up from his wax tablets. 'Senator Lepidus expects your immediate attendance.'

Seneca sighed with familiar acceptance. As usual, there was to be no ceremony, no honour guard or even acknowledgement, just protocol. But that was exactly the way they liked it.

A few minutes later, the rest of the Occultum dispersed into the labyrinth of streets that defined the Eternal City. Seneca had granted them several weeks' leave to rest, heal, and recover, an indulgence earned not through rank but survival. But his own task was less forgiving and once he saw the last of his men disappear, he turned back to the task in hand. Reporting to Lepidus.

The Palatine loomed ahead, white marble gleaming in the sun, its pillars and terraces proclaiming Rome's eternal glory. Here, power resided in comfort and senators debated the fate of nations while slaves fanned away the heat. To most of them, Africa remained little more than an abstract. To Seneca, it had become a graveyard of forgotten worlds.

He was received in a modest chamber by Senator Lepidus, who rose at once upon seeing Seneca.

'By the gods, you made it,' Lepidus exclaimed. 'It has been so long since we received any reports, we thought you were all dead.'

Seneca bowed slightly.

'Our difficulties exceeded projections,' he said evenly.

'Casualties were severe and many never made it beyond the outer deserts.'

'Tell me everything,' Lepidus said, fetching a bottle of wine and pouring two cups. 'From the beginning. Leave nothing out.'

What followed was a delicate operation. Seneca walked the razor's edge between fact and fabrication, threading a narrative that satisfied bureaucratic curiosity without triggering the kind of interest that could doom another generation of soldiers. He spoke of scorching deserts, treacherous jungles, savage warfare, and the slow unravelling of an already fragile mission. He told of Panthera's people, the Makatani, and the eventual betrayal that fractured the mission from within.

When he reached the part concerning Scipio, Lepidus's face darkened.

'A camp prefect... murdering his legatus?' he whispered, barely able to process the idea. 'Stealing from those who had saved his life? Such dishonour... It shakes the very foundation of discipline.'

'There was no ambiguity,' Seneca confirmed. 'Flavus was killed by Roman steel, but the stolen treasure was recovered from Scipio's corpse after Panthera's men caught him attempting escape.'

Lepidus leaned forward, brows furrowed.

'Tell me about this treasure for Claudius will demand an account. Rumours still persist of wealth enough to finance a new province. Did you find any such evidence?'

Seneca did not flinch.

'Only a small coffer,' he said, truthfully in tone if not in fact. 'A few trinkets, jewels of minor note. Nothing more than could be expected from any minor tribe in Gaul. What Scipio took was all that was found.'

'And Panthera's people?'

'Gone. Their city destroyed. What we encountered was not an empire in waiting but a civilisation in its twilight. Wise, yes. Noble, but poor and broken. They've now vanished into the wilds and what little they left behind will fade.'

The lie passed easily. It was not cowardice but stewardship. Seneca knew what Rome would do if it discovered the truth. Panthera's city would be razed. Its children enslaved. Its treasures melted into coins to pay for more legions and more conquest.

'The emperor will be disappointed,' Lepidus muttered, already calculating how to dress failure as success. 'But confirmation of the Twenty-First's fate and a warning against further expeditions may be sufficient justification for ending this quietly.'

'That would be wise,' Seneca agreed. 'There is nothing but death the further south you go.'

'Remain in the city,' said Lepidus eventually, 'and draft a full written report. Claudius may request a personal audience, but I'll be in touch either way.'

Moments later, Seneca left the Palatine with a sense of unfinished business weighing heavily on his mind but at the base of the stairs, a familiar figure emerged from the shadows.

'How did it go?' asked Sica.

'We're safe for now,' replied Seneca. 'The official story is that we found nothing worth Rome's trouble.'

Sica gave a slow, deliberate nod.

'Good, then it's time I told you something I should have mentioned sooner.'

He reached beneath his cloak and drew forth the object he had kept hidden since that fateful moment beneath the panther statue. Sunlight struck the pendant and jewels sparkled as the golden panther seemed to breathe in the Roman air.

Seneca inhaled sharply.

'By the gods, Sica,' he said, 'where did you get that?'

'Panthera showed me the truth,' Sica said, his voice low. 'The real treasure chamber. Not the bait, but the truth. Gold, gems, and artefacts beyond value, enough to rival even the hoards of Alexandria. He offered it all to me as a reward for saving the life of his son, Seneca, but I took only this.'

Seneca stared at the pendant, his mind replaying every carefully crafted word he had just spoken to Lepidus.

'If this is revealed,' he said grimly, 'Claudius will do everything in his power to find the source. He'll send ten thousand men if need be. And they'll burn everything from here to the ancient city.'

'Those people deserve more than that,' replied Sica. 'They deserve to be forgotten.'

'What do you want to do with it?'

'I don't need it,' Sica said simply, holding out the pendant, 'it's yours to do with as you wish.'

'I can't accept it,' Seneca whispered, stepping back. 'It's... too much.'

The two men stood in silence, the pendant gleaming between them like a judgement, neither knowing what to do next. Finally, Seneca broke the silence.

'Come with me,' he said. 'I think know who can make this right.'

They walked together through the heart of the empire as Rome bustled around them, oblivious to the burden they carried. The pendant, hidden once more, seemed heavier now, a secret so volatile it could shatter legacies or buy new ones.

The Forum opened before them in all its splendour, temples, columns, arches, all proclaiming Rome's eternal dominion. But Seneca led Sica past the seats of power and wealth, guiding him toward something older, something sacred, the Temple of Vesta.

'Wait here,' he said, striding forward toward the temple gates.

Sica watched as his commander approached the temple guards and after a series of discussions, a messenger was sent into the temple.

Several minutes later, an elderly woman emerged to talk quietly with the Occultum leader. Her bearing radiated quiet strength and though she was obviously not one of the exulted priestesses, her clothing proved she was one of their many trusted servants who dedicated their lives to look after them.

The conversation between the two was brief but intense and a few moments later, the woman extended her hand as the pendant passed into her grasp.

To a bystander, it was a simple offering. To Sica, it was the disposal of a secret which could have toppled dynasties, but would now vanish into the discreet hands of those who served gods, not men.

When Seneca returned, his expression had changed, and he looked across to Sica.

'It's done,' he said. 'She'll see that it's sold quietly, likely to traders from the East. The profits will feed the poor, heal the sick, and care for the widows of dead soldiers. I think Panthera would have approved.'

Sica nodded and cast a final glance back at the woman still standing on the temple steps.

'She's still watching you,' he said. 'How do you know her?'

Seneca paused, a flicker of something private crossing his face.

'I've known her all my life,' he said quietly, looking back towards the woman. 'Her name is Celia… *and she's my mother.*' And with that, Seneca turned away to walk back into the city.

Chapter Fifty-Three

Rome

A few weeks immersed in the comforts of Roman civilisation had worked their subtle magic on bodies once broken by hardship. Rest, rich food, and unbroken nights of sleep had restored a measure of strength to the men of the Occultum, though nothing could entirely erase the toll taken by their ordeal in the African interior.

They gathered outside the Forum Romanum beneath the bright Roman sky, their posture once more casual, their expressions relaxed enough to resemble the men they had once been before their journey into the unknown had reshaped them. Their cheeks carried the healthy flush of men who had eaten well and slept deeply.

They leaned against the marble pillars that edged the Forum, lounging in quiet camaraderie as the great city swirled around them. Street vendors cried their wares in nasal, sing-song calls, slicing through the din of a thousand conversations as perfumed matrons and toga-clad magistrates threaded through the teeming crowd, their entire worlds bounded by appointments, favours, and fleeting prestige.

'Like watching children play with toy soldiers,' Marcus muttered under his breath, his gaze following a heated argument between two red-faced senators. 'After what we've seen... their concerns seem almost innocent.'

'They haven't seen what we have,' replied Decimus, idly inspecting the edge of his gladius. 'Still no word from Lepidus?'

Seneca shook his head, casting a glance at the sun's position as it climbed higher in the sky.

'Imperial summons rarely arrive with clarity,' he said, 'it

could be a commendation, it could be another assignment. Or simply a whim that's caught Claudius's attention.'

'Where's Sica asked Decimus, scanning the crowd for their missing comrade.

'He went to fill his water flask. He shouldn't be long.'

A heartbeat later, the sharp rhythm of hobnailed caligae striking stone reached their ears. The sound, ordered and unified, did not belong to civilian life and the men of the Occultum straightened as a full century of Praetorian Guards emerged from the crush of the Forum, sunlight gleaming off polished armour and crested helms. Their approach was swift, purposeful, and left no doubt that this was no ceremonial display.

They halted before the Occultum and turned to face them as Seneca rose slowly, his instincts prickling.

The centurion in charge stepped forward. His face was scarred, weathered by years of service. This was no palace soldier, he was a killer.

'Which one of you is Falco?' he demanded, his voice devoid of warmth.

Falco stepped forward with the unshaken confidence of a man who had faced death too many times to be intimidated by rank.

'That'd be me. What can I do for the Praetorian Guard?'

'The emperor wants to see you personally,' the centurion said, and with a flick of his hand, a dozen guards moved into place around Falco in a formation that was less escort and more containment. 'You'll come with us. Now.'

Falco turned slightly, his eyes seeking Seneca's.

'Wait,' Seneca interjected, stepping forward. 'This man is under my command, and I demand an explanation.'

'I am not informed of the emperor's reasons,' sneered the centurion. 'I just follow orders. Perhaps you should do the same.'

The insult was deliberate, and Seneca's eyes narrowed, but before tempers could ignite further, Falco raised both hands in mock surrender.

'Relax, lads,' he said with a smirk. 'He probably just wants to ask about my legendary success with women, or maybe he wants to hear how I once killed a Numidian lion with nothing but a half-eaten loaf of bread. Either way, I'll see you at the tavern later.'

With that, the twelve guards closed in around him and marched him off through the Forum, disappearing into the sea of white marble and crimson cloaks, as the Occultum stood in uneasy silence.

'What about the rest of us?' Seneca asked eventually, addressing the centurion. 'Do we wait for his return?'

The centurion's lips twisted into something resembling a smile.

'You'll find out soon enough,' he said coldly. Then, more sharply: *'Seize them.'*

The command landed like a thunderclap and in an instant, the Praetorians moved. Trained to subdue assassins and traitors, they struck with speed and efficiency and Seneca barely had time to react before three of them had grabbed him, forcing him down to the floor. Around him, Marcus, Talorcan and Decimus were similarly overwhelmed and within moments, all were tied securely, their binds already cutting into their skin.

'What's the meaning of this?' Seneca bellowed as rough hands forced him back to his feet. 'We are Roman soldiers! We serve the Senate and the emperor!'

The centurion offered no reply, and the crowds parted

in silence as the bound men were dragged away. No one interfered and the forum swallowed them, its pillars bearing mute witness as yet more honourable men disappeared into the grey machinery of imperial suspicion.

But Seneca's eyes caught one final, flickering moment of clarity before they were taken.

Across the square, half hidden in the shadows of a portico, Sica stood watching. His water flask now full, his hand gripping its leather strap tightly. He made no move to intervene, he couldn't. But as their eyes met across the crowd, understanding passed between them. This wasn't over.

Epilogue

Rome

The tavern hunched at the edge of the Subura like a festering sore, a disreputable blot upon the face of civilisation. Its cracked plaster walls, blackened by smoke and years of neglect, exhaled the fetid breath of old wine and sweat. The clientele were precisely the sort imperial officials pretended didn't exist, runaways, murderers, deserters from far-off legions, petty debtors, and professional cowards, men whose crimes had blended so thoroughly with their survival that they could no longer tell the difference.

It was here, amid Rome's diseased underbelly, that Sica had disappeared, not out of fear, out of necessity.

Five days had passed since the Practorian Guard had descended upon his comrades in the Forum. Five days of silence and careful, calculated inquiries that had produced nothing but blank stares, evasive shrugs, and in one case, a knife in the ribs of the man he questioned. Word of his search had spread faster than answers and whispers followed him through the markets and alleys, through wine shops and gambling dens. But the kind of whispers that cautioned, not the kind that informed.

He sat alone in the corner of the tavern, his back to the wall, his wine untouched, his eyes constantly scanning the room's dim interior. Shadows shifted in the corners, men spoke in low tones and every glance lingered too long.

He had passed through the farthest reaches of Africa, had stood toe to toe with death and laughed in its face. Yet here, in the very heart of civilisation, he was paralysed, not by what he knew, but by how much he didn't. He had become invisible. Alone, and dangerously so.

The wine before him was little more than ritual, just enough to keep up appearances. It no longer warmed or soothed. It served only to give his hands something to hold while his mind spiralled through thoughts that refused to settle.

He had scoured every contact from his mercenary days. Old fixers, disgraced centurions and informants who once knew when provincial governors sneezed. But all were useless, and each had denied knowing anything. His comrades had vanished without a trace and that silence was not natural.

The logical response, the survivor's instinct, was to leave. Rome was a city of a million faces, and the empire even more so. He could change his name, grow a beard, vanish into the eastern provinces and sell his sword for silver. He could start again in Antioch, or Palmyra, or beyond. He had the skills, and he would survive, but the idea tasted like poison.

He had bled beside those men and loyalty wasn't a coin to simply change hands, it was a bond forged in the crucible of fire, of dirt, of shared hopelessness. To walk away now would be to dishonour that bond, to become the very thing they had always fought against.

His jaw tightened and he lifted is wine to drink deeply. Five days of failure. Five days of nothing. He had reached the end of the map.

And then, as the last drop of wine dripped down his chin, a memory returned. Not a revelation, but the merest fragment of an idea. A light glowing inside his mind like a spark in dry grass.

He froze, his eyes wide, heart suddenly hammering. There was one contact, one person he hadn't followed. Someone who could reach into the places even the Praetorians feared to go.

The idea chilled him. To speak to this person was to risk everything and if he misjudged, he would be killed without mercy. But what choice did he have?

The path ahead did not promise safety. It plunged into darkness, into secrets buried too deep to forgive discovery, into dangers that would not relent until they had swallowed him whole. Behind him lay the temptation of vanishing into obscurity, of letting the world forget he ever existed. But ahead… ahead lay the most perilous road he had ever faced.

There was no turning back. No more hesitation. No more waiting for fate to choose.

He stepped into the reeking alleys of the Subura, the filth clinging to his boots as the city's heartbeat quickened around him. Each shadow seemed to watch. Each whisper carried the weight of unspoken threats.

He was the last of the Occultum now. And that legacy demanded more than survival, it demanded truth, it demanded justice, and if all else failed, it demanded vengeance… cold, ruthless, and absolute.

And though nobody knew it yet…vengeance was coming.

The End

Next Book

Follow the Occultum as they are plunged into mortal danger, fighting not just Rome's most dangerous enemies, but the full force of those men in power who hold a grudge against them.

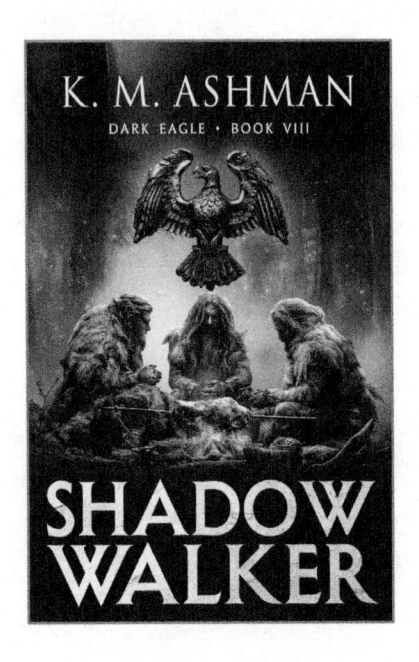

Author's Notes

Roman Governance of Egypt

Egypt became a Roman province in 30 BC following the defeat of Cleopatra VII and Mark Antony by Octavian (later Augustus). Unlike other provinces, Egypt was governed directly by a prefect appointed by the emperor, reflecting its strategic and economic importance to Rome. The prefect held the formal title of Praefectus Alexandreae et Aegypti (prefect of

Alexandria and Egypt), emphasising the distinction between Alexandria and the rest of the country. Alexandria served as the focal point of Greek culture on the Mediterranean and the nexus of Roman trade routes to the deserts, inner Africa, and the East. Roman administration was largely concentrated in the major cities, whilst rural areas retained much of their traditional Egyptian character. The province was defended by auxiliary forces, with three or four alae of cavalry and seven to ten cohorts of infantry, totalling around 4,000-5,000 men. This relatively small garrison reflects Egypt's generally peaceful nature under Roman rule, as the province understood the economic benefits of cooperation with Rome.

The City of Alexandria

Alexandria was founded by Alexander the Great in 331 BC and quickly became one of the greatest cities of the ancient world, serving as Egypt's capital until the Arab conquest in 641 AD. By the 1st century AD, Alexandria contained over 180,000 adult male citizens according to a census from 32 AD, with total population estimates ranging from 216,000 to 500,000, making it one of the largest pre-industrial cities ever built. The city extended about 40 kilometres along the Mediterranean coast and was divided into distinct quarters for Greeks, Egyptians, and Jews, with royal palaces occupying nearly a quarter of the urban area. Alexandria was famous for the Lighthouse of Alexandria (one of the Seven Wonders of the Ancient World), the Great Library, and magnificent temples like the Serapeum dedicated to the god Serapis. Under Roman rule, Alexandria became the focal point of Greek culture in the Mediterranean and served as the nexus of trade routes connecting Europe with inner Africa and the East. The city's cosmopolitan character and cultural ambivalence - extending along a spit of land with its back to Egypt and face to the Mediterranean - made it as much a part of the wider Mediterranean world as of its Egyptian hinterland.

Transport on the Nile

River transport was the primary means of long-distance travel in ancient Egypt, with the journey from Alexandria to Syene taking approximately 10-12 days by boat when sailing upstream against the current. The Nile's geography provided excellent conditions for navigation: boats travelling north went with the current, whilst those sailing south could use sails to catch the prevailing north winds. Egyptian boats were built without nails, using planks of local acacia wood or imported cedar that were joined together with pegs, notches, and rope bindings. These vessels lacked keels but were held firm by tension and water pressure. Cargo barges were capable of carrying enormous loads, including massive stone blocks and obelisks weighing hundreds of tons from the quarries at Aswan to construction sites throughout Egypt. Boats typically carried large crews in case there was no wind, or it blew in the wrong direction, and depictions show vessels having pilots in the bow using long poles to measure water depth. The Nile truly served as Egypt's main highway, too wide to bridge but perfectly suited for the movement of people, goods, and armies throughout the kingdom.

The Monuments of the Nile

The journey from Alexandria to Syene (modern Aswan) in 44 AD would have taken travellers past some of the most magnificent monuments in the ancient world. The stone quarries of Syene were celebrated for their granite, including the famous red granite called syenite, which provided the colossal statues and obelisks found throughout Egypt. Temples dedicated to gods like Serapis, Isis, and various pharaonic deities lined the Nile's banks, many dating back over a thousand years before the Roman period. The massive stone sphinxes, towering obelisks, and elaborately carved temple complexes that Seneca and his men would have witnessed represented the accumulated architectural achievements of three millennia of Egyptian civilisation. The islands of Elephantine and Philae, near Syene, contained particularly important religious sites, including temples of Isis and monuments dating from the Old Kingdom through the Roman period. These monuments would have created a profound impression on Roman soldiers, demonstrating that Egypt had achieved architectural mastery when Rome was still a collection of mud huts on the Tiber.

The Southernmost Border

The Roman frontier in Egypt was established at the First Cataract of the Nile, at Syene (modern Aswan), where the emperor maintained a permanent garrison. This imposing fortress served as both a military outpost and a customs station, where tolls were levied on all boats passing along the Nile in both directions. Roman soldiers, most probably from the III Cyrenaica legion, were stationed here to guard the border. At least three detachments permanently garrisoned the southern border around Philae and Syene, protecting Egypt from enemies to the south and guarding against rebellion in the Thebaid. Beyond Syene lay Pselchis, which housed only an isolated outpost with a token garrison that may not have been continuously manned. The choice of the First Cataract as a border made practical sense, as the rocky rapids created a natural barrier to navigation and military movement.

Primitive Tribes in Africa (1st Century AD)

During the Roman period, much of sub-Saharan Africa remained inhabited by diverse tribal societies whose technological and social development varied enormously across the continent.

Archaeological evidence suggests that many groups still relied on stone tools, wooden weapons, and fire-hardened spears, whilst others had developed sophisticated ironworking traditions that produced high-quality weapons and tools. The practice of ritual scarification and body modification was widespread, serving both aesthetic and social functions that marked tribal identity, rank, and spiritual significance.

Cannibalism, whilst not universal, was documented among certain groups as both a warfare practice and religious ritual, often believed to transfer the strength and courage of enemies to those who consumed their flesh.

These societies possessed intimate knowledge of their environments that allowed them to thrive in conditions that would prove fatal to outsiders, using natural toxins for hunting and warfare that could paralyse or kill with remarkable efficiency.

Hidden Cities and Lost Civilisations

Africa's archaeological record contains numerous examples of sophisticated civilisations that flourished in regions later forgotten by external observers, only to be rediscovered centuries later by European explorers and modern archaeologists.

The Kingdom of Kush, centred in modern Sudan, maintained advanced urban centres and monumental architecture that rivalled contemporary Egyptian achievements, whilst the later civilisation of Great Zimbabwe demonstrated remarkable stone-working capabilities in structures that mystified early colonial investigators. The Aksumite Empire controlled vital trade routes and erected massive stone obelisks that still stand today, proving that sub-Saharan Africa possessed engineering knowledge that could create monuments designed for eternity.

Natural geography often protected these centres of civilisation, hidden valleys, difficult terrain, and hostile environments served as barriers that kept advanced societies isolated from outside interference for centuries. Archaeological discoveries continue to reveal evidence of sophisticated urban planning, advanced metallurgy, and artistic achievements that challenge assumptions about African technological development during the classical period.

Roman Knowledge of Africa

Roman geographical knowledge of Africa beyond Egypt was extremely limited during the 1st century AD, based primarily on second-hand reports from traders, occasional military expeditions, and the accounts of travellers whose reliability was often questionable. The Empire's southern frontier in Egypt extended only to the First Cataract at Syene (modern Aswan), beyond which lay territories that appeared on Roman maps as largely blank spaces marked with warnings about hostile tribes and impossible terrain.

Pliny the Elder and other classical authors recorded fantastical accounts of African peoples and geography that mixed genuine observation with mythology and speculation, creating a literary tradition that portrayed the continent's interior as a realm of wonders and terrors beyond civilised understanding.

The practical difficulties of desert crossing, combined with formidable geographic barriers and genuinely hostile populations, meant that systematic Roman exploration of sub-Saharan Africa remained virtually non-existent throughout the imperial period.

Military Practices and Equipment

The Roman military system described in this novel reflects documented practices from the mid-1st century AD, when legion organisation had evolved into the familiar structure of cohorts and centuries that would dominate imperial warfare for the next three centuries.

The testudo formation and other tactical methods employed by the expedition represent genuine Roman military doctrine, adapted here to circumstances that would have challenged conventional approaches to warfare. Equipment descriptions, from Lorica Segmentata armour to gladius sword techniques, are based on archaeological evidence and contemporary accounts that demonstrate the sophistication of Roman military technology during this period.

The concept of elite units operating independently from main forces, whilst not explicitly documented under the name 'Occultum,' reflects the reality that Roman armies included specialists and scouts whose missions often required unconventional methods and extraordinary risks.

Go to KMAshman.com to follow for more in this series.